WHY I HAVE SO MANY NAMES

MY MEMOIR

In memorial of Bertha Dean

SAUL HENRY BETHAY

Copyright © 2018 Saul Henry Bethay
All rights reserved
First Edition

PAGE PUBLISHING, INC.
New York, NY

First originally published by Page Publishing, Inc. 2018

ISBN 978-1-64350-484-1 (Hardcover)
ISBN 978-1-64350-485-8 (Digital)

Printed in the United States of America

> "But now, O Israel, the Lord who created you says: 'Do not be afraid, for I have ransomed you. I have called you by name; you are mine" (Isaiah 43:1).

This memoir, *Why I Have So Many Names*, is a personal and interesting one with humorous and serious anecdotes about Saul and his life experiences.

The language and expressions are of the African American and Southern culture, with grammar and dialect of this period.

If there are errors, please accept them, and my apologies.

James R. Jarrell*, Editor
Retired Librarian

Dedication

This book is dedicated to Mrs. Zipha Lee Bethay Bryant Goins, Class of 1958, "The Shoulders I stand On," and my many friends.

Acknowledgments

It was Anthony Hardie who put my typed manuscript onto a disk for Anthony Chiappette to put into his computer for us to edit and to see if it made sense to an Italian who knew nothing about the South's segregation at the time. The encouragement I received from Alline Culmer, Zipha Goins, and Patricia Harden as I wrote the draft of each section kept me writing—thank you. My thanks also to those of you I called for accuracy. Dee Catarina's editorial approach was invaluable.

SHOULDERS I STAND ON

James and Mary Bethay Baker	Grandparents
Ludie and Marie Bethay	Parents
James and Dot Bethay	Uncle and Aunt
James and Edith Williams	Uncle and Aunt
Mrs. Roda Tyson	First Landlady, Fort Valley
Dr. and Mrs. O. E. Hicks	Extended Family Parents/Teacher
Tony Grant	Friend
Dr. James N. Mitchell	Friend/Mentor/Advisor/Educator
Alfred Hicks	Special Friend/Brother/Cook
Lionel F. King	Dear Friend
Dr. Claude Saint-Come	Foster Son/Educator/Professor/Writer/Researcher
Hiram Culmer	Brother-in-Law
McKinley Smith	Friend
Edward B. Joyner	Friend
Monroa B. Goutier	Friend/Brother/Cook/Professor
Russell Bethay	Dear Brother
Helen Russell	Special Friend/Professor/Nurse
Charles Ludie Bethay	Dear Brother
Lucille Howell Hagwood	Dear Friend/Teacher
John Blanding	Brother/Father/Friend

Because of them, I became a son, grandson, nephew, uncle, cousin, student, teacher, counselor, dean, director, coordinator, researcher, speech maker, writer, cook, swimmer, entertainer, housekeeper, pool player, and best friend.

May they rest in peace.

I am still being supported in so many ways (carried) by my family, relatives, friends, former students, and colleagues!

I am the richest person alive without money. Money cannot replace what I had and have, thanks to my Guardian Angels!

Contents

Foreword	13
Immediate Family Tree	15
Introduction	17
Cook County Training School	27
My First Real Dates	32
The Bethay Family Tree	44
The Chandler Family Tree	49
My Family Tree: A Little Information about My Siblings and Me	52
Fort Valley State College, September 1950	61
FVSC, Math—Mr. Crofton	67
Sophomore Year at FVSC	70
Junior Year at FVSC, 1952–1953	75
Senior Year at FVSC, 1953–1954	79
1954	87
Tokyo and Fuchu, Japan, 1956	101
Hawaii, 1957–1958	107
April 1958	112
Michigan State College, June 1959	117
Edward Waters College, 1960–1961	129
Mississippi Valley State College (MVSC), September 1961–1962	137
Columbia University, September 1963	146
Englewood Junior High School (EJHS), 1964	151
Personal Data Sheet	157
1964–2017	165
Joseph Paige, 1964–1965, and 232 Rutland Road	170
Purchasing the House	172
John Wesley Jordan*	176

Mama and Victor Bryant Sr. Visit and the Bikes	180
Cars	181
Engle Street School	182
Janis E. Dismus Middle School and Mrs. Sarah Cheatham	186
Highlights in Englewood	194
Mrs. Mary Eason* (Just died September 15, 2017.)	196
Car Burning and Mr. Samuel Wynn	198
The Wallet on the Top of the Car	199
Brooklyn College, 1985	203
The Weekend College Students	212
Highlights at Brooklyn College	214
Dr. Steven B. Carswell, Ph.D.	218
Dissertations	221
Highlights of My Part-Time Jobs	223
Vicarious Education	228
One Year in the Life of Saul Henry Bethay, 2003	231
Some of the Worst of Times	235
How Do I Cope?	236
Awards Committee at Fort Valley State University, July 31, 2006	237
Our Responsibility to Our Youth	238
I Sang for My Father	249
The Fort Valley State College (University) Alumni Association	252
The Mississippi Valley State College (University) Alumni Association	257
Pool (Billiards)	259
Let's Not Forget . . .	262
Unpublished Writings	271
Other Family and Dear Friends	274

Foreword

THIS IS NOT HOMEWORK. This is not an assignment. This is not a term paper. This is not a thesis. This is not a dissertation. This is a sum total of my experiences (personality) over the first eighty years of my healthy life to the best of my remembrances. It should be read as such. Any mistakes or omissions should be charged to my age and head and not my heart or anyone else.

Immediate Family Tree

Caesar Bethay and Mary Inman
Jack Bethay
Nettie Bethay McGee
Arthur Bethay
Jeff Bethay
Walter Bethay
Sula Bethay Williams
Gary Bethay
James Gene Bethay
Ludie Bethay
Henry Bethay
Ludie Bethay (date of death [DOD]: February 4, 1962) and Marie Williams Bethay (DOD: January 13, 1994)
James Baker (DOD: June 1943) and Mary Inman Bethay Baker (DOD: January 1963)
Annie Mae Bethay Jackson
Vincent Ulysses Jackson, Annie Mae's son
Unnamed sister died at birth
Alline Bethay Roberts Culmer
Calloway X. Roberts., Evelyn Roberts McKenzie, Rollie Byrd Roberts Jr., Larry Roberts, Patricia Roberts Baptiste, John Henry Robinson, Hiram Culmer Jr.,* and Harold Culmer (Alline's children)
Charles Ludie Bethay (DOD: January 29, 2013)
Gregory Cooley (Charle's son)
Russell Bethay, Sr. (DOD: January 27, 2007)
Yvonne Bethay,* Russell Bethay, Jr., Geraldine Bethay,* Glistene Bethay, and Alfonzo Bethay (Russell's children)

SAUL HENRY BETHAY

Saul Henry Bethay
Dr. Claude Saint-Come* (Patricia)*, Dr. Steven B. Carswell (Melissa); Ryan and Aidan Carswell, and Pamela Sue Rivers, (Saul's family)
Zipha L. Bethay Bryant Goins
Victor Bryant, Sr. and Keith Goins (Zipha's children)
Marian Marie Wilson
Antoine Wilson, Lorenza Wilson, and Paul Wilson (Marian's children)
Robert D. Bethay
Darryl Bethay, Sr.* and Sonja Bethay (Robert's children)
Gloria Jean Bethay (DOD: June [?] 1943)

INTRODUCTION

I WAS BILLY UNTIL I was twelve years of age. I was the sixth child of Ludie and Marie Williams Bethay; the second, a girl, died in childbirth. At my birth, I had two older sisters and two older brothers: Annie Mae, Alline, Charles Ludie, and Russell Bethay. We lived on Mr. Copper's farm near the Cecil sawmill, sharecropping the farm. Daddy was always an excellent, if not one of the best, farmers during his farming time. There was not anything I felt he could not do farm-wise—from raising crops to building things, constructing anything from outhouses to smokehouses.

We had no running water. The outhouse had Sears Roebuck and Company catalog, brown paper bags, or corncobs, as I remember. The water from the well was kept in the bucket with a dipper and a washcloth hanging on a nail nearby along with the wash pan and a bar of soap—octagon or potash. That bucket of water was for drinking and washing the hands and faces. Our Arm & Hammer baking soda had many uses other than for those biscuits served three times a day: it was used for upset stomachs, as toothpaste and deodorant, and mixed with honey, for scrapes, bruises, and burns. Castor oil, 666, Black Draught, turpentine, hog huff tea, liniment and Epsom salt were some of our medicine.

Baths were taken in the tin number 3 tubs on Saturday nights during the cold months. Other times we boys bathed in the pond, creeks, or rivers nearby. We all used the same comb for our hair.

Clothes were washed in the number 3 tin tubs and boiled in the black washpots using lye and potash soap. The clothes were then scrubbed on those tin washboards until they were free of dirt or stains of any kind—white clothes were *white*. Clothes were then hung on those outside wire clotheslines in the sun to dry. The "wash" was ironed with the "smoothing" irons heated either by the fireplace in the winter or on the wooden stove in the kitchen at other times.

We were always clean because our hands and faces got washed three times a day—breakfast, dinner, and supper. And sometimes our feet got washed too at night. The other parts of our bodies were washed on special occasions or when we went fishing or swimming and before going to town on Saturday to the movies, eating popcorn in the balcony. On the street walking around the courthouse square, we ate ice cream on the cone and Ike and Mike cookie bars. We washed this down with a twelve-ounce Pepsi Cola. Adel was our town on Saturday.

We kept the dirt yards swept with those brush brooms from the woods, too.

Yes, at the time, my underclothes were made from the flour sacks, but no one could see them under the overalls I wore. Kerosene oil lamps were our light to study and do other things at night. There was no electricity or telephone or fax or e-mail or typewriter or computer; we bought penny postcards and three-cent stamps from the mailman, who came Monday through Friday each week. I do not remember holidays during the week then.

Back to the family and my earliest recollection. As I remember or was told, Russell was responsible for me with Charles's help. I was to never be left alone. Grandmother Mary Baker, my daddy's mother, was married to her second husband, James Baker, Grandpa Beck. He married her with ten children at the time. He was the only grandfather I ever knew on either side of my family.

At four or five years of age, I remember Grandma sitting under the walnut tree as we cracked the walnuts with a brick, telling me about the facts of life in her own way; many things I did not fully understand until much later. But telling me things before my time was not unique with my grandmother. Everyone always took me to be much older in sharing things with me. I was always a good listener and did not repeat what was told to me. I had the makings of a good counselor even then.

My grandma told me about all our neighbors. She even told me or I thought she did of the behavior of a married family of men who liked men sexually. I later learned that to be true.

Grandma Mary was known for her tea cakes, and when I visited, I would say "I smell tea cakes," and before long, I would have one or two to eat. I always felt to be the favorite child, grandchild, brother, nephew, cousin, uncle, or even friend. I was and am still treated as such.

Alline told me later that one of her early jobs was to keep flies off me as a baby. Two more sisters were born, one in December 1936 and the other one in March 1938. Now there are seven of us. In July, 1940 another brother was born, Robert Don Bethay (Bobby), and in 1943 another sister was born, Gloria Jean Bethay, who died from pneumonia three months later.

Back to my beginnings. Being born in January 1934, I was able to attend school in September of my fifth year at County Line Elementary School, Adel, Georgia. It was a rural church school with two teachers—Miss Burke and Miss Lawrence.

One of the worst fights I have ever experienced in my total life took place one day at that school because of me. There were two students with mental or emotional problems—Theodore Jackson and Riley Shaw. Neither of them would be accepted in today's "normal" elementary schools. One day at school, Riley took my brown bag lunch from under my seat (church bench) and I told Theodore Jackson. In Theodore's attempt to get my lunch back, they began to fight. No one at the school was able to stop them. Finally, one of the teachers had some other students go get Theodore's father, who lived the closest to the school. It was Mr. Pete Jackson who stopped the fight which had dragged on all morning without any schooling taking place at any time.

Before I was six years of age, Charles, Russell, and I were burning or smoking some rabbit tobacco in this old car Daddy had parked outside the house. I do not know even if it would run. It caught fire and burned. Daddy came home and whipped Charles and Russell, and I thought I was out of it until I passed the room and he drugged me in and gave me a few licks with his belt—my first remembered whipping.

The Bethays all came to our house each year to celebrate Grandpa Beck's birthday. That was the time to see all our aunts and uncles and cousins and so on. It was more like a family reunion, as I remember it.

The next thing I remember was December 1939. We moved 'cross the river (*rivers* because there were two but we never referred to them other than "cross the river"—connecting the two counties Berrien and Cook).

We lived in "the country" on Miss Susan's place, sharecropping still. Miss Susan had one sister and two daughters living with her.

Back to the farming. This land we were on could grow any and every thing: cucumbers, strawberries, okra, squash, tomatoes, peas, beans, sweet corn, sweet potatoes, and white potatoes (ice potatoes) in the garden and in the fields sugarcane, watermelons, cantaloupes, field corn (for our meal for bread, dressing, mealing fish, and food for the farm animals), tobacco, cotton, peanuts, and velvet beans in the fields. We raised chickens, hogs, and cows for some of our meat. The other meat came from goats, turtles, rabbits, squirrels, possums, coons, robins, blackbirds, sparrows, doves, and fish. We had our own eggs, lard, milk, butter, and syrup we made. On the outside, we had pecan, peach, fig, pear, walnut, and pomegranate trees. In the woods, we had grapes, blackberries, raspberries, huckleberries, and plums. Mama canned anything she could in those Mason Fruit jars. We were never hungry and we always had some type of food to eat.

Soon after we moved 'cross the river our grandparents, Mary and James (Grandma Mary and Grandpa Beck) moved near us. Our grandmother always wanted to be near my daddy, Ludie. Our house had a wood fireplace in the living room only—no electricity or telephone. Living nearest to the Side Camp Elementary school, the teachers always stayed with us. It was a one-room, one teacher elementary school with never more than twenty students at a time enrolled. With the teacher living with us, sleeping in the only room which had a fireplace, displaced my parents, and they shacked elsewhere within the house with the rest of us for a $1-per-week rent during school months. I think the teachers got $4 per week if that much.

Miss Fry, my second known teacher at the new school, was a "pretty thing." She and the family sat around the fireplace during the winter months and talked about everything going on in the neighborhood—talk that children could hear in those days in the presence of grown folks.

During the winter months, we shelled peanuts for planting in the spring. We parched some too and made peanut candy out of some. Good!

I also remembered that time one night Miss Susan and her crew were over at our house sitting around the fireplace, and Miss Susan's sister was chewing some bubblegum. I wanted some and asked her for it. She took it out of her mouth and gave it to me. Daddy gave me that look of displeasure and disappointment but did not say anything then or later. Maybe because they were White and he did not want any disturbance among us. But I later knew that I should not have had done that. It was one of my childhood experiences.

We were the only Colored family to have a battery radio, so Colored neighbors came to our house to hear Joe Louis fights. At times, that station played three Colored songs during a fifteen-minute program, which called all the names who had written in for a requested song during the fifteen-minute Colored program. The program was more about hearing someone's name over the radio than the song he finally played. But it was the Grand Ole Opry on Saturday night, which was a must after we came from town (Adel) with our soda crackers and cheese before bed and after we had cleaned those mullet fish for Sunday morning breakfast to go with that grits, biscuits, and syrup.

Side Camp Elementary School was my school for the next six and half years. I had one classmate—a girl named Doris Williams—in my class the remainder of my elementary school years. This school, Sanctified Church of God in Christ, was a small potbelly one-room building—a schoolhouse during the months between September and May and a church on Sunday year round. The pastor came on the fourth Sunday and they would have dinner on the ground, as it was called then. Each household brought cooked food to eat—fried chicken, potato salad, collard greens, and cakes. Children did not eat plain or pound cake; that was for grown folks.

One Sunday at Side Camp, I asked this lady for a nickel to buy an ice cream cone, and she said, "I am going to give you that nickel but don't buy ice cream, buy yourself a pocket handkerchief, something you can keep." Can you imagine? I am eight years old; no money, and she was telling me to buy a pocket handkerchief, especially when I was still probably wearing flour sack drawers. That lady was Miss Henretta Nesmith.

Before Mama joined that church, I would go on fourth Sundays just to eat. Not being members, we still participated in Sunday School and programs which included children. I always gave the same welcoming address for all occasions as long as I was around and attending the affair:

> Dear friends, we bid you welcome to this our [*Holiday*] day.
> Just sit still and listen to what we have to say.
> And if we happen to blunder, just sit still and say,
> I know that child is excited because
> this is our [*Holiday*] day.
> Thank you!

Back to school. One teacher had to teach seven grades reading, math, English, and spelling. We had no other subjects taught. We had recess for gym. At twelve o'clock, we who had them ate our brown bag lunches. Students who had corn bread or crackling bread hid their lunch in the ditch until they were on their way home. We would be their friends then and help eat the lunch they were ashamed to bring to school.

In my fourth grade I told the teacher why not start at the back of the books because we never get to half of any book during the year. My mother asked me that night when did I became a teacher?

Our books were the books gotten from the Whites' schools after they were used for at least seven years. We had no space in the "write your name" section of the book for our names. Any books which had colored pictures we called library books, and they were put on a wooden rack, which we called our library. We had a pump outside for water. We had the outhouse for you-know-what. And occasionally we got a crate of apples and some canned milk, probably from the White school near if they had more than they would eat before the food became spoiled.

I was educationally reinforced by hearing everything taught seven times regardless of the grade, and I tried to know as much or more than any other student regardless of his/her age or grade. I was considered a smart boy. I was good in the math and spelling. The school had grade-level arithmetic only.

When my oldest nephew (Carroway X. Roberts) was being born, we had to stay with our grandparents and we did not have our books for the next school day. I do not know why the teacher did not know this or why she was not there unless she knew about the pending birth and was staying someplace else.

But we were questioned by her about not having books without an answer we could give. We could not tell her about the birth of our nephew at the time.

Now I must tell you about my second whipping on one hot summer day. Daddy, Russell, Grandpa Beck, and I were at the tobacco barn while the tobacco was cooking inside the barn. My grandfather asked me to go get him the ax. I said, "Good gracious, old man, don't you see any "boudy" else around this barn other than me?" By this time, Daddy had a tobacco stick running toward me. I was a fast runner, but when I tried to jump 'cross the ditch on the other side of the road, I fell in and Dad in on top of me; he came with the tobacco stick. A few licks and that was that. It hurt my grandfather more than it did me. He kept saying, "If you didn't want to get the ax, why not say nothing? Now see what you have caused yourself to get." I know I was Grandpa's favorite grandson. It was me who he would want to miss town on Saturday to go fishing with him. I never told him that I'd rather be in town looking at Roy Rogers or Wild Bill Elliot or Dick Tracy, and eating popcorn in the balcony. I loved him too much to say no when he wanted something from me other than the ax time.

Another time, Daddy asked me to go get a plow scrape from the back field. I had learned my lesson somewhat about expressing my feelings verbally. On my way back to the house, I poked holes in every watermelon in my path. Sometime later Daddy noticed this and asked me to fess up. I lied. I said the crows had done it. He said, "No crows made tracks like yours." Off went the belt.

Another time we had moved from our original home to Miss Susan's house, and the well was near the old house. My sisters kept knocking the dipper against the bucket, telling me that they needed water. Daddy heard this and came in and asked me if I did not hear my sisters asking me to get some water. Again, I said, "Daddy, how many children do you have? I am beginning to think that I am not your child." Need I say more. I got more whippings than all the others put together. I only remember my oldest sister, Annie Mae, getting a whipping once, and we boys lied about leaving a tin tub in the pond and said Zipha and Marian did it, and Mama whipped them for that.

Another incident you need to know. My brothers, not Bobby, and me would get a sheet of tin and go on top of the tin top crib and slide down onto the ground. Daddy saw us do this one day and said, "Boys, stop doing that, you're going to kill yourself."

Sometime later, one Sunday, before we went to County Line Church with Mama, who was still a member, H. S. and Joe Fleming—our lifelong neighbors and friends at Side Camp—came by. I had to show them my flying trick. Dressed in my short pants for church, I got the piece of tin and got on top of the crib, and down I came like the Wright brothers. Soon after, Joe said, "Billy, look at your leg!" I was bleeding from my right knee down to my socks. I began crying, looking for Daddy. I located him, and in his excitement not knowing what had happened, he immediately took me to the back porch and began cleaning me up, trying to stop the bleeding. He put some cotton on the cut and tied it up. Off we went to church, but I could not walk. I stayed in the car until we got back home. I still could not walk. Daddy picked me up in his arms like I was a baby and took me in the house. (That alone was worth the cut. I will never forget that feeling being in his arms. Daddy was never a touchy, feely man toward his boys. As I grew older, I better understood him and his show of love for us.)

Sometime later, Daddy went outside to the castor bean tree and got a leaf from it. He took that leaf and put it over the vinegar-and-clay mixture and placed this over my cut and tied it. That leaf turned as if it had been out in the sun. The next morning I could walk again and have never had any problem with that cut or leg anymore. Thanks to "Dr. Ludie."

Now, at the beginning of my seventh grade year at Side Camp Elementary School, my youngest brother, Bobby, entered school. At some point, he had done something the teacher did not like and was about to whip him. I said, "Don't hit that boy. If you have to hit on someone, hit me, not him." I scared her so badly until she did not hit either of us, nor did she tell my parents what I had done. That teacher, Miss White, was the sister of a schoolmate I had in high school and my senior year at Fort Valley State College—Robert White.

Now it is May 1946. Graduation time. Valedictorian. The teacher told me to write my graduation speech. I suffered about two weeks, not knowing what to do, because I had never had any teaching about writing speeches. The final week she came up with the Gettysburg Address for me to recite from memory. I had to learn that in about a week. I still remember most of it today—"Four scores and seven years ago . . ."

Now what. Nashville, the county seat of Berrien County, only had a ninth-grade school for Colored students. What was one who wished to finish high school to do? Being the person I was, I got on my bicycle and rode round trip about forty or fifty miles each day for the next three and half years. As I remember, my parents always let me do what I wanted to do without discussion or approval. They stopped me when they felt I had made the wrong decision or choice. Those were the times I got those whippings. I knew I deserved them because I knew my father and mother really and truly loved me and would not do anything out of their way to hurt me or let anyone else hurt me.

(Before Daddy was killed by the car accident in 1962, I felt he wished he had been me and had the opportunities which were open to me that were not available during his day. If he could not afford it and I found my way to do it, he did not stop me or get in my way. In his way, he always encouraged me and helped me in any way he could even if it meant his last dollar. He lived vicariously through me, I believe. I wish he could see me now and see what I achieved because of him.)

On my own and on the bicycle Russell got rid of when he wanted a blind horse, I arrived at the Cook County Training School in Adel, Georgia, to enter eighth grade. I am now twelve years old. Many of the Colored high schools were called training schools rather than high schools. (I was questioned about coming from a training school at Columbia University in 1961. In New York, these are the schools for delinquents.)

Without parents, birth certificate, or transcript, I was enrolled into the Cook County Training School. When asked my name, I told them Saul Henry Bethay—the beginning of being called Saul. My first cousin Dorothy was in that class. We had been together for four months at the County Line Elementary School where we entered in 1939 and before we moved 'cross the river. Her brother, Willie James (W. J.), was already in that high school in Adel. They came by school bus from their "country" house in Cook County.

In September 1946, a new set of teachers at Fort Valley State College came to work at the Cook County Training School in Adel. This was my first knowledge of college, Colored or White. In that day, few Colored children finished high school, including my two older sisters and my two older brothers. Neither of my two older sisters and brothers even went to high school. I am happy to say they all did well without it or in spite of it. Alline did take courses after she was married with a family. I am proud of her achievements.

I was the first in my immediate family to finish elementary school. Later, my younger sisters finished college—Zipha at Fort Valley State, four years after me and Marian later in Miami (she ended up working toward her PhD). Bobby too finished high school in Miami and joined the Army.

Cook County Training School

The Cook County Training School was a school which housed first grade through the eleventh. We had one main building with an auditorium on the second floor. We had a home economic building; we called it the Home Make Building. We had no gymnasium, just an outside basketball court for the team to practice and play its home games. We had no other physical education sports like track, tennis, volleyball, swimming pool, etc. We did not have a cafeteria; everyone brought his/her lunch or missed eating lunch if they did not have one to bring. That was the case for many students. Lunchtime was our time to go outside for an hour midday and mingle with the other students.

I remember when I was in the eighth grade, I was talking in my math class and the next thing I knew Mr. Nance had hit me with the ruler. He took up five minutes apologizing for what he had done or what I had made him do because I could not keep quiet while he was teaching; somewhat like when Granddaddy had asked me to get the ax at the tobacco barn and how it upset him that I got a whipping.

In the eighth grade, boys had to take homemaking (home economics.) One Friday the teacher left an eighth-grade girl, Arvenia Nash, in charge of us while she did something out of the classroom. A student held her and asked the class, "Who want to kiss her?" I remember holding up my hand but not getting out of my seat. Arvenia grabbed a chair and started swinging it. It hit Curtis Nesmith on the head and it started bleeding. The next thing I knew, Mr. Jerry Powell, Sr.*, principal, came in and said, "I will see you all in a week."

I got home that evening and Daddy said, "Boy, you got to stay home next week because I need you to help dip tar" (from the pine trees). He should have known something was wrong because I said nothing, no complaints. I stayed out of school that week without any argument or questions or mentioning school. My parents never knew I had been suspended that week. Charles and Russell had left by this time, and Bobby was too small for that type of work. We did have a boy, Joe Daniel, living with us and helping Daddy with some of the farmwork and other tasks. He lived in Valdosta, and every time I see him, he says Daddy still owes him some money. One day I am going to give him a few dollars to shut his mouth.

(I just learned that he is deceased at the time of this writing.)

Dipping tar was one of our sources of income when we had no cucumbers, beans, watermelons, cantaloupes, tobacco, or cotton to sell. Selling barrels of tar was good money then. It was a sticky job if you forgot and turn the tar bucket on the wrong side next to your overalls, carrying it from tree to tree. I did that many a time.

In those days, parents were not involved as to what took place in school like my being able to register without them or they having to come back to school after my suspension or even getting a letter telling them that I was suspended.

Another time, a boy kept picking on me and would not stop. A senior girl, Evelyn Penny, grabbed that boy and beat him up. Miss Nash (all female teachers were called "Miss" like we called White ladies "Miss" whether they were married or not) told Evelyn that girls don't fight and she should be ashamed of yourself being a senior, too.

That did not bother Evelyn, and I was thankful because it saved face for me. I was never a fighter, just play fighting as a boy growing up, not ever angry fighting. Being whipped by Daddy was enough for me. Some years later, I was visiting Ralph Williams after they had moved to Adel, and we tousled in the dirt for more than two hours. We were so dirty when we finished until you could only see our eyes on our faces. Boy, were we dirty.

During my bicycle days, a few days I would leave my bicycle at these White people's house and take the bus almost from the beginning of the route about 6:00 a.m. and ride all through the county, including by my cousins Jesse Lee, Dorothy, and W. J.'s house, just to be with the other students on the school bus and not always being by myself riding that bike all those miles. I would be among the first students to get on the bus from where I got on. It was near the rivers, about five miles across the rivers from where I lived. Anything for a change.

When I did ride the bike all the way to school, most days I would be the first one at school. When I had a nickel, I would stop at a store in Adel and get me a donut for extra breakfast or have it for lunch. That was often because I kept a little spending change. We took our lunch to school in brown bags, as I remember. Leaving home so early to get to school, I always had some breakfast before I left.

While waiting on the school bus one morning at these White folks' house where I left my bike, the lady of the house asked me if I would see if I could help her son with his math homework. In less than five minutes, he understood what to do. She said, "He should be going to the Colored school. They are teaching you better than they are teaching my boy at his school."

I stayed at school one afternoon to watch a home basketball game. It was nearly dark when I was nearing the rivers. A White man who lived in the last house before the rivers saw me and said he would take me home in his truck because I should not be going across those river bridges at night. He took me home.

One White lady told me before I graduated from high school that she could not get anything done in the afternoon until I had passed on the bicycle on my way home.

There were many White people who cared but could not do anything about the segregated system at the time. (East Lansing, Michigan, was where for the first time I was affected by real prejudice. At twenty-four, we had to show our ID to enter a bar when the eighteen-year-old White boys could just walk in. Then too I had not tried to go into an all-White establishment in the South before. I "knew my place.")

One afternoon on the school bus on our way home after school, Dorothy kept thumpting Clifford Alford on the head, trying to wake him up. He woke up and hit her hard. W. J. said, "You deserved that lick, you should've left him alone."

From time to time, we would have several fights on the school bus or there would be some student causing a disturbance, as I remember. Mr. Connie, our bus driver, would put students off the bus and drive off a distance and stop the bus and tell someone to go get that person and tell him/her to get back on the bus. It was one of my other cousins, Son Foster, who was often put off the bus. Son was always a playful kid with a good heart. Always joking around, laughing.

Son and an older man, Buddy Harris, started hanging out together going to "jook joints" drinking, smoking, and the like. Son was not even old enough to be in some of these places. One Sunday night, they were in Ray City 'cross the track in one of those joints. They got into it over something. Son was just a kid, maybe fifteen years of age, always kidding around, as I said. I guess from drinking, Buddy stabbed Son, killing him dead, as we would say then.

(Briefly about Ray City. I was on one of those boat trips one night around Manhattan in New York City and started up a conversation with a man on the boat who was visiting from Los Angeles. I asked him where he was from? He said, "LA." I said, "Is that home?" He said, "No, I am originally from Georgia." I then perked up. I said, "Me too. What part?" He said, "Ar, you would not know, it's just a small place." I said, "Try me." He said, "Ray City." I said, "Do you know where Nashville is?" He could not believe it. Nashville and Ray City are about eight miles apart and in Berrien County, too, but there was no Colored high school. Side Camp is about five miles from Ray City. A small world even then.)

Back to Son and Buddy. About 11:00 p.m. that Sunday night, Buddy came knocking on our door, waking Daddy and some of the others of us up. He was scared, crying, telling Daddy what he had done. Daddy asked him where Son was? He said, "He's out there in the back of the truck." Then he asked Daddy what he should do? My daddy was always calm, unless it involved me. He said, "You got to turn yourself in." Daddy got dressed, went with Buddy and the dead child in the back of the truck first to Son's parents' house, and left him there. Then they went to the sheriff's office in Nashville, where Buddy turned himself in.

That killing was the talk of the neighborhoods for a long time—Side Camp, Ray City, Nashville, Hahira, Valdosta, Cecil, and Adel, where Son was a student with us.

I do not know Son's parents' reactions. But just imagine someone waking you up on a Sunday night with your child lying dead in the back of his truck.

They themselves were a little strange. They had their own place and sold brush brooms on Saturday in Adel for some extra change. I did not see any of them before the funeral. They were not the type people visited anyway. They were my relatives but we were not close. We all were at the cemetery in Cecil, Georgia. They had no funeral for Son, just a simple graveside service. During the service, it started to rain and I gave Miss Mollie, Buddy's mother, my raincoat to put on her shoulders. She looked so sad. When they began lowering Son's casket, Miss Mollie began screaming, crying to the top of her voice. Someone had to help her to her car. You would think that it was her child, not the other way around.

Buddy served his time on the chain gang. When he was released, he married my only elementary schoolmates, Doris Williams (later Doris Harris). They reared a big family after that in Valdosta. I would go by to see them from time to time when I was in Valdosta.

Back to the bus driver. Mr. Connie was a good man. He cared for the students. He was the only bus driver we had as long as I knew; in fact, we only had one bus. This bus passed several White schools before it got to our Colored school in Adel. Cecil, Georgia, did not have a school either, and the bus had to pick up the Colored students from that town, too.

Just imagine only an elementary school in "the country"—county for Colored students and one "every grade, first through eleventh" other school, the Cook County Training School.

My First Real Dates

When we started going to Nashville on Saturday and I got to know people in the town, I met this cute young thing that I began seeing on weekends. She lived with her grandma in Nashville on the White side of town. Only a few Colored people lived in that section of town. Most Colored lived 'cross the tracks in "the bottom" where the happenings were.

That Colored school, grades first through the ninth, was in that section of town, 'cross two sets of railroad tracks. The joints and everything else Colored were there, too.

I had this dance in Adel for us to go. The grandma had said no. All her aunts and her mother got together to convince Grandma to let Dorothy go. She finally gave in and let me know that I could pick her up. When I went to pick Dorothy up, all the relatives were there on the porch to see their thirteen- or fourteen-year-old daughter, niece, and granddaughter take off on her first real date—and off we went to Adel to the dance.

I could not stay awake unless I was dancing; thus, I was home early. Everyone thought I was a good boy and did not stay out late at night. They did not realize that I could leave early, do my do, and be home before 10:00 p.m.

I had another similar experience. I had a date in Lowndes County, probably arranged by Charles because this time it was the girlfriend of Charles's girlfriend, Claytis Carter.

When I went to call on her and we were about to leave, her granddaddy said, "Who did you say Claytis was going out with?" One of her brothers told him, "Saul Bethay." He said she might as well go back in her room and take off her clothes because no granddaughter of his is going out with a Bethay. Her grandma pleaded with him to let Claytis go out that night with me. He still insisted that she was not going anywhere with a Bethay. This time the mother, who lived not too far, just on the other side of the fields, was sent for.

The mother came and tried to reason with her daddy. He said no to her also. Then her mother wanted to know why. He mentioned my "drunking" uncle, Uncle Coot, who lived in Valdosta and was always drunk on weekends and hanging around other people's houses, including Miss Bolder's, until she put a stop to it.

Claytis's mother told her father that what his uncle does has no bearing on this boy, and she was to go.

That relationship continued throughout our college days. Claytis went to Albany State and I went to Fort Valley State; graduating the same year I did and at the same age. I was six months older than she. I went to her Junior-Senior Prom in Albany in our senior year.

We remained friends throughout her lifetime. She married and left the Valdosta area and lived between Macon and Atlanta until her husband died, and then she returned to Valdosta and brought her own home and taught in the city until her retirement, sickness for many years, amputation, and finally death.

After she returned to Valdosta, I would visit her each time I was in town, and many times I stayed with her. I am still friends with the family. Her mother recently died (January 2014) and her stepfather did 2013. Her parents always it seems to have owned the only Negro dry-cleaning business in Valdosta until they could not do it any longer in 2013.

Before all of this dating took place, I had my own car, and previously Mama and I went to Nashville and got our driving license at the same time. I am now fifteen, and I did not want Daddy to cut my hair with those scissors anymore.

I would be into a good play in the yard, and he would say, "Boy, go get those scissors." He would sit down, and I had to lie 'cross his legs while he cut my hair with those scissors.

Being the person I said Daddy was, he could get that looking glass and cut his own hair with those scissors. He shaved with a straight razor and used that shaving brush with some bar soap to lather with.

Now I began getting my hair cut in the barbershop on Saturday in Nashville. I had my own money from all those aforementioned jobs in addition to other jobs, sometimes depending on the season, pulling tobacco plants, harvesting cabbage plants, or washing car dealers' store windows on Saturday mornings in Nashville when we did not have work to do at home.

My big thing was during the summer in the fields cropping tobacco. I first drove the sled for a $1 a day. But that was not enough. The older boys and men got $5 a day. I told whomever that I too could crop tobacco at ten years of age. I would take three leaves off the bottom of each stalk, whether they were ready or not. This way I could be fast doing it. I did not have to look at each leaf before I decided which one was ready.

Now that I was really dating, I needed my own money and I had it. I did not have to go to Mama or Daddy for any more money—they could keep their fifty cents. Ha-ha!

I dated other girls while in high school. In fact, I dated Arvenia Jackson in our junior year. Arvenia was the granddaughter of the richest Colored man in Adel, Cook County, Georgia. He was Mr. Dave, as he was called by Coloreds, or just Dave by Whites. He always wore overalls and went barefoot. He brought corn and cotton from the farmers, and he would ground your corn for meal and grits. The grits was so "husty" until it took about a bucket of water to wash enough grits for twelve people. I do believe he also brought livestock from farmers as well, especially hogs.

My sister Annie Mae married one of Mr. Dave's nephews, Ulysses Jackson. Mr. Dave had two sons and two daughters. One of the sons was Arvenia's daddy, Mr. Ellis, and one of his daughters, Grace Jackson, taught elementary education at the CCTS. Arvenia had two stepsisters who were twins—Mary and Martha. I could only tell them apart when I could see Martha's mole on the left side of her face. As I remember, Arvenia's other uncle's name was Buddie Jackson and her aunt's name was Doris Jackson. They all live in the big house on their big business lot as one entered Adel from the south on Highway 41.

One day I was in Adel and telephoned Mr. Dave's house for Arvenia. Mr. Ellis answered the phone. He asked who was it? I gave some girl's name and quickly hung up. That so-called courtship did not last long. Later I started going with Arvenia's cousin, Lola Mae (I don't remember her last name—). After graduation some of my family and I were invited to Lola Mae's house, where we ate dinner and took graduation pictures of me and with me. I still have some of those pictures from May 1950.

Later years, Lola Mae married one of my sister Annie Mae's brothers-in-law, Alfonso Jackson (Six Degrees of Separation). Alfonso was in school with me at my first school. In fact, it was his daddy. Mr. Pete, who stopped Theodore Jackson and Riley Shaw from fighting about my lunch at the County Line Elementary School in 1939.

During my four years of high school, I had English, math, science, biology, a month of literature, and a semester of French I. I have never had the following courses in any of my schools: penmanship, physical education, art, music, foreign language as a course, algebra, trig, or physics. In high school, other classes were taught some of the traditional subjects, but my class was taught differently each of our four years We had no physical education building either; thus, we had no gym classes. I still do not know why we were also treated differently during graduation exercises.

During my high school years, when it rained, three times the two rivers flooded. One time I was able to cross by taking off my clothes and pushing the bike from the far edge of the bridges in flowing water up to my knees. (I was never fearful and I always thought that I was a good swimmer. I was the one who had to see if the rivers were safe to dive in before the older brothers did.)

I learned to swim at seven years of age, two days after my older two brothers had learned days before, just one day apart, too. We all learned to swim the same week. We learned to swim in a swamp where one had to pull leaches out of his legs, and there were snakes and turtles in that swamp, too. My brothers and I did not have to go to church on Sundays. We would use that time to hunt, fish, or swim. One Sunday after church, H. S. and Joe Fleming went with us to see the new swimming place we had found on the creek. Rushing to get in the water, Joe's shirt got caught on his heel and it went into the water with him. We stayed at the creek as long as we could, trying to let the sun dry his shirt. But that did not happen. We later took Joe home with some lie as to why the shirt was wet. His mother said that story did not hold water. I am sure he was whipped that Saturday night after he had had his tub bath. This was the Fleming tradition—beatings saved up from the week's wrongdoings.

I was almost drowned one Fourth of July celebration on one of those rivers mentioned earlier. I dove in one of those same rivers to see how far I could go and stay under the water without coming up for air. Mr. Johnny McSwain thought that I was drowning because I was under the water so long. He jumped in on top of me just as I was about to surface. Mr. Johnny almost made me drown and he went around saying how he saved me from drowning. I could swim better than him (he).

During high school, the rivers never flooded where I could not cross when I was on the home side of the rivers. Following a bad flood, as much as two weeks having to stay away from home without clothes, I stayed one week with my cousin/classmate Dorothy's family and the other week with another cousin, Ralph Williams, who lived on the same school bus route at the time.

At night, I would wish my clothes and dry them by the fire using up all the family firewood. My cousin Dorothy's daddy (Uncle Gene) got up one of those mornings and went hunting for a rabbit for meat for breakfast. His only son Willie James (W.J.) told his daddy that he liked Billy better than he did him because he never got up to kill a rabbit for him.

Another time Russell and I were spending a night at this cousin's house, and I was sleeping in the middle of them. I wanted my cousin to move over in the bed. He did not want to move and I told Uncle Gene. My uncle told him to move. W. J. told his father that he was not going to fall out of the bed for Billy. (My older relatives still call me Billy today.)

Even before high school, it was in 1941 that my favorite Uncle Gene died. His untimely death would not be the case today, but then Colored people were not readily admitted or treated at the "Whites'" hospitals.

One Sunday at the County Line Methodist Church, Uncle Gene became ruptured. His brothers, included my daddy, tried to help him recover by laying him upside down on the back of a chair. The more they rubbed his stomach, the more and louder he screamed in pain. They then rushed him to Valdosta's hospital, where he died two weeks later.

I could not stop crying at his funeral back at the County Line Methodist Church. This was a new church, a replacement for the burned-down one Dorothy and I started to school in 1939. It was the first time I saw my daddy cry. Daddy helped gather Uncle Gene's crop that year.

Following are more of my highlights during my high school years between September 1946 and May 1950.

There were times when something was happening at school at night and I would stay in town with another cousin, Emanuel Durden, a cousin on my mother's side of the family. Emanuel was also in my high school class—not too smart but a lover. All the girls liked him. He was one of four boys in my high school class along with twelve girls. Emanuel worked at the same lumberyard all his adult life, the same mill I worked at briefly.

Manuel, as we called him, reared a nice large family. He had about six lovely children. He and our cousin Ralph, my second cousin and Emanuel's first cousin, became the weekend drunks, going several times back and forth to the County Line liquor store to get whiskey. Cook County was a "dry" county for the sale of alcohol at that time. Lowndes County (the county Valdosta was in) was not.

Emanuel was killed riding his bike one day by the son of the owner of the plant he worked in. No charges were ever filed because the driver of the car which killed him was the son of the owner of the plant where Emanuel worked. Emanuel's wife, Helen, had died a few years earlier from cancer.

I always wanted to have my own money. I did not mind working for it. I would hire myself out to other farmers, doing farm chores for $3 per day. During the Second World War, the German prisoners who were brought back here to the States were hired out to the farmers to do farmwork. I, at about ten years of age, was there to work, but the prisoners could not understand this kid out there trying to do what they were doing. They would not let me work. They made me stay in the shade of the trees, and they gave me some of the best sandwiches for lunch each day. A summer I shall never forget.

I am sure my daddy did not know about the Germans out there either. Also during the World War II, sharecroppers were hired by the Federal Government to help build runways for the airplanes to land and take off at Moody Air Force Base in Valdosta, Georgia. My daddy helped build the runways off season.

Also, during President Franklin D. Roosevelt's time, we got ration stamps for sugar and shoes. We sold our sugar stamps to Whites because we ate syrup instead of using sugar, and we had honey from the bees. There were the CCC camps for boys and WPA workers for men (I don't remember what those stood for). We collected and sold scrap iron for a little extra cash, also.

I even worked at a lumber mill during high school, and when I got my first pay of $15, the family came to town thinking I would have the money for groceries, but I had spent it on those crepe-soled shoes. I guess in those days, Colored people could not take things back and my parents never confronted me about that. They took it as if they knew that was my money to spend any way I wanted to.

Not having had any geography in school, in 1941, when the Japanese bombed Pearl Harbor, I thought Berrien County would be next. I did not know the distance Hawaii was from Side Camp. During the war, I loved looking at the parade of airplanes going and coming 'cross the sky.

Another time during high school, my brother Charles had come home to visit from Miami and had lost his license. He asked me to drive with him back to Miami, and he would send me back to Valdosta, Georgia via bus (there was no bus to Nashville then). When we reached the city limits of Titusville, Florida, I became tired and Charles began driving. Apparently, he was driving too fast and the patrolman pulled us over, with Charles having no license driving. They took us to jail. I went too because I had no other place to go, and I was not driving on to Miami without Charles, inasmuch as that was our reason for being there in the first place.

We had to spend three days in jail until our sister Alline got a copy of Charles's license and brought it to us.

There was no fax or anything like that at that time. The guys in jail said that they were going to beat us up unless we gave them some money. Charles said we had no money and turned his ring around on his finger to begin fighting. I began crying and one guy said to leave those boys alone because they looked like good boys. Which they did. The jailers let me help in the kitchen, and I would fix Charles's food. This may have been my first real cooking experience because I did not have to cook at home.

We got the license. They let us out. We drove on to Miami. My first trip. Charles worked at the Hialeah Race Track, taking care of the famous horses. I visited the stables and looked at all those fine horses for hours. The racetrack is a beautiful place even today. My sister Alline had to house me and wait until she got paid on the weekend to send me back to Georgia.

On the way to the bus station, I was able to see that part of Miami but was afraid because Alline had fallen asleep and I felt we would miss our stop. But that was not the case. We got there, and while in the bus station, a Colored man got down on the floor and crawled to the back of this lady's seat of this lady who had her pocketbook on the floor. I saw it happening but did not know what to do. I did or said nothing. I knew when to keep quiet unless it was my father I was talking to. I learned that too later.

Now on the bus to Valdosta, Georgia, my seatmate was a lady who had left her husband for a while and was on her way back to him in Jacksonville; the town I had to change buses for Valdosta. Before we reach Jacksonville, Florida, she had told me her whole life story in detail, and she said she had never told anyone all the things she had told me, but she felt better after having done so. Maybe that was another counseling experience like cooking in jail was my first cooking experience.

During summers, my nephews and nieces would come stay with us. I always kept candy and they would ask for some. I would say, "Call me Uncle Saul and I will give you some." They would say, "Uncle Saul, give me some candy." I would give them some candy, and as soon as they had it in their hands, they would say "Billy" and run off laughing.

Now let us move to my senior year at the Cook County Training School. By this time, Charles was working in a hat factory in Connecticut. He would come home with his name in his new hats.

Charles also had a white convertible car with a black top. He decided to give it to me to drive to school the last part of my senior year. One day a teacher asked me to drop off her clothes at the cleaners on the way home. I forgot, and when I reached home, a neighbor was there and he saw the ladies' clothes in the back seat of the car. He told Daddy that Billy girlfriend left her clothes in his car. He was just playing around with me.

My daddy had taken my grandmother to Jacksonville to visit her blind, sick sister. We had to pick him up in Valdosta on his return. We went to town that Saturday to get Daddy. When we got there, I asked Mama for some money. She tried to give me fifty cents. I told her if that was all she had, she needed it more than me. The others got their little money and went to the movies and ate popcorn, ice cream, etc. I sat pouting. Daddy got there and they shopped for the flour, grits, fish, and other needed things for the house. When we got home, I jumped out of the car without taking any groceries.

My daddy came in and said, "Young man, can't you help take the groceries in the house?"

I said, "Daddy I have decided that if I work all week and come Saturday and all you have for me is fifty cents, then I am not working anymore."

By that time, Daddy had his belt off and hit me about three times. Then he stopped and said, "I am never going to whip you anymore, you are not learning a damn thing in school and you are not going back. You will stay here and work from now on."

I am a senior ready to graduate in May, and that man said I was not to finish high school after all that bicycle riding, crossing those rivers, and staying away from home for weeks without a change of clothes.

He let me suffer all Sunday and get dressed for school on Monday. I picked up the car keys and my books, waiting any minute for him to tell me, "Boy, do you remember what I told you Saturday night?" I walked to the car. I got in. I cranked the car and drove off.

Now it is two weeks before graduation. Dorothy came to me and asked if anyone had come to me about the valedictorian speech. I said no. "What about the salutatorian speech?" She too said no. I said, "I hope they don't think that I can write a speech and deliver it in two weeks."

The next week our advisor took us across the street to the church we were to have our graduation in because our auditorium was under renovation. Our advisor left a copy of the graduation program on the bench and Dorothy got it. She showed it to me and not only were we not valedictorian and salutatorian, we were only listed as graduating. The rich Negro in Adel, Pete Jackson's granddaughter Arvenia, was listed as first honor and another girl, Ollie Pearld Holmes, was second honor.

Arvenia was smart but had completed only two years of high school at the Cook County Training School. She did not meet the qualifications for valedictorian for that reason alone; traditionally the graduating class would have a valedictorian, a salutatorian, and first, second, and third honors—not this graduation.

Traditionally, some of the White store owners would give a few dollars to the girl and boy in the class with the highest averages. That year Mr. Deloach, our principal, gave two students in the graduating class (girls) top "honors" which had nothing to do with their averages. Dorothy and I had the top grades.

Mr. Deloach gave Willie Frank Elliott, a junior in the school with the highest average, the White folks' money at my graduation from the Cook County Training School in Adel, Georgia.

During the Commencement Exercises, Willie Frank was so confused when the principal called him to come up each time to the podium to get the money. He was dressed in a suit because I do think he was an usher at the ceremony.

This scene caused such a disturbance in the audience until it continued when the speaker tried to deliver his speech? The speaker finally stopped and sat down because no one was listening to him after that money scene.

One teacher did get up and take off her robe after about the third time Willie Frank Elliot went up to the stage to get money, which I should have been given.

After we marched out, Willie Frank came up to me and said, "Take this money, I am not graduating until next year."

I said, "Keep it until then and then you will have double."

I had no bad feelings toward Willie Frank. He had nothing to do with this. He did what he had to do at that time. (I saw Willie Frank in an Air Force drilling squadron passing when we both were in basic training in Lackland Air Force Base, San Antonio, Texas, in September 1954.) Dorothy said after graduation that she got what she came for and that was the diploma. So be it.

That was the good part. I applied to my teachers' alma mater, the Fort Valley State College (FVSC), for entrance in September 1950. Come August, I had not heard from them. I stopped my daddy from working when I got the letter from FVSC, stating that they had not received my transcript. Daddy did not know what a transcript was but knew it was something needed to get into college. We put the mules in the stable and got in the car and went to Adel, looking for the principal. He was nowhere to be found until about 5:00 p.m. My daddy said, "My boy said you were supposed to send something to college for him."

He said, "I did not think he was going."

My daddy pointed his finger in the principal's face and told him, "Send it!" And we got back into the car and went over those rivers, going home.

Soon thereafter, FVSC informed that I had been accepted for the September 1950 class but Sears Roe Buck and Company said I did not get the $100 scholarship because I did not have agriculture in high school.

Here I am after sixteen years on the farm, learning by experience more than any high school would ever be able to teach me, getting turned down. But like everything else before this, this did not stop me. When I got to Fort Valley, I had already declared my major as agriculture, trying to get the scholarship, and I did not change it. Otherwise, I would have been a biology major.

Agriculture turned out to be the best major for me as I will explain in detail when I get to college.

Before I go further, let me shake the family trees.

The Bethay Family Tree

Mary Inman Bethay Baker and Grandpa Beck

Grandma Mary was the center of the family. All the family affairs centered around her. And we got to know her well and best because she always lived near us until Daddy and Mama and the rest of my family moved to Miami in 1954. She then moved to live with her daughter, Nettie, in Valdosta, who had a house full of grandchildren all the time. But that helped her live over a hundred years of age.

Grandma Mary did not live a full year after my father was killed. He was working under the car I had left for them, and the jack fell. Down came the car. More later on this.

When we lived near Cecil, Georgia, Grandma was near. When we moved across the river, they moved and were near. Before my grandparents moved across the river, the biggest annual family gathering was Grandpa Beck's birthday celebration at our house in the front yard.

All her living children, my uncles and aunts, helped with the arrangements. We had dinner on the ground, as it was called then. Everybody bought food—fried chicken, chicken and dumplings, potato salad, black-eyed-peas, pies, corn bread, collard greens, rice, etc. The aunts made their favorite cakes and pies. We children did not eat plain or pound cake; they always had to be layer cakes and homemade icing in the center and on top, with no jelly filling. Jelly was for "poor" people who did not have eggs to make cake fillings.

Grandpa Beck

I have told you most about him already. He had no teeth but could bite an apple and that was the thing he would do to make us children laff.

He did leave Grandma Mary for another woman he had met in Nashville for a while. I cannot remember how long. We had to stay with Grandma a lot of the time during that period. Lucky she only lived 'cross the field from where we lived, and we took care of her.

As we got older, we started going to Nashville on Saturdays to do those things we used to do on Saturday in Adel. Nashville was closer and had more juke joints than Adel. Now I don't remember Adel having any joints at the time. Nashville had three and we would go from one to the other, eating and dancing after seeing the cowboy movie and serial in the balcony with the popcorn.

I danced. I was a good dancer, and the girls and ladies loved dancing with me. I did not drink, but Russell and Charles did.

We would see Grandpa Beck in town on Saturday afternoons. One time, he had bought a big bag of mullet fish for his new family and we told Grandma. Much later, he came back sick to live with Grandma. She took him back and took care of him with all the old "home remies." We had not stopped loving him. I don't think my family ever hated anyone; we did not practice that.

Grandpa Beck remained in poor health until he died in 1943.

We had his funeral at County Line Church and buried him in the cemetery there, also. I remember crying at his funeral too. I guess you say I was a crybaby. I cried at my baby sister's funeral as well, either a few weeks earlier or after.

I cried also because Mama was crying so—crying when Gloria Jean could hardly breathe and those ladies were trying to give her some type of medicine which she could not take. A hospital was not an option. Gloria Jean could have been alive today if things were different among the races—prejudice and segregation, just pure racism.

Aunt Nettie Bethay McGee

Aunt Nettie and Uncle Sam had the most children among their siblings. They had fourteen.

When Uncle Sam died, we did not fully undress because we thought we would be going back to Aunt Nettie's funeral soon. They had never been separated for any period since they were married. When you saw one, you always saw the other one soon—a devoted couple throughout their married life.

They buried Uncle Sam, and soon after, Aunt Nettie could be seen everywhere. She took on a behavior of a younger person. I believed she too lived near, if not over, one hundred. At the time of this writing, I believe there are only one boy and one girl living, George and Viola ("Sister")—George in Miami and Viola in Valdosta.

Dorothy and I were at their house on the day of Aunt Nettie's funeral. I remember the cops outside telling every driver to park on only one side of the street (road). Later they began telling the newcomers to park on both sides because they were more than four or five blocks away from the house now.

Dorothy said let us go ahead to the church; otherwise, we would not be able to get in. To our surprise when we got near the Mount Ollie Baptist Church, one would think that it was on the fourth of August. Each year, hundreds of people all over the place, near and far, would be selling everything from homemade ice cream to corn liquor (moonshine brew). They had church for some, but most of the people and activities were outside. The big thing was waiting for the drunk Sonny Register, driving his car as fast as it could go, to run it into a tree across a ditch. This would happen every year. He acted as if he were on a program for this scary moment. Everybody knew when anyone yelled "Sonny is coming" to get out of his way.

Mount Ollie Church was located about ten to fifteen miles north of Valdosta between Hahira, Cecil, and Adel to the west and Nashville, Ray City, and Side Camp to the north.

Uncle Jack

Skin color and hair type were the two characteristics which determined one to be pretty. The lighter the skin and the straighter or curlier the hair, the prettier one would be. Uncle Jack was pretty.

I don't remember much more about Uncle Jack other than he was always well dressed and did not live on the farm or do farmwork. He had four daughters: Leola, Thelma, Rosa, and Ella Mae and one son, Rollie Bethay. I would see them at Grandpa Beck's birthday celebration each year at our house. (Ella Mae later married Thelpo Slater and had five children. Charlyne is in charge of the Bi-Annual Bethay-Inman Family Reunion in Valdosta as I write this.)

The Bethay boys would get off to themselves and talk in a circle while the womenfolk prepared the food for serving. When one of them wanted to pee, he just took it out and peed.

(Charlyne's brother Joe started the reunion. He always did an excellent job too, but he got tired of that hard work and decided to give it up and that is when Charlyne took it over. Another Cousin, Lee Walker, Sr. wanted to do it one year, but it was not too successful. If it were not for Charlyne, we would have had a disaster. More about the reunion later.)

Sula Bethay Williams

Sula Bethay Williams was the seventh child, and her brothers were Jack, Walter, Gary, Coot, Jeff, James, Ludie, and Henry.

Aunt Sula was married to James "Jim" Williams until she died of breast cancer—the first family member I knew who had cancer.

They had thirteen children, and only one is living (Annie Lee Hunter) at the time of this writing. Jim was the oldest boy who worked at Sears in Valdosta as long as I knew him as an adult. He had a good job during that time. He was not farming or sharecropping anymore like my daddy and Uncle Gene. Uncle Jim died first, as I recall, and we did not see much of this family after we moved 'cross the river. They all ended up living in Valdosta, and we would see some of them some time or when we were at some type of gathering, which brought some of us together.

Uncle Walter (Walt)

I knew Uncle Walter and his family best for a time. We would go by their house occasionally when we were in Valdosta where they lived.

James Gene Bethay

My favorite Uncle.

Uncle Gary

Uncle Gary and his family lived in Quitman, Georgia. I never knew the rest of his family, only him by seeing him at Grandpa Beck's birthday.

Uncle Coot

The only thing I remember about Uncle Coot was that he was the Saturday-night drunk and would go by the house of Miss Bolder (Miss Viola's sister) and hang on her porch and clown and sing. She broke that up by putting a white sheet over herself and went out the back door and came around the house waving her arms like a "hant" (ghost).

Ludie Bethay

My father.

Uncle Jeff

Uncle Jeff was dead.

Uncle Henry

Uncle Henry was away in Florida, unable to return to Georgia. I was given his name for my middle name.

The Chandler Family Tree

Grandma Chandler and Grandpa Chandler
(deceased prior to my birth; I never knew him)

Children

Annie Chandler Williams (my grandmother, Marie Williams Bethay's mother)
Edith Chandler Williams (Ralph and Alfred's mother)
Rachel Chandler Durden (Emanuel's mother)
Arbelle Chandler Williams

Charlie Williams and Annie Chandler Williams, my grandparents

Children

Marie Williams Bethay (my mother)
Partene Williams
Mary Lou Williams Utley
Alma Williams Miles
Lillian Williams Houston
Wilbur Williams
Charlie Mae Williams

I REMEMBER VERY LITTLE about Grandma Chandler. Grandpa Chandler was dead before I got here. I do remember that they lived on the road between Adel and Nashville. Special family functions were held at her house when all the children and grandchildren were present: birthdays, funeral repasts, etc.

The next thing I remember about Grandma Chandler was when she came to live with one of her daughters, Aunt Arbelle, before she died. It was there where I saw and remember her the most. We would visit them on some weekends and times when we would stop by coming from Adel on Saturday.

We had to get off the main road and go through some winding road with space enough for one car to Uncle Golden and Aunt Arbelle Williams's house. They were among the few Negroes who owned a farm with all its attachments, barns, cribs, livestock—you name it. (They were like Claytis Carter's family in Valdosta.)

One Saturday afternoon, we were on our way there to see Grandma Chandler when as Daddy made one of those curves in the road, Robert White's family was in their car coming toward us. The two cars collided; we had an accident. The broken window knob on the door made a big cut into Mama's right arm. We had to go back to Adel for the doctor to sew or tape it up. The arm healed, but when Mama died, she had that scar on her arm.

I do remember Robert White getting out of their car after the accident and began running until someone stopped him. I do not know what he was scared of or running from. Even today, he says he does not remember that accident. It was before his sister, Miss White, taught at the Side Camp Elementary School and before Robert and I were in the Cook County Training School together.

I also remember that Charles, Russell, and I were about to jump into that river near Uncle Golden's house when he stopped us before we dove in. Uncle Golden told us to wait a minute and let me show you boys how deep that river was, as if we did not know. But he was under the water a long time. That did not stop us.

It was at Aunt Arbelle and Uncle Golden's house where some of our best family cookouts took place. This family was the best cooks in the world. The family reunions were held there until our cousin

Grace Durden started having them at her house years later. Then after Grace died, our cousin Jack and Florrie (King) Thomas starting having them at their house out in the country near Aunt Arbelle's place. The men, including Ralph and Emanuel, would drink and barbeque that meat all night.

For many years after Jack Thomas died, Florrie still held the family reunion at her place. It was just a few years ago (maybe at the turn of the century) that she stopped trying to do that each year.

Mama's people mostly lived in Florida, Saint Petersburg, and Tampa. I remember once Grandma Annie came to visit us. They had to buy Shredded Wheat for her. We thought it was so funny seeing her eating "hay," as we thought it was. One Christmas, Mama, Zipha, Marian and Bobby went to St. Pete to visit Grandma Annie and the other family members living in Florida.

Daddy, I, and a boy from Nashville who had been helping us dip tar before Christmas took them to Valdosta to take a bus to St. Pete. After they left, Daddy gave me a handful of money and said to take the boy home (Nashville, Georgia). This meant I spent that Christmas alone. Mama never knew about this, but I remember crying on my way home from Nashville with just money and no family. It was almost as bad as the Christmas in 1956 in Tokyo with just Airman Robert J. Small. I'll tell you about this later.

One summer, Aunt Alma and her two daughters at the time came to visit us when we were at the Nix's place. It was great having them with us for a while. We always saw each other afterward at the family reunions and funerals.

I never got to see Mama's brother Wilbur and, Aunt Partene was dead before I was born. Aunt Charlie Mae died while I was in the Air Force. I saw Aunt Lillian and Aunt Mary Lou at funerals when the funerals were not theirs. It all depended on who died first or last. It either had to be a family reunion or a funeral for us to get together.

(When I was in college at Fort Valley, Aunt Alma and Aunt Lillian would put me a five- or ten-dollar-bill in an envelope and send me occasionally. Now you can see why the students thought I was too rich to live on campus my freshman year.)

My Family Tree: A Little Information about My Siblings and Me

You will be better able to understand me and appreciate from whence I came.

Annie Mae Bethay Jackson* and Ulysses Jackson

The oldest sibling living at the time of this writing, died in August 2017, Annie Mae married Ulysses "Ula" Jackson, and they had one son, Vincent, and he had two boys and three girls.

Ula was home from military leave and was helping Daddy tow a car back to the house when the towed car was hit by another car coming fast across the hill. The car Ula was in turned over several times. Everyone thought Ula was killed. They were near the house when this accident happened.

Ula survived the accident. He and my sister moved to Miami. They accumulated several houses there in Miami. Years later in Opa-Locka, Florida, it was Ula who told my daddy not to go under the jacked-up car until he got back. Daddy did not listen, and before Ula got back, he heard the car fall and Daddy was under it, crushed to death. They took Daddy to the hospital nearby, but he was dead on arrival. More later about Daddy's death.

On my tenth birthday, I was having a few friends in for a party, and Annie Mae made me a white-icing layer cake. When she finished it, the guests were there and she wanted the icing to harden some before cutting it. She put it in the icebox on top of the block of ice. Not knowing this, I went in the icebox to get some ice, and out comes the cake on my feet. Annie Mae said, "You all are going to eat it as it is." She scooped it up and we ate it with a spoon. It was delicious. We had an icebox by then.

Annie Mae was always an independent businesswoman. With the least years of formal education, she was always able to keep a job; most of the time working in you know who houses.

It was one of her houses our parents lived in in Opa Locka, Florida, when we moved from Brown Sub to 153rd Street. She lived in her other house on 163rd Street in Opa Locka and owned the lot across the street in front of the house our parents were now living.

A house became available two lots from the end of her property. I did not know about buying on credit and paying all of that interest over many years, and I said no to my parent. One of my brothers-in-law, Hiram Culmer, helped them get the house. I always sent them money to help pay the mortgage once they got it. When I went into the Air Force after college, I had an allotment made out to my parents for $50 each month for the four years that I was in service. So they and I always knew the mortgage would be paid. I became a Tenant in Common with Rights of Survivorship. Thus, when Mama died, I became sole owner of the property in Opa-locka.

I was going to buy the house next to my house in Opa-locka, but a storage bin had been built on the property and the city of Miami wanted me to pay years of back taxes for the bin—almost half as much as I was going to pay for the house. No way, Jose. Otherwise, I too would be the owner of two houses next to each other in Opa-locka, Florida.

After many a year living in one of Annie Mae's houses, we have her to thank for helping our parents get settled in their own house until they both passed away. This was the first and only home my parents ever owned.

Alline Bethay-Roberts-Culmer

Alline was the first sibling to have a child. She had eight in all. One is dead. It was this child who was born in our house on Miss Susan's place when we could not get our books. That oldest nephew, Carroway X. Roberts, became a famous singer and recording artist, owning his own band and performing around the world, including New York City, and opening for Moms Mabley. He has performed with the best.

When Cal was little, Alline needed someone to help her with him. Mama agreed with her that I should go. I had no say in the matter and really did not want to go. I hated it. I missed being home with my siblings and friends cross the river.

The first day I was playing in the backyard and ran into the water pump handle and burst my face above one eye. I cried, hoping that would get me back home. But it didn't. She put some white tape over some cotton and that was that.

Like Daddy's watermelons, Alline had a beautiful white suit in her clothes closet. I took some scissors and cut a piece out of one of the sleeves. I said the rats had done it. I cannot remember how long I had to stay, but I do know I was back home for school at Side Camp.

Alline and I have always had a good relationship. And she has always been proud of me and my achievements in and out of school. I must say none of my siblings every seemed to envy whatever I did or whomever I helped. I can say they all did well themselves; they all ended up owning their own homes, and most of them always had more than one. I am really proud of my entire family. I tell everybody that I have and always had the best family. I would not change that for Oprah's money.

Charles Ludie Bethay

Charles has always been my big brother. We have always had a good brotherly relationship. He was always concerned about me and my welfare. I credited him with making sure that I learned to be an independent boy and man. He taught me everything he knew: swimming, hunting, and the facts of life.

We were night fishing once and we had set lines. My cork was bobbing when Charles came by. He pulled up the line and a catfish was on it. I was most concerned that everyone knew it was my fish Charles had caught, and I kept telling him on the way home that it was my fish he pulled out of that river on my line.

The "Rolling Store" man came by the house during the summer once a week. One could buy dry goods, groceries, and candy from him, and he also had a fish tank on the back of the store/truck. We could buy fish from him, which we did when we did not have time to fish on our own. One day after our purchases and he was leaving, Charles and Russell stole some more fish from his fish bin off the back of his rolling store. I guess we needed the fish bad enough until Daddy did not say anything or beat them because he knew where the mullets came from and he had not brought them,

One Saturday Daddy, Charles, Russell, and I had gone to Adel. After all the stores were closed, Daddy was nowhere to be found. We waited as long as we could, and Charles said we better start walking home—it was the distance I had to ride that bike each day going to school. It was just when we got near home, about 1:00 a.m., Sunday, that Daddy drove up, too drunk to come into the house without staggering all over the yard, even falling down. Before Daddy had come, I was so tired walking those twenty or more miles. I began crying. Charles comforted me.

Another time Cousin Dorothy was in a play at her school—County Line Elementary School—and we wanted to see it. For some reason we did not have transportation, and I do not know why because Daddy always had some type of car or truck; in fact, he took his car and took an ax and cut that car in half and made him a truck. I said that he could have been an engineer if he could have had the schooling. He had the brains for it.

At any rate, after we finished our field work and got dressed, we three boys started walking from Side Camp, where we live, to Dorothy's school, about ten or more miles. Dorothy and the cast were doing their last number when we got there. Immediately we had to walk with them to their house, which was near the rivers. Again, I was so tired until they had to almost drag me. That is why I do not like walking or riding bicycle today. I have five bikes in my garage at the writing of this section.

It was Charles who gave me a car to drive to school in my last year of high school. Charles too was pleased with my interest in education, and he did everything he could to help me in any way to achieve. Can you imagine how popular I was with my own car at fifteen, picking up my own dates in a black-and-white convertible before I graduated from high school?

When Charles was dating his wife, who had a younger sister, he tried hooking us up. We had a few dates and went to each of our proms the same night. What a disaster. She was unhappy when she was at the Cook County Training School Junior-Senior Prom in Adel. I was equally unhappy when we went to her Lowndes County High School Junior-Senior Prom out from Valdosta, in the country.

We spent more time between the proms on the road than we did at the proms. In addition to my being too immature for Elizabeth, I feel the proms did the most damage to our relationship.

Charles, you tried. Elizabeth and I remained good friends even to today. Her sister Mae and my brother Charles were married for many years. May they both rest in peace! It was they whom I spent Thanksgiving with in Flint, Michigan, the year I was at Michigan State College in East Lansing. It was Michigan State College when I was there from 1959 to 1960. More about MSC later.

Russell Bethay

Russell was the quiet one. You never quite knew what he was thinking. Let me share with you a few additional experiences we had growing up. It was he who took advantage of Daddy's kindness. He seemed to have been able to get away with more things than anyone else without any type of punishment other than the few times already mentioned.

Russell wanted a dog. Russell got a dog. When Russell got tired of the dog, it became my responsibility. Russell wanted a bike.

Russell got a bike. Russell wanted a blind horse. Russell got a blind horse. Billy got the bike. That was a good thing because the bike was my transportation to high school for three and a half years.

Russell and I almost killed Charles. We were in the cotton house playing on the pile of picked cotton. We covered Charles's head with cotton and sat on it. It was only when he stopped moving that we realized he was in serious trouble. We did have the sense enough to slap his face until he came to.

Another time we were helping one of our neighbors pick cotton—the family whose boy's shirt went into the water on his heel. Russell took a match and lit a boll of cotton. It started burning his finger and he dropped it. He was standing near a sheet of cotton and the burning cotton fell on a sheet of cotton and that set the whole cotton field on fire.

I do not know how Daddy dealt with Mr. Cary about this because Mr. Cary too was a sharecropper. The White man had to have been concerned, too. But to the best of my knowledge, Russell was not even reprimanded.

Like Charles, he tried to hook me up with the sister of the girl he was dating at the time. That never got off the ground. I knew I was too inexperienced for her. I spoke at this girl's funeral in February 2014—Dorothy Stubb Pruitt. We too remained friends and Russell married her sister, Ella Mae Bethay* (died January 2018). They had five children.

Later in life, he and Ella became separated and he moved to Miami to be near his four sisters. Russell suffered with a stroke, which affected his mobility. Zipha and Alline were his health overseers, especially Zipha. It was she who brought Russell in from the nursing home he was staying after he could not live any longer alone. She and Robert took good care of him up to his unexpected heart attack one morning in their home which caused his death,

Russell looked forward to my annual visit to Miami. We spent some of my days there on the beach together. We would see each other every even year in Valdosta at the Bethay-Inman Family Reunion.

Our relationship was such that he made me trust of his financial affairs before he died. May he too rest in peace.

Zipha "Zip" Lee Bethay-Bryant-Goins

A Capricorn. It seems as if we have and have always had more in common among the siblings.

Where do I begin trying to explain that? The best place is to begin at the beginning.

Let's start with Side Camp Elementary School. I am certain that she started school at five years of age as I did because of her December birthday. But we got separated four years before 1954. Why? And how? I finished a seventh grade elementary school and Zip finished a twelfth grade high school while I finished an eleventh grade high school - all the same schools. That was some of the distance. Enough about that.

We are the only two who attended the same schools throughout college. Zip entered Fort Valley State College the September following my June graduation in 1954. She graduated June 1958.

I got out of the Air Force in time to attend her graduation. I had not been back on that campus since my graduation four years earlier.

Let's back up. I remember our being together in elementary school. We participated in programs and plays. But after my graduating from elementary school at twelve years of age, our time together got scarcer and scarcer.

Though we were not physically together, I always was kept abreast of what she was doing and where she was, especially when she got to college. I knew she was among the best-dressed students on campus because when she needed a dress she would end up with more than one sometimes. Dresses coming from Mama, me, and some of the others. I know Mama and Daddy sent her that $50 allotment I sent them while she was in college to make certain she had what she needed or wanted.

I was a member of Alpha Phi Alpha Fraternity while in college, and she joined Alpha Kappa Alpha Sorority. She went into education to be a teacher. So did I. I ended up teaching at the same school she did her student teaching—Maggie Califf Elementary/High School, Jones County, Gray, Georgia. I could not stand the principal, Mr.

Crofford. Neither could she. She became friendly with the same family in Gray as I did—Mrs. Eppie Hammock and Emory Lamar.

When I graduated from college; I did not go immediately into teaching I joined the Air Force. When Zip graduated from Fort Valley State College, she did office work for many a year before she began teaching. She enjoyed her teaching, and so did I. Zip ended up bowling; I got into shooting pool.

Zipha was always the one who looked after our parents. She is the one family member who has never been far away from them more than a week, if that long, even after marrying and moving out. It was she who took care of Mama's personal needs, church needs, social needs, and more importantly, her medical needs and ended up housing Russell from the health facility he was in until his untimely death in her home—all at the same time taking care of her family and teaching until partial retirement. She is now a business lady. Could one ask any more from one person?

Marian Marie "M" Bethay Wilson

Marian was always called the baby girl since our last female sibling died soon after birth. This position she took seriously. She married. She had children, three boys. She traveled abroad with her military husband, who was on leave and was killed in an auto accident only a few blocks from their home. She too ended up with more than one home.

Left to rear these three small boys, she established an early learning center for two- to three-year-olds. She had those kids doing things first-grade kids were not doing in some of the Black schools in Miami.

She ended up working on her PhD, taught in colleges and universities, and wrote a book (*Facing My Fears with No More Tears*), all after she stopped being a coast guard off the Miami waters, swimming underwater strapped with a tank on her back.

Read her book and you will see why I am so proud of her!

Robert Don Bethay

When Bobby was born, I was seven. We spent only one year together in school (1945–1946). I went to high school in another town (Adel), which meant that I left home before he got up in the morning, and he was in or ready for bed when I got home.

He was too young to work much on the farm before I left at sixteen; thus, we spent very little time together. After that, I went to college. When I graduated from Fort Valley in June 1954, he went into the Army and I went into the Air Force.

We were never home together on leave during my four years in the military. Bobby made a career out of the Army.

I saw him at Daddy's, Mama's, and Russell's funerals—all in Miami. He and his first wife and their son stopped through New York on their way from Germany one year. It has been just the last five years that we have tried to stay in contact. I saw him at two family reunions in Georgia and he has been in New York two Christmases.

Our phone contact has diminished recently. But I am happy to report that he has done well and is doing better now that he is retired and has nothing else to do but play the horses. He retired from the Army and the Post Office and was affected somewhat by that Agent Orange when he was in service. Need I say more?

Bobby and his present wife, Su, own their own business in Chicago, which is doing quite well. I was out there a week after our brother Charles died in Flint, Michigan. I flew to Chicago and stayed with them, and we, Bobby and, I drove to Michigan for the funeral. That was the longest and the most time we had spent together since he was ten. I have been to Chicago twice; once to attend the aforementioned funeral and once on a vacation with my friends Cecil G. Smith and Lloyd Matthew from Bermuda.

Fort Valley State College, September 1950

I GUESS MAMA HAD been talking with Miss Viola because some how she knew about my plight about where I was going to stay when I got to Fort Valley now that I had been accepted—no Sears $100 scholarship, which I was counting on. I do not ever remember applying for campus living anyway. Maybe it was because I was not sure how I could afford just being there.

As my Guardian Angels would have it, Miss Viola told Mama that she knew a lady in Fort Valley who lived alone and maybe she would let me stay with her. With no telephone, the Sunday before freshmen were to be at Fort Valley that Monday, Mama, Miss Viola, Daddy, and I got into our old car with my suitcase with my few clothes—no flour sack drawers among them. Charles used to send me clothes when I was in high school too, so I had clothes. Also, I had purchased a few things by now from having my odd jobs here and there; especially once I began courting in high school. I do not know how much of my own money I had, but off we went. Fort Valley is 150 miles from Side Camp.

It was not hard to find the lady's house once we got in town and asked someone because she lived just off the main street from downtown and just a few blocks (streets) from the campus.

We got out and knocked on the door. This somewhat heavyset lady opened the door and came out on the porch. Miss Viola greeted the lady and introduced us and told her why we were there. "This boy wants to go to college and has no place to stay, so I told them that you might let him stay with you." Miss Rhoda Tyson looked at Miss Viola. She looked at Daddy. She looked at Mama. Then she looked at me for the longest, I thought. And she then started the looking process all over again. I started to feel a little nervous by this time.

Miss Rhoda finally said, "There is just one problem. I work on premises and I am home every other weekend and I would not be here with him or be able to cook for him." We were just lucky that was the weekend for her to be home.

Mama spoke up and said, "That would not be necessary, he can take care of himself." I never knew Mama felt that way about me, too. Boy, was I jumping with joy inside.

Then Daddy said, "How much?" The looking started all over again, and finally Miss Rhoda said, "Could you afford $15 a month?" I knew I could make that much with a cup on the street. See, I used to beg for pennies when I went to church on Sundays both at County Line and Side Camp to buy homemade ice cream cones and punch that candy card board; whatever price you punched, you paid that much for a bar of candy, from one penny to five cents, never more.

Back to Fort Valley. Daddy gave the lady the $15 and me $100—the only money he had cleared from the sale of his share of tobacco that summer. I still do not know how they were able to buy gas after that and get home and live thereafter.

They left. I am now feeling lonely already, almost like I was feeling when Alline made me stay with them to help take care of Cal when he was a baby.

Miss Rhoda showed me to my bedroom, a house with a living room, two bedrooms, a kitchen, front and back yards, and a front porch, as I had said. I cannot remember what type of fuel she had. I think it was oil, electricity and an indoor toilet with white toilet paper—from rags to riches in one moment.

I think Miss Rhoda offered me dinner with her. Afterward, I went to the sawmill grocery store, which was open on Sunday because the mill was open on Sunday, as I remember. I purchased some grits, cornflakes, milk, white bread, and some franks, sausages, bacon, cold cuts, and eggs. I was used to seeing Mama shop on Saturday in Adel and Nashville so that was not new to me.

I put the meat in the refrigerator (not icebox)—did I say refrigerator?

Now it is Monday morning. I got up. I took a bath in the bathtub with running hot and cold water. I dressed for college. It was Freshman Orientation Week

I walked the several blocks to the campus and saw all the other students all over the place—the most Negro people I had ever seen in one small area at the same time. I remember going to the auditorium where the other freshmen were in line. I got in line and someone asked me my name. I said proudly, "Saul Henry Bethay." She looked my name up on her list and said, "Yes, Mr. Bethay, here you are." It was my first time ever remembering being called Mister. What a ring. Then she asked me what was I majoring in. I had never given that any thought beyond the Sears's application for the scholarship. I said Agriculture. She gave me a list of my classes for the three-quarters my freshman year. In my day, you did not choose your classes; they were in the catalog for you to take each quarter, depending on your major.

The courses I was taking were English, Math, Freshman Orientation, Farm Machinery, and Introduction to Education. I needed books only for English, math, and education.

(This was the first year beginning Agriculture [Ag] students did not take English and math with the other students. Ag students were always too "dumb" to be in classes with the other students. The French teacher, Mr. Hicks, did not have his required number of students for French, so the administration told him he had to teach that "dumb" class of freshmen Ag students.)

The English requirement was that students had to write a theme (paper) each week. After the first week, Mr. Hicks said we would write the same theme each week until we got it correct—rewriting the weeks' corrections without being graded. I wrote "My First Trip to Miami" every week for that first quarter. When he first gave the paper back to me, it had more red ink on it than it had blue ink, and that was the case for many a week.

Mr. Hicks also required us to buy a workbook for grammar. He taught us the eight parts of speech and everything anyone needed to know about English and writing—not literature. I enjoyed that class so much until I kept taking other grammar courses until I had enough courses (credits) to declare a minor in grammar and writing.

I am getting ahead of myself. Let's get back to the first day. I walked out of the auditorium, and those football boys asked me to sing the school song. I said that I had just gotten here and did not know the school song. Then they said, "See that tree out there in the oval?" I said, "Yes." Then one of them said, "See that squirrel up that tree?" I said no. He said, "You will bark like a dog up that tree until that squirrel comes down." (Male freshmen were called dogs.) I went to the tree and began barking. Finally, one of them came over and told me to stop. He further said, "But the next time we see you, you better know that school song."

I got off that campus as fast as I could back to Miss Rhoda's house.

We had to take some type of placement test to see if we needed remedial subjects. That did not affect Ag majors too much because we took most of our classes by ourselves now.

The next day on campus, the administrators met with us freshmen and gave us the introduction and welcomed us to the college. We were told that everyone is called by his/her last name here with Mr. or Miss before it.

I was only sixteen years old and the president, Dr. C. V. Troup, introduced himself, and afterward I told him my name. He then told Dean W. W. Blanchet standing next to him to meet Mr. Bethay. That introduction went down the line as I met all the administrators and top officials of the college. I felt like a real man; no one questioned my age or size.

I was a small 130-pound freshman. I grew until I was twenty-four years of age. They took me as I was and acted as if they were glad that I was there.

Some days later, I went to the bookstore to see about my books. As my Guardian Angels would have it, I started talking with an older student (twenty-four years of age). During our introduction and conversation, he asked me what books I needed. I told him and he said, "I am a veteran and we can get all and any books, including the books you need."

For the first time I had my own books and no other name was written in the "Write your name here" section. That began a friendship and a pattern for the next two years and a friendship which lasted many years later.

He adopted me as his little brother from then on; he told other students that he was my big brother, too. He even told his own family that. After he graduated in 1952, he lived near the campus and made sure that I got any school needs I wanted or needed. His name was Losey J. Keene.

Now to Mr. Anderson. Mr. Anderson, my freshman orientation teacher, lived only two houses away from Miss Rhoda's. One of the requirements for the class was that we had to visit all department heads and college officials and introduce ourselves again personally. We had to keep a record of all the activities we participated and attended in the orientation notebook.

Ulysses Williams*, a classmate, asked to borrow my notebook about a week before the class ended and I did not get it back until the day before I had to turn it in. It had fingerprints and even grease spots throughout. Mr. Anderson circled all the prints and gave it back with a grade of C. He told me when he handed it back, "I hope this will teach you to keep your notebook to yourself from now on."

Diagonally across the street from Miss Rhoda's house was my neighbor, Mr. O. E. Hicks, my English teacher as I mentioned before. I had his class the first thing each Monday, Wednesday, and Friday at 8:00 a.m. Once he realized that I lived behind his house across the street, he said I could ride to class with him each morning. I first said no. It was odd for a sixteen-year-old freshman riding to school with his professor.

In October, Mr. Hicks began asking me if I would like to rake up his pecan tree leaves? Knowing me I like to make money, I said yes to that and did it. The pecans had begun to fall and I picked them up as well. When I would finish each week, he would ask me to go with him to sell them. He would give me half of the money—in college and still a "sharecropper." Also, he and Mrs. Hicks would try to get me to eat dinner with them after any job I did. That was really out of the question at first, like riding to class with him three times each week.

They had two daughters, Marian and Carolyn. They started asking me to babysit for them when they had to be away at night, but

I had to get there before dinner. This was their way of trying to make sure I got a decent meal once in a while. (He told me this many years later.) They could not understand how this young little boy who was eating nothing more than potato chips and drinking Pepsi Colas, not to mention living alone, was faring. That was the beginning of my becoming Hicks's boy at school as well as in the neighborhood. The daughters took me as their big brother, too. They called me Bethay.

Back to college. During orientation week, I leaned that they had work-aid jobs even on the farm. I applied and was hired immediately, making $15 per month. Yes. I was able to pay my first room rent in October and pay it the rest of that year.

I was assigned to work in the Horticulture Department under Mr. Stallworth. By working on the farm, I could bring home anything grown on the farm such as eggs, vegetables, fruits, etc. I now had plenty fresh food to eat all the time.

I always liked to cook since my experience in jail in Florida. I did not know at the time that it was just the beginning. I was never a restaurant person. I always liked my own food better.

Two Home Economics majors lived next door to me, and they began having dinner with me on Sundays. They were the majors in cooking, yet I did all the cooking at my house. I even tried a layer cake but got it a little too dry. But the white egg icing was good and sweet. We ate it as if it were okay.

When classes started that quarter, I began noticing that some of my classmates had reading and I was not given reading. I followed them to their reading class one day and asked the professor why were they having reading and I was not? She said, "One was assigned to this remedial class based on his/her test results from that test you took when you first got here." I told her I didn't read any better than they do and I wanted that class, too. She said, "I just told you how one gets assigned to this class." Then she said, "I do not believe this. Here I am standing here arguing with you about why you cannot get in this class when everyone else wants to get out. Young man, do you see that seat there? It is yours. I cannot put you in my roll book and I cannot turn in a grade for you because you are not officially in this class, but that is your seat as long as you want it."

FVSC, MATH—MR. CROFTON

LIKE MY ENGLISH PROFESSOR, Mr. Hicks, Mr. Crofton, an Agronomy teacher, had to teach us "dumb" Ag boys math. Why I remember this class so well is because Mr. Crofton would have one of us work a problem on the board, and when he finished, he would ask the class, "Boys, is that problem correct?" Right of wrong, some of the students would say, "Yes, Mr. Crofton." And they would be laughing behind Mr. Crofton's back.

If the problem were incorrect, I would say so and the other students would get upset with me. I told them I was doing it for their benefit because I knew how to work the problems. But Mr. Crofton went along with the students when they said the problem was correct, when in fact it would be wrong many times.

Because of this, I was not liked among my classmates in this class or any of the others we had together. (We were together as a class the entire four years.) Also, I too was the second youngest in this Ag class. Ulysses Williams* was the youngest, the one to whom I lent my Orientation notebook in Mr. Anderson's class.

Mr. Crofton was being evaluated one day by Mr. Anderson, who was head of the Education Department in Agriculture. A student was asked to work a problem on the board and he worked it incorrectly. He did not do this on purpose; he just did not know. Mr. Crofton asked the class, "Class, is that problem correct?"

The class said, "Yes, Mr. Crofton."

I said, "No, Mr. Crofton."

Then Mr. Crofton began to say, "See, Mr. Anderson, we have this young man who always tries to keep the class back by finding fault with the problems."

Mr. Anderson asked, "Mr. Crofton is this an example of what he does?"

Mr. Crofton said, "Yes, Mr. Anderson, I am glad you can see what I am talking about."

Mr. Anderson said, "Are you sure this is the example you want me to see?"

Mr. Crofton again said, "Yes."

Mr. Anderson told Mr. Crofton that he had never seen a problem more incorrect than that one on the board. He then walked out.

Mr. Crofton then said, walking around with both hands together behind his back as he usually did, "Boys, we got to be more careful." Then the boys told me that I was going to get an F because no one embarrasses a professor and gets away with it. I told them that if anyone gets a grade higher than I did, I was going to the Dean and let him give us a test to see who knows math in this class.

Mr. Crofton began respecting my assessment more in class; in fact, I received an A each of my three quarters in math my freshman year. That math book was written by Dr. Joseph Fuller at Tuskegee Institute in Alabama. I still have that book.

Later I had an Agronomy class with Mr. Crofton and got my A there also. He was a better Agronomy teacher than he was a math teacher.

We had Chapel every Monday, Wednesday, and Friday in the auditorium before lunch; we had assigned seats, and attendance was taken at each gathering. We had Vesper at 4:30 p.m. every Sunday. Attendance was required whether you lived on or off campus.

Each day at Chapel, someone or some student organization was in charge of the program. Vesper was more like church in that we always had a speaker, and most times, it was someone from another college. I got to meet most of the college presidents of the Negro colleges at this time. Each student was introduced to the speaker before he/she could get that cup of punch and two cookies.

I was a joiner of organizations. I first was a member of the Agridemic Forum. I later joined the Players Guild. During the winter quarter from January to March, I attended all the Greek fraternities' smokers. I just knew that everyone wanted me, so at the last minute I pledged Alpha. The other students had been accepted and presented to the student body, and I had not heard from the Alphas.

Mr. Hicks was an Alpha and my advisor. I went to him and told him that I had not heard from them. He said not to worry about it, but it was getting more embarrassing each week. Everyone was saying why wasn't I in one of the pledge clubs with my academic average.

Finally, I got a notice to meet with the Alphas. I was asked, "What do you have to offer Alpha?" I said that I was on the honor roll; I had perfect attendance in my class and at all the school affairs, programs, etc. students were required to attend. All the administrators, teachers, students, and workers on the campus and on the farm like me.

Sophomore Year at FVSC

I COMPLETED MY FRESHMAN year very successfully; I was on the honor roll all three quarters. I only made two Cs that year. Luckily, I made As to balance them. I was inducted into the Sphinx Club of Alpha Phi Alpha Fraternity. I was voted to become vice president of the Players Guild, an English major position, and my classmates had begun respecting my scholarship and seriousness of learning. They did not mind my telling them to be quiet if they were talking when the professor was trying to teach, and if I could help them with something they could not understand, they did not mind that either.

Awaiting me at home that summer was picking watermelons and cropping tobacco. The cotton was not ready for picking before September. Thank God! I never could pick one hundred pounds of cotton my whole career. That was the expected minimum amount one should be able to pick in a day. Some people have been known to pick up to four hundred pounds; a bale of cotton weighs five hundred pounds.

The Alphas had told me that I had to return in September knowing all the chapters and their location. Zip and I spent the nonworking hours learning the chapters. Would you believe they never asked me to name one of them? Zip should have been made an Alpha too from all that studying with me. But it was not all to no avail; four years later she became an AKA.

I do not remember why I did not return to Miss Rhoda's that fall. I roomed with three roommates; one of them was my bed mate, and the other two were brothers, Lucius and Henry Skrine. My bed mate was Thomas Nails from Waycross, Georgia. Henry looked like a White boy, hair and all. The landlady worshipped him; she gave him the biggest portions of any meal she served. She gave Thomas the smallest; he was paying the same as we were, and he always left the table upset. She fed us breakfast and dinner. That was the end of cooking for me for a while

Let me share some of my academic experiences my sophomore year. I leaned to candle eggs for hatching and I learned that one did not need a rooster for a hen to lay an egg; in fact, it is better if they were not around if the eggs were for eating. I learned also that one rooster could fertilize the eggs of twenty hens. Baby chicks are called bitties, then pullets for female. Adult chickens are roosters and hens (Poultry 101).

In Agronomy, I learned terracing and how and when to rotate the same crops. In Fruit and Nut Production, I learned how to prune trees. I learned how to cook, eat, and enjoy asparagus—a long way from cabbages, rutabagas, turnips, mustards, and cauliflower.

Business English was required. We had this recent graduate teaching it. He wanted me to help him after class and the boys began teasing me. I stopped. Afterward, I could not do anything right in class, including reading for him. I knew I was the best in that simple English subject but he gave me a C.

I went to Mr. Hicks and told him what had happened and asked him what we were going to do? He said, "Nothing." I said, "Nothing!" Then he said, "I told you to leave it alone, didn't I?"

(I was at a party in Newark, New Jersey, in 1968 and there was a man there who looked familiar but I could not place him and he got annoyed when I kept trying to figure out where I knew him from. Through the process of elimination, he said he had taught at Fort Valley State College one year. I asked him if he remembered a student named Mr. Bethay? He said, "I cannot believe this after all those years.")

Our chemistry teacher was being evaluated by Mr. Anderson and no one knew the answers to the simplest questions he would ask, except me. I had memorized Charles's and Boyle's Laws and I could balance an equation or two. I knew some of the elements from the periodic table, like sulfuric acid, H_2SO_4. The professor said after Mr. Anderson left, "You damn boys acted like you never heard any of this shit. What are you trying to do, get my ass fired? If it were not for Mr. Bethay, my ass would be gone."

In spite of the B I got in chemistry, I feel I learned the least in that subject—not because of the teacher's teaching; I just could not get it. More about this in 1965.

In the fall, the high school bands from throughout the State came for a Clinic. There were buses and band members all over the campus. We had an excellent band, too. In fact we had an excellent music department. One could learn playing in a band, singing, or directing. Our choir broadcasted on the Macon, Georgia, radio station each Sunday morning

Another big annual event was the Ham & Egg Show. Farmers brought their prize ham and dozens of eggs to be judged for first, second, or third prize. One would never see this many hams and eggs anyplace other than a meat market or poultry market.

Socially, my sophomore year, I still held my position by being able to dance on all numbers during the evening. I was known even as a freshman to dance with all the female teachers, including Mrs. Troup. We had a fat African teacher this year, and every time a rumba number came up, we took the floor. My eyes were looking at her tits as we danced.

If you brought a date to the dance, you had to have the first and last dance with her. If a girl refused you a dance, she could not dance with anyone the next dance.

Traditionally, the two biggest balls held each year were the Ag and Alpha balls. That year after our induction into Alpha, most of the Alphas were Ag majors. We for the first time had the highest averages among the majors and fraternities. No other Greek-lettered organization had a separate ball either.

Dr. Troup decided this year that we should not dominate; we could still have the Ag Ball, but not the Alpha Ball since we mostly had the same students for both.

We began having a Panhellenic Ball—all the Greeks together from then on. I still was the "ball" at both.

The president of the Players Guild got pregnant and did not return to school that year, and I became president. The first of

October, Mr. Adkins, the advisor, came to me and said that I had to participate on a symposium at Florida A&M College next month. I asked him what a symposium was? He said I had to make a speech with a group from the different colleges. He taught speech, but I was to take that course my junior year.

Here now I am an Ag major. I never had a speech class and was about to participate in a symposium at another college. I asked him what was I to speak on? He said, "The Universality of Classical Drama." I said to myself had he lost his mind. I had only had about one month of literature in high school and he was talking about the classics.

Off I go to Mr. Hicks. I told him my situation, expecting him to get me out of this impossible dilemma. He said, "You can do it." Now there are two people who have lost their minds, and they wanted me to lose mine trying to do this.

Mr. Adkins's wife worked in the library and was a Classics major in college. Mr. Hicks told me to go to her and tell her my topic and ask her to get me seven books on classical drama.

I got the books and took them to his house that night. He told me which one to start with and he would quiz me after I read each. I said, "What about the speech?" He said he would take care of that, too. He would give Mrs. Adkins an outline for her to write the speech. In three weeks, the Greek characters were coming out of my "ears"—Medea, Oedipus Rex, Antigone, and Agamemnon, among others.

Now it is the day to leave Fort Valley for Florida, A-&-M College in Tallahassee, Florida, I had not seen the speech. Mr. Adkins handed it to me once I was in the car. On the way down to Tallahassee, I rehearsed the speech over and over. I was familiar with the plays and their characters, so all I had to do was rehearse the written speech.

We are now at FAMC and they had not made provisions for all the participants from the different colleges. Once the Alphas learned that I was an Alpha and that there were others from the other colleges, they made their Alpha pledgees give up their bunk beds for us. I told him, the young man who was to give his up for me, "No, let's share it." I know he got no sleep that night, making sure that he did not touch me or pull the blanket. His name was George Mims. More about him in 1963.

We learned that they had assigned a girl from Tennessee State the same topic to speak on.

Being a lady, they let her go first. It was embarrassing when they got through with her with all the questions she could not answer; Mr. Hicks had prepared me for them. That gave me the confidence I needed. They gave me a standing ovation when I finished my speech and another round of applause when I did so well with their questions. I was asked if I were a classics major? When I said that I was an Ag major, they could not believe me.

The head of the Classics Department of Tennessee State College, whose name escapes me at the moment, told me that I should change my major to the Classics. When I told him Fort Valley did not have that department, he could not believe me again. My Guardian Angels were at work again. I was a star the remainder of the visit.

We had a very good Players Guild. We performed some of the best plays throughout my college years—*Joan of Arc*, *The Glass Menagerie*, *The Willow and I*, *Dear Ruth*, and *Smiling Through*.

I tried acting too. In my freshman year I was in a play and forgot my lines. I took one of my hands and hit my forehead. The director told me I should have just stood still until it came to me. I was nervous at the time. I was one of the kids in *The Willow and I*.

Junior Year at FVSC, 1952–1953

THE MEN'S DORMITORY WAS ready for occupying the fall of 1952. The men had lived in Ohio Hall up to that time. This year I was ready and able to live on campus. I do not know where the extra money came from, but I was one of two to be the first to occupy room 210. That was my number which I shall refer to later.

I was made dormitory director for the next two years. This meant that I had to work closely with the dean of men on all the activities affecting the men in the dorm.

Each dorm, male or female, had a matron who lived in the dorm with an apartment. Anytime I wanted a snack while in the dorm, I just had to go downstairs and she gave me full run of her refrigerator or anything else she had in the kitchen. She would let me cook food from the farm there, too. I had open access to the apartment of the Dean of Men, who also lived in the dorm.

My grades improved each year after the problems I had earlier with professors. I was always on the honor roll. That Spring I was taking a course in Fruit and Nut Production under Mr. Stallworth. When I got my grades, I had an A in every class except his. I went to him and told him that he had made a mistake in my grade. He laughed and said, "Mr. Bethay, I did not make a mistake. How would it look and what will the men say when they see that you got the only A and you work for me?" I said, "See what they are going to say when I don't come back to work anymore." I did not work the next quarter and missed the honor roll for the first and only time during my four years of undergraduate college.

In another class with Mr. Joyner, I earned the only B in his class, I think, and he had no problem giving me the only B. He was a tough professor, too. One day he was late for class and we left the classroom after fifteen minutes, but we had sense enough to not go too far from the classroom. Someone looked in the window later and Mr. Joyner was writing a test on the blackboard. We all rushed in and he said, "You still just have the same amount of time if you were here, you should have waited."

Living on the campus, I now ate in the dining hall. We ate family style. We rotated being host and hostess. The host sat at the head of the table and served the meat; the hostess sat at the foot of the table and served the starch. Any other dish was served by the one who sat nearest to that dish when the plate got to him/her. The stack of plates was near the host. He placed the meat on the first plate, which was his, and started it around the table to his right for completion.

Mrs. Juanita Frambro was our dietitian. She was very strict. One had assigned tables and had to use proper etiquette at all times. She had a chime she would hit three times when she wanted the dining room quiet. One could not pick up his/her fork and the napkin that had been placed in his/her lap until announcements had been made and the blessing said by her:

> *God bless this food.*
> *Give us love and peace in our hearts.*
> *And make us thoughtful of others.*
> *Through Jesus Christ, our Lord.*
> *Amen.*

After she was finished with the blessing, one could not begin eating until the host started.

James Horn, my classmate in Ag, came in after the acceptable time and wanted to stay. She told him to get out. He was too late. He went and got Dean Blanchet. She told Dean Blanchet that he better take him to his house and let his wife cook dinner for him because he was not going to eat in here today.

Dr. Blanchet, like a dog with his tail under him, left with James.

The football players ate later than we did during the season. One day they were too noisy and would not settle down for her and she refused to feed them. It took the coach and the president for her to give in and let the football players eat. That was Mrs. Frambro.

For special occasions and special honors, Mrs. Frambro could prepare some delicious meals. Students had jobs as waiters and waitresses. And they worked as professionals all the time. It was their jobs to bring the food to the tables and clean up after us. That is why it was call a dining hall rather than a cafeteria.

One morning we had franks (wieners) for breakfast. I was talking and cut up both franks in small pieces. I heard the bell tolling three times, and I knew it tolled for thee. Mrs. Frambro could see anything wrong going on from the center of that dining room. She said, "Mr. Bethay, you will eat all those franks before you eat anything else." The franks turned to rubber as the eyes were watching me chew.

The following thing was happening before I moved on campus my junior year; it was some of the young men's practice to get with their girls Sunday morning after breakfast in the auditorium or in the chemistry lab on the second floor across from the balcony during the dances or (sock hop).

One night I was in the staircase at the far end of the auditorium when I began feeling that someone was watching us. I jumped up, turned around and there stood Mr. Crofton looking at us perform our sex act. He asked, "Mr. Bethay, what are you doing?"

I said, "Nothing, Mr. Crofton."

Then he asked, "Young lady, aren't you a freshman?"

She sheepishly said, "Yes."

Then Mr. Crofton said, "Mr. Bethay, I think you two better get back into that dance." Whew!

Also during my junior year, there was an old lady who lived next to the college farm and walked with a cane. She would walk into town almost every day during the week. One day we were in lab, as we called our Ag classes on the farm, when we saw a tornado coming through the farm area. We thought it was coming directly toward us and started to run. A man who worked on the farm with Mr. Stallworth said, "Stay still, you do not know where or which way it was going." To us it looked like it was coming directly toward us.

Lucky it did not but it leveled this lady's house flat. We all ran over there after the tornado had passed looking for her. We just knew she was dead under all of that debris. Someone said that she might be in town because we could not find her.

We began leaving but my GuardianAngels told me to go back and look just one more time. As I walked across the rubbish, I saw these fingers piercing out from under the boards. I called Mr. Stallworth and the others back, and we lifted the boards off her. She had fallen between the two trunks she had on each side of her fireplace; the chimney fell the other way, and she was knocked between the two trunks without a scratch.

Now the bees. There were beehives on the college farm, and one hot spring morning, this idiot decided to bring one of the hives across the campus. Out of about one thousand students, I was the sweetest. I got stung. My face swelled up so bad that I could not attend class for several days. That is the only time I missed any class other than the times I was away on school business, like going to FAMC in Florida and when we took the play *Smiling Through* to Albany State College in Albany, Georgia.

Senior Year at FVSC, 1953–1954

My senior year was routine, just repeats of many of the same things I was involved in the other three years with a few new exceptions.

I learned about forty years later that Robert White from Adel had lived on the third floor of Jeans Hall above me and kept away from me all my senior year and his freshman year. He did this because when he got there and told them that he was from Adel, everyone said he had to be a good student like Mr. Bethay. And Robert said that he could not go anyplace without hearing about this student Mr. Saul Bethay, and he was not to have anything to do with him or try to be that perfect student he was—Mr. Bethay this, Mr. Bethay that. Robert even changed his name while I was there and I did not recognize him because he had grown to be the size of the football player he was. I knew him as Bruiser only. I was so busy trying to graduate when he got there. Freshmen did not matter too much unless one of them had a problem in the dorm.

One day Mr. Rutledge, my sociology professor, and Mr. Stallworth were on the outer porch of the academic building when someone came by and told me that I was going to be late for the Ag program? When I stared to leave, Mr. Rutledge asked why was I going to that Ag program. I told him that I was an Ag major. In surprise, he said, "Are you sure?" Mr. Stallworth said, "Take a good look at Mr. Bethay. He has farming written all over his face." By the way, after I missed the honor roll, I began working with Mr. Stallworth again until I graduated.

We had most of our classes in the Academic Building because the Ag building burned our sophomore year. But when we came on the main campus for our other non-Ag classes, we were always appropriately dressed. In fact, we were among the best dressed men on campus. By looks, no one could tell that we may have just come from the farm earlier—we dressed for our Ag classes, too.

I had not fully learned my lessons yet. We had a Friday night hop and I took this girl into the chemistry lab to "run an experiment." Ozias Pearson was known as the kisser. He and this girl were in the hallway kissing, and we did not want them to see us coming out the chemistry lab that time of night. They kissed and they kissed. Finally, their tongues got tired and they left. We thought they had gone back into the dance. We waited a few minutes until we thought the coast was clear before we came out. When we came out, we did not hear any music. The hop had ended at 11:00 p.m. instead of midnight.

We rushed downstairs, and who was getting her mail out of her mailbox? Dean Lyons, the dean of women. She did not say anything but her eyes followed us until we exited the building. We did the hundred-yard dash to Ohio Hall where this girl was housed. Lucky for us, Ozias and his girl were still kissing with his foot in the door. Had the door been closed, this girl would not have been admitted in. My Guardian Angels again at work.

The next day, Saturday morning, I went to the Hicks's for something. When I got back on the campus, everyone was telling me that Dean Lyons had been looking for me all morning and had told everyone to have me come to her office as soon as they saw me. I said to myself, "Why did she not suspend us last night before the whole campus knew about us? And too, why is she involving everyone in having me come to her office?"

Puzzled, I did not know what to do. I knew Mr. Hicks could not get me out of this with my foolishness. What made my imagination worse was the thought of my writing Daddy to come for me for such foolishness, and I had two more quarters before graduation and one of those quarters was student teaching.

I delayed seeing Dean Lyons as long as I could. I reluctantly went to her office. She said, "Mr. Bethay we have been looking for you all morning."

I said, "We?" I just knew *we* was the administration and she waiting to get us together to suspend us.

Then she said that Mr. Somebody had taken ill last night and he was in the AKA's Jabber Walk skit for tonight. "Everyone said only you could take that part and be ready by tonight."

Before I asked her what the part was or how long, I said, "Yes, Dean Lyons. I will do it."

She then said, "They are waiting for you in the auditorium."

I said, "Yes, ma'am." And I got over to the auditorium as fast as I could. We won second place that night in the skit. That was my "Academy Award" performance while at the Valley.

Now it was the winter semester and time for student teaching. I and another classmate had been assigned to Millen, Georgia: I was assigned to the Millen High School to do student teachings and Son Wright to another high school nearby. Arrangements had been made for an apartment for us. This lady cooked and did our laundry. In addition to my high school classes, I had two adult classes of farmers each week in the evenings. One of our adult students needed a porch built. I was excellent in making out the order for the build of materials, and Mr. Wright was the best in building.

We built my adult student the porch, which he invited everyone to come by and see while we were still in town.

Mr. Anderson and other agriculture education officials from Atlanta were visiting all of us in the county who were doing their student teaching that quarter. Mr. Wilson, from Atlanta, asked us if we needed any help? Before any of us could say anything, my critic teacher, as they were called then, Mr. Briggs with his big, heavy self, got up and said, "My young man will not let me help him with anything, he knows it all. When I try to help him with his lesson plans, he will not let me."

Then I said, "I had to do them the way Mr. Anderson had taught us to do them, and it would be he who would be grading them."

Mr. Wilson said, "Show me what you all are talking about."

Mr. Briggs said, "Mr. Bethay put one of your lesson plans on the board."

I said, "I will only do a new one, one you all want me to demonstrate."

One of the officials gave me one to do. I took up about four blackboards with all the (1) Job, (2) Objectives, (3) Skills, (4) Procedures, (5) Tools, (6) Evaluation, etc. to the best of my knowledge now—close if not complete.

Mr. Wilson told all the other student teachers to take out a pen and pad and copy Mr. Bethay's lesson plan and when he next visited, they all had to be done that way.

The next morning at school, Mr. Briggs told me that I did not have anything else to do if I did not want to. I had my A. He also said he had never been so embarrassed before.

That did not change anything with me. I have never been disrespectful and would not start then. I had nothing else to prove. I continued to try to do my best. It was for the students anyway—high school and adults.

I wrote a farming skit (short play) for the high school boys to perform, which was successful. And when the farmers listened to me telling them how to rotate crops, candle eggs, select seeds, spray for insects, and castrate hogs and cows for meat, they were as attentive as they could be. For the first time the farmers gave a student teacher (me) a banquet for the job he had done, and the farmer whose porch we built told the others at the banquet that he did not have enough wood left over to start a fire. We had done such a good job. Thanks to Mr. Wright in this one.

When I think that I celebrated my twentieth birthday while I was doing my student teaching, it scares me even today—just five and a half feet tall and weighing 130 pounds. What a celebration it was, cake at my landlady's house on the nineteenth and other celebrations, including my first Broadway live play in Augusta, Georgia.

Back to Mr. Briggs and Mrs. Briggs, too. They lived in one of the nicest houses I had ever been in or seen even in the movies or anyplace else. The Briggses would invite me over for socializing, including during my birthday. But most of all they were friends with the Hornsby family in Augusta, Georgia, who owned the Negro Insurance Company in Augusta and one in Atlanta.

One Saturday, Mr. and Mrs. Briggs invited Mr. Wright and me to visit with them to the Hornsbys. The Hornsbys had chauffeurs, butlers, and maids. I tried to hide my argyle socks.

It was the first time I had ever been served hors d'oeuvre before a meal. After dinner, one chauffeur took all of us in a limousine downtown to see a Broadway play, Mary Martin in *South Pacific*. (I have seen that play twice since I have lived in New York but with a different cast.)

We had to sit in the balcony; Mr. Hornsby could buy that theater with his money. They had a six- or seven-year-old little girl who kept giving me parched pecans (my first of this, too) in the dark during the performance.

My last quarter at Fort Valley was very exciting. The Dean of Men took several of us to Camp John Hope, swimming. It was the same camp which I was initiated into the Alpha Phi Alpha Fraternity in 1951, and thereafter, I was voted vice president and dean of pledgees for the remainder of my stay at Fort Valley. A long jump from almost not even getting in.

After having been such a devoted Alpha in college, I have never been active a day after I graduated. Why? I do not know. Everyone thought that I was going to become the National President of Alpha.

One day I was walking on campus toward the Academic Building and I saw Mr. Hicks approaching me. I knew he was angry, and I knew he was angry with me before he got too near me. He had this sheet of typed paper shaking it in my face, saying, "Read this! Read this! Read this! Don't you ever put another notice on that bulletin board without reading it! Do you hear me?" I had no idea what he was talking about because he gave me no chance to read it before he left it with me as he walked away, disappointed.

Announcements were left on a bulletin board in the Academic Building. I had placed this on it:

> ***There will be an importance Players Guild meeting Thursday evening at 7:00 p.m.***

Mr. Hicks had given me three As in English and I had made one of the highest scores on the Sophomore Comprehensive English exam in writing and grammar in 1953 and now a senior using a noun when I should have used an adjective—"importance" instead of "important." I would be scared to death for him to read *this* writing after fifty years. I am too old and too far removed to pick up all the mistakes I know must be within. One has to take all mistakes for love now.

Mr. Hicks was my advisor, and each quarter one had to meet with his/her advisor to check all the things he/she had done during the quarter in all areas. One could be evaluated from the Scope Chart if he/she had been honest. I had to go to church to make sure I could be true in the Scope Chart. The girls could go off campus on Sunday to one of the local churches. That was my way of being with my girlfriend legally and doing for once what I should be doing and not in the staircase or the chemistry lab when I should have been dancing.

At the zero hour, I went to Mr. Hicks and said we had not marked my scope chart and he said he had hoped that I did not come to mark it just to see if they would keep me from graduating. I told him that I will not be the guinea pig for this. We marked it and turned in my last one. I had done this for twelve quarters.

Now I am waiting to receive Mrs. Frambro's invitation to the seniors' banquet. Her invitation was the college's way of letting seniors know that they had met the requirements for graduation. I had no doubt, but I still wanted it to display when I moved around campus the last few days. Also, I did not want Mama and Daddy to drive up here June 6, 1954, in vain.

We wore our caps and gowns on Sunday at 5:00 p.m. and on Monday at 10:00 a.m.—"Land of Hope and Glory," *Pomp and Circumstance*. Our caps and gowns were black with gold tassels. Daddy told me later that I was the only one he recognized.

I was awarded the Al Knox Award for $10. I learned later that the faculty was split 50/50 between Donald C. Graham and me. Dr. Troup, our president, voted for me. He said Mr. Graham physically could not have been able to do half of the things Al Knox did in college before he died; only Mr. Bethay came closest, and it was an award for a student's accomplishments, not one of sympathy or pity. Mr. Graham had to walk on crutches. He once had infantile paralysis.

They called my name again and I came back on stage, and Dr. Blanchet said, "Receiving the Bachelor of Science Degree in Vocational Agriculture, Mr. Saul Henry Bethay." I took the degree with my left hand and shook Dr. Troup's hand with my right one and went to my seat with my heart pounding through my shirt.

After the ceremony, 250 students marched out, following the administrators and faculty. We were greeted by our parents and congratulated by our classmates, many we were seeing for the very last time.

Mr. Hicks congratulated me and chatted with us for a few minutes and said, "I must go because we are preparing lunch for you all." You all meant Mama, Daddy, and me.

The Alma Mater

Fort Valley State, Fort Valley State!
Our lives to thee, we dedicate
Our Souls we blend to sing thy name
Eternal praise we do proclaim.

Faithful and true, Fort Valley State
We at thy call, forever wait
We lift our hearts in thankfulness
For loyalty and thoroughness.

- *William H. Pipes*

We love to hear thy sweet name called;
Thou art the dearest school of all.
Our hearts to thee will e'er belong,
Thou art so steadfast, brave and strong,

SAUL HENRY BETHAY

We love thee so, Fort Valley State,
Our loyalty we dedicate;
Thy name forever we proclaim;
Fort Valley State, We love thy name.

- Odessa Hardison McNair '54

1954

It was June 7, 1954, and I was cropping tobacco with a BS Degree in Vocational Agriculture. I had not gotten any offers to teach, nor had I put out any feelers either. I do not remember why. Was I expecting things to automatically happen for me as they always did? Where were those guardian angels? When I walked in those hot summer fields and looked down, I saw only one set of footprints. Four years later, I realized that that set of prints were my Guardian Angels.

I must have heard it on the battery radio that the Air Force was looking for new recruits. The next thing I remember, I was at the recruitment station in Valdosta, ready to sign up for the Air Force. I was told to bring my degree and a limited amount of changing clothes. Daddy had to take me to Valdosta because I would not have had any other way to get down there. That meant that he had to stop working to do that for me. (I did not have to spend four years in college to go the Air Force, but I never did what everyone else did, and I was not old enough earlier. I needed Fort Valley State and still do.)

The recruiting officer took my degree (which I never got back) and I completed a form. We six were given some instructions as to taking the bus from Valdosta to Atlanta and someone would meet us there. And we six must stay together at all times. I looked at him because there were three White boys among the six. How were we to stay together on that bus and stop in Macon, Georgia's bus station and eat lunch together?

I figured out that he must know what he was doing. He spoke to the bus driver when the bus came. We boarded the bus for Atlanta. When we got on the bus, both Negroes and Whites looked at us without saying anything—the Negroes were in the back of the bus and the Whites were in the front of the bus.

They must have known that we had to be "special" to be integrating the bus in 1954. But I do believe that the military had integrated before then, and anyone who wanted that military money had to conform, public transportation included. Anyway, we ate together in Macon and arrived safely in Atlanta.

We were taken to this large building not too far from the bus station. (I saw this place many times after I had gotten out of the Air Force because I would visit Atlanta each summer after our Family Reunion in Adel, and I would stay nearby with my friend A. J. Stafford, who is deceased now.) It was the Air Force Recruitment Station. There were thousands of young boys of all colors. For the first time, I felt older because most of these boys were just turning eighteen and were graduates from high school; I was twenty, a graduate from college, a college only a hundred miles south of Atlanta, the Fort Valley State College.

In an open bay sleeping area, we all spent the night and had breakfast the next morning. We took some type of recruitment test for placement in the Air Force. I wish I had known what this test was for. Maybe I would have taken it a little more seriously. It was the test to determine what you would be assigned to do once you got out of basic training.

My next remembrance was that a group of us were at the Atlanta Airport getting ready to board this two-propeller airplane for Houston, Texas. The airports, Atlanta and Houston, only had one tower each at the time. You should see them now. What about how full the air is today with all type and size of planes? My first airplane ride.

We were met in Houston and taken in this Air Force bus to San Antonio, Texas, where the Lackland Air Force Base is located. I thought there were a lot of people in Atlanta, but really this time, I had never seen this many people together in my life, all dressed alike in those fatigues and "farming"-looking black boots. I did not know that the next day one could not tell me from the others because they had given me my issue of Air Force clothes, too.

A new set of military clothes and a blanket were not all we got; we got those clean haircuts, and the White boys looked like us now head-wise. It did not bother me because I was wearing my hair cut close anyway. I really did not need that haircut, but I know the barber got paid by the head.

Now I am an airman. Airman Bethay. For the next four years no Billy, Saul, Dog, or Mr. Bethay. It was Airman Bethay.

The next six weeks is known as Basic Training. One learns about the Air Force and the role he/she is to perform while in it. After breakfast, we would march (drill) until about 10:30 a.m. Then we would go to one of the base theaters to watch films of the Air Force story. My new friend, Hubert McManus, could not stay awake during the films because he was up all night selling the candy his mother would send him. More about that later, too.

The reason we did not drill beyond 10:30 a.m. was because the temperature outside was more than one hundred degrees in July and August every day. At night, you would see why they gave you that stupid blanket when it was over ninety degrees during the day and dropped below sixty degrees at night.

We would have breakfast, lunch, and dinner each day. There was one of us called the chow runner. It was his job to get our place in line for the mess hall three times each day. He took that job very seriously. If he came for us and one or two of us were not ready, he would get angry. The chow runner always wanted us to be on time to be able to eat among the first groups. The last squadron to eat had to be on the drill grounds soon after they ate. If we ate early, we could go back to the barrack for a while and fool around if our areas were clean for inspection—daily.

One day we were marching and I saw and recognized Willie Frank Elliot. He saw and recognized me also, but we could not break rank and we had no way of looking each other up during basic training or thereafter. Willie Frank was the young man who was given the money I should have been given at my high school graduation. At that time, the only communication tool was the telephone on someone's desk; there was no cell phone yet.

Hubert McManus would wake the boys up after the lights were out and sell them candy on credit. When payday came, some of them would not want to pay. I became the strong-arm man to get his money. We would be sent to the First Sergeant for discipline afterward. The first sergeant would assign us to KP duty in the mess hall.

The second time we were sent to the mess hall for discipline, the Mess Sergeant said, "Weren't you boys just here?" We said yes. I told him that the reason we were sent there was because our troop sergeant did not like to see Negroes and Whites friends, and this is his way of dealing with it. This sergeant was a Negro and said, "I will fix that SOB. You boys sit over there and you do not have to do anything."

When our group came to chow, they saw us siting around just eating anything and everything in the kitchen. (The Air Force served the best food I had ever eaten my whole four years.) Someone went back and told the sergeant what they saw and the first sergeant stopped sending us to KP for discipline.

Each six weeks the base had a competition among the squadrons to see who knew the Air Force story the best. My squadron chose me to represent it. I told my sergeant that I would not do it unless Hubert be excused along with me to study the Air Force Handbook.

We were sent to the first sergeant for permission to be exempt. When we walked in, the first thing he said was, "Not you two again. I don't know what I am going to do with you."

We said, "Sir, we are not here for discipline."

Then he said, "Then what else in the hell would you be sent to me for?" I told him about my having been chosen to compete in the competition and he said, "Have they lost their cotton-pickin' minds?" He shook his head and finally said, "Okay, I sure hope they know what they are doing."

For the next two weeks, Hubert and I had no duty of any kind. I studied the Air Force Handbook and Hubert would quiz me. Something came up on the day of the scheduled competition, and it had to be postponed until a later date. I had shipped out before it was rescheduled. My Guardian Angels at work again.

Before that, it was bivouac time. This is the week new airmen go into the woods and try to act like real soldiers. You packed your gear and marched about five miles to the campsite. It was the Wednesday before Labor Day 1954. We arrived that afternoon and ate and got assigned to our tents. If you thought the meals were good back on base, there was no comparison to bivouac's meals. The first day we had barbeque steaks and all its trimmings. And the food got better each day thereafter—chicken, ribs, and pork chops, just to mention some of the meats.

I went on the firing range for the day's practice and I realized that I was not putting any holes in my target. So the next day, I looked for the marksman in my group and lay down next to him to do my firing. I told him that I needed three bull's eyes on my target to qualify. He took my weapon (rifle) and *bang, bang, bang* and I got my target and got the hell off that firing range. Whew! One could not leave until he qualified. I would be still on that firing range now if I had to qualify shooting that weapon. Maybe if they had given me a sling shot, I would have been able to hit that target.

In September, the grounds in Texas were parched. We were supposed to be crawling under this barbed wire in the mud but there was no mud. The ex-Army sergeant who was now in the Air Force to train us said what we were doing was a disgrace to the military, performing that exercise as if we were too good to get dirty, let alone get wet. We could not stay out there until it rained because it might never rain in August and September.

We had to leave bivouac on Friday because it was Labor Day on Monday. So we went back to our barrack for the weekend and went back out again on Tuesday morning. We had to leave bivouac on Wednesday morning because another squadron was coming in that afternoon. My Guardian Angels again at work.

Lackland Air Force Base

Squadron 3723, Flight 729
San Antonio, Texas
September 1954

Some autographs I received upon completion of my Air Force basic training:

SAUL HENRY BETHAY

Airman Bethay,
Happiness to a guy that is making the best of luck from the bottom to the top.
A pal, Red Mack

To my swell pal & talking mate,
May your service be enjoyed & I hope I see you before and after we get out.
Roy Williams

Good luck to a pal - Aggie Weldon

To a real nice guy, and a good "airman." Keep it up pal, you'll go a long way.
Lots of luck and Best Wishes when and if we separate.
A Buddy, Buddy Vaden

Going to say good-bye to such a swell friend, but this is the Air Force. Best of luck.
Ronald B. Burgess

Good luck to a good airman. - Jerry Schueller

Good luck and best wishes from a pal to a pal - J. D. Greene

To Saul, a good fellow to have for a friend. When your spirits are low, just think of Lackland some more - Narwood

Airman Bethay,
Give the best to the Air Force and the best will come back to you.
A friend, Walter E. Tootle "Tenn"

WHY I HAVE SO MANY NAMES

<<Autographs Page 2>>

Lots and lots of luck to a real Great Guy. You have made Basic worth going through - David Barth
Good luck to you always - Billy D. Winfee

Here's to the future holder of the American Spirit of Honor Medal. - Von Miller Doc"

When we all go different ways may our friendship always go with us for the fun we had at Lackland. I shall never forget. Best of luck from a Yankee Pal.
H. A. Johnson "Chow Runner"

Lots of luck in everything you do - Jerry Lawrence

Best Wishes for 4 years that will be well spent. Your Pal, Earnest Fairchild

Best Wishes to a real cool Cat, to a Cool Pal - Henry A Cohen Jr.

Keep a Head with the women - Your pal, James Luckett Jr.

Best Wishes Saul - Your Pal Wm. A. Hall

"Do right to the next 4 years in this chicken Shit outfit, HA" Larry Ball

Dear Joker, Best of luck in whatever you do. Your buddy Vernon G. Hittle

Lots of luck to a very Brilliant Airman - Russel Housel

Just think only 3 yrs. and 10 mo. in the Air Force. Your Pal Clarence Dixon

SAUL HENRY BETHAY

Saul,
I hope you will make a good airman in every way and get your rank fast.
Then you want have to work so hard. "Ha Ha" - Miller Stewart, Jr.

WHY I HAVE SO MANY NAMES

<<Autographs Page 3>>

Dear Saul,

I will say one thing, if there are better friends, it will have to be proven to me. I would trust you with anything that belongs to me. May I take this opportunity to wish you the greatest of success and happiness in life.

Hubert McManus (Deceased 1993), Hamlet, N. C.

Hubert was my best buddy and we were never in touch after this experience. However, I found his address, which kept going to the wrong place, and it was after his death a cousin wrote and told me that my letter kept coming to her address but he never got them. Somehow, I feel that he too was trying to do the same but did not know where to begin. A dear friend during our basic Air Force training. I write about him in *Why I Have So Many Names.*

Now my basic training is over and I got my assignment to go to Laredo Air Force Base in Lerado, Texas. My Air Force Special Code (AFSC) was Communication Clerk. That meant that I was assigned to an office with a desk, typewriter, and telephone for the remainder of my Air Force career. No matter where I was to be stationed, I would always be in an office only.

There was a scheduled parade as soon after I had arrived at Laredo. Having to be inspected with an unironed uniform on, I was "gigged" and pulled out of rank.

I told the officer that I had just gotten there from basic training and had not had time to have my uniforms cleaned. That made no difference to him. (I should have never been required to participate inasmuch as I had just arrived on that base.)

I was the Chief Distribution Clerk for Base Publications. All the Air Force manuals came through my office for distribution throughout the base. There were a sergeant and an officer assigned to my division along with two other airmen who ran the printing presses for the base. The other two airmen did the packing and shipping for publications and printing. I had no lifting to do of any kind; at least I did none.

If someone needed a regulation (publication) and it was not in stock, it was my job to order it and let them know when it came in. With nothing much to do, I read many of the publications and taught myself to type. I learned more about the real Air Force then than I did when I was at Lackland Air Force Base.

Because I had a degree, I was not sent to a technical school after basic training for my AFSC. This AFSC requires one to be able to type over thirty-five words per minute to make a stripe and get promoted.

I got a typewriter and a typing book and taught myself to type. I did everything the book asked me to do. I ended up being able to type sixty words per minute including being able to type numbers, which very few secretaries are able to do.

I made my first two stripes on schedule, one after the other, and then my AFSC was frozen (closed) the remainder of my stay in the Air Force. (I was separated with only two stripes in four years.) I did not want to go to an Officer Training School. I did not join the Air Force for that. I needed time to grow up without Daddy having to further pay for it or whip me. The Air Force was the best way for me as I saw it.

I had one of the nicest, best, cleanest rooms on base. We could fix our rooms up anyway as long as they looked presentable and in keeping with the Air Force regulations. I even brought some cheap curtains. I always got top praises during barrack inspection. That is until this airman moved in with me. He was a White boy from the Midwest who had no personal hygiene habits or was not apt in keeping the room clean and in order.

We got gigged during one of our inspections. I told the captain that I wanted to move. He said, "No." "I know what the problem is. The other airman is moving. Not you." I had my own room the remainder of my stay at Laredo. I was never assigned another roommate, and my room was the one to be used as an example for the others.

They had bingo on base each week and I was lucky about winning. Some of the prizes were shirts. I became stocked with civilian shirts. And one day I was in the Service Club and in walked my roommate, before he moved, with one of my favorite shirts on. He saw me and got out of there. He had not taken a bath or used any deodorant. I threw that favorite shirt in the garbage.

I played bid whist on base. At Christmas, my sergeant invited the office staff to his house for dinner. He could not leave me out without showing his prejudice. I was the only Negro in my section. I had a nice time at dinner. His family accepted me and made me feel welcome. Another first for me. Now I am eating with the White folks in Laredo, Texas.

That was the end of the mixing for a while. We had to cross the Rio Grande to Nuevo Laredo for our dancing and you-know-what. Some of the Mexican women did not take to us too readily unless they thought we were going to spend a lot of money on them. There was a section in Nuevo Laredo where the women stood in front of their little room door and beckoned you to come in for pay. Most of them were the fat ones who would respond to you. That or they were not my type. We had to pay five cents to get into Mexico and two cents to get back across the Rio Grande River. Laredo and Nuevo Laredo were separated only by the river. I crossed it many a weekend during my eighteen-month stay at Laredo Air Force Base.

I had a good friend in Personnel and he called me one day and told me that they needed my AFSC in Tokyo, Japan. He had told me earlier that my captain was leaving for France soon. When I went in to see the captain and told him I wanted to take that assignment, he said, "First, how did you know about the assignment?"

Then he said that I was needed at Laredo more because they had no one available to replace me. And too that I was the only one on base doing what I was doing and I knew the job well and was doing a good job. BS. I said, "Am I needed more than you?"

He said, "Airman, get out of here and start packing."

Another friend of mine was from New Orleans, Louisiana. We had planned on my taking a leave in February and go to Mardi Gras. But that was not to be at this time. I took my thirty-day leave to visit with my family in Miami before I shipped out to Tokyo.

I was bored in Miami. I took a busboy job at Cookie's Restaurant over the beach. It paid $25 per week. We were supposed to be getting 15 percent of the waitresses' salary too, but the boss took it from the waitresses and made up our week's pay with it. It was after I left there that I learned that we should have been getting some of that tip money each night because the waitresses had to turn that part of their tips in each day. The cheapskate.

I had to take two buses from Opa Locka to the beach. I spent more money on transportation than I really was making. But this time, it was not for the money. I wanted something to do while I was on leave and I got to eat good food. I was in good with one of the cooks. He would cover my meat (like steaks) under that garbage we were fed.

Mr. Hicks was now in New York at Columbia University working on his PhD degree. He asked me to stop by and see him on my way to Japan. Can you imagine how excited I was to be able to take him up on that offer. My Guardian Angels at work again.

I got my ticket for New York and on to Burbank and then Oakland, California.

I stopped by to see Mr. Hicks who was staying in Whittier Hall on Amsterdam Avenue in Harlem really. We had a good father-son reunion. We went out to eat, but he was too busy and I did not have the time to see the city. But my purpose for being there was fulfilled. I saw Mr. Hicks. I spent some quality time with Mr. Hicks. Now Tokyo.

When I finally got to the processing center in Oakland, I thought I had seen crowds of people before, but it did not match the crowd of airmen in this place. We were to be processed to take a ship from California to Japan. At dinner that evening, ten names were called from among those thousands of airmen. Airman Saul H. Bethay's name was among them. We were told to report to Personnel after breakfast the next morning. I could not sleep. I had been told that if they saw an AFSC among the group they wanted to keep on their base they could. I just knew they wanted us ten.

I prepared my speech to let them know why they could not keep me there. I had left a good job at Laredo Air Force Base to go to Tokyo, and I did not want to be kept in California.

I skipped breakfast and went directly to Personnel as soon as it was open. Before I could get out my anger, we were told to be ready for air lifting to Tokyo the next morning at 8:00 a.m. Whew! No ship ride for us.

The most airplane riding I had ever had, all in such short period of time. We had to stop in Honolulu, Hawaii, for refueling and to pick up more boxed lunches. We tried to leave Hawaii four times. All on the eighteenth of January. We would get out over the Pacific for one or two hours, and the captain would announce over the speaker that we had to turn back because of some type of trouble with the plane. The fourth time we were told that if any of us wanted to wait on another flight, we could, because he knew some of us were scared.

Not I. I did not want anything to keep me from Tokyo and of all places, Hawaii. There was not any more trouble with the planes but those boxed lunches were tearing my stomach up. I had cramps all the way there. That did not matter as long as I got there. But when we arrived, I realized that I had not had a birthday that year. It was skipped because of crossing the International Date Line.

We arrived and went to our temporary quarters on the outskirts of Tokyo for two nights. The next morning about 3:00 a.m., I went to the latrine. We were on the third flood and I looked out of the window at the trees. They were all white with "rain." I did not know that they had different rain in Japan than we had in the States. I kept looking at this in such amazement for an hour or more. Then another airman came in to use the latrine and said, "Boy, it is snowing out there."

The coldest it ever got in Georgia, to the best of my remembrance, was eighteen degrees. We had heavy dew once which froze and we thought that was snow. But now real snow. I could not wait to get out in it and touch it. But I could not let the others know that I had never seen snow before, so I was walking with the others to breakfast when one of the airmen picked up a fist full and made a ball and threw it at someone. We started a snow fight and never made it to breakfast.

The first morning at my permanent station in downtown Tokyo, we were having breakfast. As soon as I put my fork of eggs into my mouth, the fork started hitting against my teeth. I said to myself, these Japanese have poisoned me. Someone at the table saw my excitement and said, "Everything is okay. It is just an earthquake. You will get used to that here."

I am in heaven now. Tokyo has everything, I learned later; New York City had just more of it. I had never really seen New York before I moved here in 1964. My seeing Mr. Hicks did not count because I did not see any of the sights at that time.

In Tokyo, we lived in apartments in the middle of town. We were near everything and only a subway, bus, trolley, or rickshaw ride away. We had houseboys to shine our shoes and keep our rooms clean. They served us in the mess hall, too.

Now let me tell you about the next eighteen months of my life in Japan.

Tokyo and Fuchu, Japan, 1956

Now my AFSC is Chief Administrative Clerk in the Accounting Division of the Far East Air Force, Tokyo, Japan (a long way from Nashville, Georgia).

My office was about ten blocks from the apartment I was housed. And on good days, I enjoyed walking through the streets downtown Tokyo among the Japanese going to work, too. The Imperial Palace was nearby across the moat. My new job was in the Accounting Division (and office) of the Far East Air Force. It had a large staff. My job was to send out completed financial report throughout the Command. I did not know that much money existed as was listed among those monthly reports. My biggest job came at the end of the month, getting the report out—mailing them, not preparing them.

My work hours were from 8:30 a.m. to 4:30 p.m. I had not been there long and decided to do something in the office one Saturday morning. I did not know that everyone left the building on my floor at noon on Saturday. Here I was left alone and did not know how to secure the office. I dialed 0 and got nothing but Japanese language. I never learned more than a dozen words of Japanese in the entire eighteen months I was in Tokyo. As my Guardian Angels would have it, one of the officers needed something from his desk and came back into the building that afternoon and found me in my desperate straits. He secured the office and I got the heck out of there.

Another day about noon, the typewriters, trays, telephones, papers, and books began flying through the air in the office. The Japanese personnel mostly began screaming and hiding under the desks, which were not moving. It was over before I knew what was going on. It was one of the big ones, not the only one. The buildings in Tokyo are built on rollers, which allow them to sway back and forth during the earthquake. A real experience being on the eighth floor at that.

One of my big thing was getting steam baths and massages. The first time I tried to get into that vat of scalding water, I thought that the skin on my feet and legs were going to peel off. I thought she was deliberately doing this to me. I kept asking her to put cold water in the vat. She kept telling me that I was ruining it with the cold water. Before I left there after eighteen months of this, I could get in any hot water without any trouble.

I now have two new American friends, one from Little Rock, Arkansas and one from Birmingham, Alabama—Lee Rayford and Theodore Reese, Jr. We tried to do everything together after duty—ice-skating, seeing "Broadway" plays and American movies, going to bathhouses, and dancing at the Airmen's club.

We had not been in Tokyo for more than a week when we decided to take a cab to Air Force Hall where the American movies were shown. This taxicab driver took us several blocks from where we were staying and said, "Air Force Hall." The building looked empty and the area deserted. We paid him and got out. Sure enough, it was as it looked.

No Air Force Hall. What a predicament. Not being able to speak Japanese, what were we to do for direction? We did not know at the time that most Japanese speak English. Before we could think straight, another cab came up and asked us where we wanted to go. We said, "Air Force Hall." He took us directly to Air Force Hall. But on the way, I recognized that it was the same cab we had just gotten out of. I told Lee and Teddy that we were not going to pay him again. The cab driver started pitching a bitch when we would not pay him a second time. But we got out, and he finally left, cursing in Japanese, I suspect.

All good things don't last forever. The Far East Air Force Headquarters, the command I was under had to give up its prime location (space) in the center of midtown Tokyo and move out to Fuchu Air Force Base in Fuchu, Japan.

This new base was in a beautiful country location—farms, trees, mountains, animals, etc. The first thing one would do in the morning was look north to see if the snowcapped Mountain Fuji was visible. Our barrack was a three-floor one. We had single rooms with a houseboy to do everything. I kept mine busy because I changed clothes every day, for work and to go back into Tokyo at night. Tokyo was about a thirty-minute train ride from Fuchu. One could time his watch by the train schedule. If you were to ask anyone how far another place was from where you were, he would say ten minutes. That meant when you got on the train you would be getting off in ten minutes. During the rush hour in midtown, persons were hired to push people into the crowded trains. Sometimes we would go down there just to be pushed into the train for fun.

The food in the mess hall got even better. We had waiters and we ordered from a menu. Getting there in the morning before 8:30 a.m. was my problem; I was supposed to be at work at 8:30 a.m. The waiters would complain about our lateness, but who cared. As long as we were at out desk before 9:00 a.m., we were okay. I don't ever remember anyone ever reprimanding me for tardiness.

I met a new friend at Fuchu, Robert J. Small. (As I draft this manuscript, his wife just died in Albuquerque, New Mexico.) I told him what I was doing when he called and told me about Mary's death. He was my partner in crime. At 10:30 a.m. he would call and say, "Meet me at the PX" (Post Exchange.) If it were not near the end of the month, I would be there on command. We always saw any new item first which came into that PX.

When I had a hot date, I would have my suit made. In one day I could be measured at 10:00 a.m. and pick up my suit at 5:00 p.m. with a shirt and matching handkerchief. I became known as the sharp dresser.

Now I had a steady girlfriend at this time. She made up for the twenty-second birthday party I did not have when I crossed the International Date Line and lost a day, my birthday, January 19.

She gave me a birthday party in one of the finest restaurants in downtown Tokyo fit for a king. I felt like a king, only better. We sat on the floor and ate from soup to nuts for about four hours. No one rushes eating in Japan.

There were pieces of meat on a stick which one could dip into a sauce, which made one eat for days. It was part of the hors d'oeuvres. I started to analyze it after I had had more than my share. Through the process of elimination, I came up with the only thing it could be—chicken chitterlings. Another first and last on the chicken guts.

One of the White airmen in my office was getting married to this Japanese woman and the wedding was on the other side of Tokyo. Lee, Teddy, and I left Fuchu on the way to the wedding, and who got on the train on the way to Tokyo? The groom. He had to stop off in downtown to get something, and he did not know how to get to the wedding site. I had learned my way around quite well by this time, and we made it on time. Once we were there, we along with all the other guests waited and waited. In about two hours, the ceremony began.

Everyone had to take off his/her shoes. The bride and groom were given small wine glasses. The kannushi, or Shinto priest, would pour one, two, then three portions of wine in each of their glasses. The bride would drink hers in three separate swallows. The kannushi would pour one, two, then three portions of wine in the groom's glass, and he would gulp his down in one swallow. The guests would just burst their sides laughing each time he did this.

If that was not funny enough, he was standing there in this tuxedo with these loud argyle socks on. (Remember me trying to hide mine in Augusta, Georgia, with the Hornsbys).

The ceremony was not long. Then we all went into the reception room. There was a big bowl of fruit on each table. We ate it along with the delicious Japanese dinner. At the end, the groom said, "We were supposed to have fruit salad, but because of the mix-up in language they thought we just wanted fruit." Then he said, "We have to leave now because you know my wife and I have a lot to do before we can go to sleep tonight." We all laughed again. What he meant was that he had just taken a house off base and the little furniture had just come that day and he was late trying to get some of it set up before he brought the bride across the door.

I had met another friend from another nearby base and he invited another friend of mine and me to come over there and go to this jazz bar for some good music. We went over and met him, I in one of my new suit outfits, shoes included. While we were in the bar, an officer and a sergeant came in and began talking to us? They were thinking we all were from their base, the base the friend we met was from. Everything was going on well until I said something about Headquarters. The sergeant asked, "Are you airmen from Headquarters?" With proud, I said "Yes!" Then he said that this place was an off limit bar and we should not be in it. The airman from Tachikawa Air Force Base said that is not true; we come in here all the time and no one has ever said that before nor was it posted.

They requested that the three of us get up and go outside. They called the air police to come pick us up. We all could not fit into the jeep, so they put our hands behind our backs and put handcuffs on our wrists and marched us through the streets of this town (I call Tachikawa) to the air base. They searched us and took our wallets and then locked us in the stockade (jail). One of the jailers kept coming back to me, supposing to search me again. I told him if he were to touch me again, he would be in big trouble and he knew what I was talking about, too.

I asked them if they notified our base to come for us. They said they had and I asked why was it taking so long. About 2:00 a.m., these officers came into our stall and was amazed to see us all dressed up and not drunk. They said only officers were on duty and that was why it took so long for someone to come for us. They then said that they thought that they were coming to pick up some criminals.

The reason they were doing this to us was because they hated anyone from Headquarters and they would do anything to show it. Our officers even questioned them as to why were we arrested. They told them that we were in an off-limits establishment, drinking alcohol.

The officers took us back to our base and one of my homeboys was on CQ that night. When they let me off, he asked what he was to do. I said he had to take my pass and write it up in the CQ book to cover yourself. More about this airman who was on CQ that night later.

That Monday morning after breakfast, I went to my commanding office and told him what happened. He said I was "grounded" for a week but I could pick up my pass at 5:00 p.m. each day if I wanted to go off base at night. I did this for about two weeks, and when I went to see why it took so long, the report had just come in. It too said that we were drinking. I don't know how he knew that I did not drink, but he said, "Those damn liars. Here, Airman Bethay, take your pass."

The young man who was on CQ that night later celebrated his twenty-first birthday in the barracks with everyone giving him beer. He got so drunk until he could not get back to his room by himself. He was from Atlanta. We kept in touch with each other after we were separated (discharged) from the Air Force. We would see each other on some of the times I was in Atlanta after my family reunions.

Now it is Christmas. Robert J. Small and I took the train downtown to Tokyo. The streets and clubs and bars were empty. We could not believe that Japanese stayed home on Christmas Eve, wrapping presents. We came back to that quiet base and went to the service club and talked until we went to bed. What a Christmas.

All was going well until the big shock—the Far East Air Force Headquarters was moving to Hawaii and I had to be among the advance party.

Hawaii, 1957–1958

I DID NOT WANT to leave Japan! I knew what awaited me in Hawaii—no more houseboy to shine my shoes and keep my room clean for inspection and take my clothes to the laundry and cleaners. I knew that I would be back standing in line for my chow and having to eat whatever was on the chow lines. (The food was never bad or a disappointment in the Air Force my entire four years. It was always good. I enjoyed the cold cuts we got on Sundays.) Now we were back having to sleep in an ex-army barrack with a small cot bed.

Hickam Air Force Base was an ex-Army base, I think. It was next to Pearl Harbor. One could not get to Hickam Air Force Base without passing Pearl Harbor and seeing the battle ships which the Japanese bombed in 1941. (When that happened, I thought Side Camp would be next. I had no geography knowledge of any kind.)

Not having any choice in the assignment, I did what I was sent there to do—set up the Accounting Office for the Headquarters Division of the Far East Air Force. I believe the Air Force had eight headquarters and I was in the Far East one.

We went sightseeing one day soon after I had arrived. We came upon this field of cabbage- head looking plants in rows like the Arlington National Cemetery grave markers. They were so beautiful, like all the other growing plants and flowers in Hawaii. I asked someone in the group what were they? He said, "Pineapples." I always thought pineapples grew on trees. See, it pays to travel. Snow first and now pineapples on the ground.

I did not like the beaches in Honolulu. They were not sandy white like the ones in Florida. Someone told us that the military had its own beaches on the other side of the island. Six of us took a week's leave, rented a cabin on the white sandy military beach, and packed our groceries for doing our own cooking for a week. I became the main cook.

Several of us made our favorite dish. I made a bowl of potato salad. When we finished eating, we noticed that no one had touched my potato salad. That was the laugh of the night. We did not throw it out. We put it in the refrigerator (not icebox) and the next day the only thing I cooked for dinner was fried chicken. After dinner that night, they were licking the bowl, wishing for more potato salad.

Potato salad and fried chicken became a part of my menu when I got out of the Air Force even today. Everyone looks forward to my potato salad and fried chicken when they visit me in New York.

Feeling lonely without a girl on the beach, I wrote in the sand, "Dear Gene." I took a picture of that writing and sent it to my college girlfriend, Emogene Carter, my partner in crime. I still have my copy of that writing in the sand. (Emogene died the early part of 2013.)

Once I had the Accounting Office set up and everything in place, again I had little to do until near the end of each month. I gave up dating because the available women were worse than the ones in Mexico, if that could be possible. I say this because only the women of the streets were interested in us and our money. Instead, I took up playing tennis, badminton, bid whist, swimming, and going back to school.

Later on, Theodore Reese was transferred to Hickam Air Force Base from Fuchu. Once he got there and settled in, he got involved with one of the Negro soldier's wife. Her husband was stationed somewhere in Europe, I think. I knew he was not on this island, and apparently they did, too.

Airman Reese and this man's wife hung out each night in the airmen's club and in town spending all that man's money. I asked Reese if he wasn't concerned that the husband might come home unexpectedly? He said that was the wife's problem, not his. I left them both on the island when I was separated the next April.

I became a decent tennis player. One morning, I was hitting a round on the tennis court when a young man came up with a tennis racket and asked if I wanted to hit a few balls with him? I just knew I was good and played well. Afterward, he asked if I played on a team.

I said no. Then he said that I should because I played well enough to be on a team. Later I went to the mess hall for lunch, and someone asked if I knew who I was playing with? I said, "No!" Then they said that was Pancho Gonzales. I got nervous just thinking that I was playing with the world's top tennis player at the time.

Badminton became my other racket sport. I played doubles with another airman. We became base champs among the airmen. We were scheduled to play the finals against the officers' top players. My partner got scared and did not show up for the final match against the officers. The game was forfeited.

Now it was time to show my skill in playing bid whist. I would play every chance I got and that was one of the other things we would do when the squadron was together doing nothing. Again, I had a partner and a good friend, I thought, until he got orders to ship to France. No one could beat Sergeant Harris and Airman Bethay. During his last week at Hickam, I took a week of leave to spend with him; packing and being together as much as possible before he shipped out, I thought. I did not realize that the pending transfer was upsetting him so. He did not want to spend any time with anyone that last week, including me or especially me. Between meals we would be in our separate rooms until meal time again with no contact—a wasted week for me inasmuch as he did not want to spend that time with me.

Remember, I learned to swim in that pond at Side Camp and I got better once I left those swamps, creeks, ponds, and rivers. I took advantage of the swimming pools in the Air Force. Diving from the tallest diving board at the swimming pools was no challenge for me. I had learned well from those tall trees on the rivers between County Line and Side Camp back in Georgia.

Still not having enough things going on in Hawaii, I enrolled at the University of Hawaii. I took two subjects I had never had. Should I fail them, no one would ever know.

I took Western Civilization and Philosophy for a semester. The requirement in both courses was an exam or quiz each week. In Western Civilization, one had to discuss a different civilization each week—Greece, Rome, etc. I got a grade of C on my first test in Western Civilization. When I went to see the professor's graduate assistant who was grading the test, she said what I did was good but I was trying to retell the book. I asked her what did she want. She said that the only thing she wanted was what "type" or "form" of education, government, religion, art, music, philosophy, etc. each civilization had. I had been trying to remember everything about a country for the exam. From then on, I just studied these things in each civilization and my studying could be done is one sitting, with little or no effort to do this. My grade went from a C to As the remainder of the course. She still gave me a B in the course.

Again, the philosophy class was just the opposite. The professor did his own grading. He would not let us ask any questions for the first three weeks. He said we did not know enough about philosophy to ask question yet. He was correct. He would give you three questions out of a possible five to answer. This course was the History of Philosophy, starting with the early philosophers, such as Socrates, Plato, Aristotle, etc. I would ace every test each week.

I enjoyed learning about the different philosophers. I spent most of my spare time now studying for both subjects. I was always an overstudier (achiever) and sometimes to my disadvantage.

On one test, I chose to compare Aristotle's Idea of the Being with that of Plato's. I knew I had done an excellent job with Plato's, but when I started to do Aristotle, I drew a blank. I had to choose another question to answer, which I was able to do without any problem. I was learning this subject well.

The professor gave me an A but wrote me a note asking why I did not do Aristotle because I had done such an excellent job with Plato? I had just crossed that one out and left enough for him to see how well I knew it. I knew Aristotle too but could not think at that time.

The final exam had to do with Plato's *Republic*. I got an "A" on my final, too. An "A" for the course in philosophy and a "B" in Western Civilization. This was to happen to me again at Columbia University in 1961. (Snow, pineapples, and now my first White American professors, both were Americans from the States; Hawaii was still a territory when I was stationed there.)

Had I stayed on in Hawaii, I would have taken more courses in philosophy. I loved it enough to take a major in it if I could have had that same professor. I do well under certain professors' ways of teaching and I do better on essay exams.

Because I did not want to come to Hawaii, leaving a place like Tokyo, I would not let myself fully enjoy anything outside of the base. I did take advantage of everything open to airmen on base, though. One of the problems was racism in Honolulu at the time, and I was not one to be where I was not welcomed, especially when I felt that I was better than they in the first place. I never considered seeing the other islands while there. I was told that the big island of Hawaii was beautiful, too. In fact, I did not try to see more of Japan either. Maybe I am a one-town person.

My Guardian Angels had someone from Personnel call me and tell me that I could take an early out if I did not want to reenlist. I never considered a career in the Air Force anyway. It had served the purpose I wanted. I am now a man. I am twenty-four with a BS Degree in Vocational Agriculture and four years of military service under my belt.

I filled out the papers for separation (discharge). When I went to pick them up the day before my flight to Miami International Airport, I saw Nashville, Tennessee. What? Some idiot took it upon himself and assumed that I had made the mistake as to where I was from when I enlisted. He should have known that any written mistake could only be corrected with a written order to change it and stating why it was a mistake. This was not done. Lucky for me, I knew how to do the correction. I had to find one of the personnel, a qualified officer to sign my discharge papers. If I did not know how to do this, I could have been kept at Hickam Air Force Base in Hawaii for God knows how long. Not my case. My Guardian Angels were there all the time. I made the flight!

Now I am in Opa Locka (Miami), April 1958.

April 1958

BELIEVE IT OR NOT, I am Saul again. Also, I am home again now, working with Daddy in his landscaping business. It is April 1958. (Daddy was out of work for a long time when he first got to Miami. It was hard for him to make the transition from sharecropping to a job in the city, which he had no training or preparation.)

When I went into the service in 1954, he realized that he could not handle the farmwork with just himself and Bobby, and the young man who was around a few years early was not there either. So after he gathered his crops, Daddy loaded up the family and off to Miami they went. Alline had gotten them a place in Brown Sub to live. I cannot remember why I knew that apartment. I do not know the time I visited it either because the family was living in the house of my sister Annie Mae in Opa Locka when I came home on leave.

I do not know either why I remember Daddy having to stand on the corner waiting for someone who needed day laborers to hire him.

His son-in-law, Ulysses, was doing yard work and he told Daddy to give it a go. Which he did. It was a very successful move. This was the only type of work Daddy did the remainder of his short life. He was just fifty-four when he was killed by the auto accident in front of the house. The car jack fell and the car crushed him. More about this accident later, too.

When I returned home in April 1958 from the Air Force, I too needed a job. I put out some feelers, but I had not heard from any of them. I applied to the University of Mexico to study biology. It was some type of program American veterans could attend free of charge. One had to stay with a Mexican family and learn Spanish as they perused their degree. It sounded ideal to me.

I was accepted and was to start in September. In the meantime, I would go help Daddy with his yard work. Daddy had clients all over Miami and Miami Beach. They all paid well and paid him when the work was done. I really learned the beach area by working with Daddy. Mama would fix our lunches after breakfast, and off we would go for the day. What a pleasure it was for me to be working with my daddy again. I was working for the joy of being with him. I got some type of "musting" out pay for a while. I did not keep the Air Force insurance either because I did not want any connection with the Air Force once I was out.

I kept getting these notices for me to report to reserve. I kept ignoring them, too. One day these two air policemen came to our house on 153rd Street in Opa Locka. I just happened to be home that day. They surprisingly asked if this was the house Airman Bethay lives? I said, "Yes, I am he." With red faces, they sheepishly said that there had been some type of mistake and left without an explanation.

I knew what the mistake was. The mistake was they thought I was White by the name. I never heard from them until later on in the year. I got a letter stating that I had been assigned to the inactive unit in Colorado. Negroes were not accepted into the active reserve in 1958.

Sometime later, a brush hit Daddy in one of his eyes. It was bleeding. I got scared. I thought he might be blinded from it. I took him to a doctor in Coral Gables. The doctor examined his eye and found it was not as bad as it looked or I thought. Daddy had to wear a bandage for several weeks. But he ended up okay, thank God!

Now it is August. Someone notified me about a teaching job in Gray, Georgia. I called the principal, Mr. Crofford, and he said yes, there was a job for an Ag teacher and it was mine if I wanted it. It paid $4,000 per year, but Ag teachers got an extra $50 each month to visit the boys' projects on the farms. He gave me all the other information I needed before coming; he even let me know that I had a place to stay.

I told Daddy about the job offer. He was pleased. I told him I needed a car to complete my teaching responsibilities. I do not know the details, but I soon had a car before I was to leave for Gray.

Gray is a small town east of Macon, Georgia. It is a farm town, like most small towns are in Georgia. I was given a room at Mr. Frank and Mrs. Mattie Pitts's. Everyone called them Papa and Mama Pitts. That was what I called them, too. They introduced me to everyone as their son, and they treated me like a son. I gladly accepted that title. But I knew no one could ever take Daddy and Mama's position; not even Dr. O. E. Hicks, who now has his Ph.D. It was awarded in June 1958 from Teachers College, Columbia University in New York, New York.

Mama Pitts cooked my breakfast and dinner; I ate lunch at school. Miss Johnnie Price, Leontyne Price's first cousin, lived there also. She was the Home Economics teacher at the Maggie Califf High School. We developed a close friendship which lasted until her death years later in Atlanta.

Miss Price brought a car and did not know how to drive. I taught her how to drive (I thought I did; one day she was making a turn, not knowing how to reverse, and ran into the corner of the schoolhouse), and later she would drive by herself to Mississippi, her home.

Maggie Califf was like the Cook County Training School, with the following exception, it had grades from first to the twelfth. There was a separate shop classroom and a room for teaching agriculture classes in the same building. Mr. Nelvin Miller and I shared the shop. It was an excellent facility, fully equipped.

I had four classes, the eighth through the eleventh. One of the first projects I assigned the boys to do was to landscape the grounds around the main building. I had a young man in the eighth grade who was a dresser. He brought all of his clothes from the well-known store in Macon. A lot of the students were "goof-offs," but every time I looked around, this young man would have a tool or rake or hoe or shovel in his hands, working in those expensive shoes and clothes. This young man's name is Emory Lamar. His mother was an elementary school teacher, Mrs. Eppie Hammock. We too remained friends until her death. I will tell you more about Emory later.

Mr. Crofford had all the teachers afraid of him, but not me. One morning he came into my classroom to tell me to have a student go get some paper out of the water fountain he had just passed. We had a custodian on campus, too. I kept on teaching. The second time he came in, I asked to see him in the hall. I said, "I need to know right now, what is more important, teaching this class or getting that piece of paper out of the water fountain? If the paper is more important, then I am at the wrong school and you have an Ag class to teach." I did not have any more trouble out of him with one exception.

Mr. Crofford had a reputation for "messing" with all new female teachers; even though he was married, that did not stop him. He was the principal. I was dating Mary Sue Jones, an elementary teacher at the school. I learned that he was having an affair with her as well. I stopped dating Miss Jones, and he had the nerve to ask me why I had stopped dating her. I told him that a horse should not have but one jockey at a time.

My sister Zipha had done her student teaching at Maggie Califf. I think she had to get him straight, too, trying to mess with her at the time. (Our educational paths followed even to Gray, Georgia.)

I had a good teaching year at Maggie Califf High School; it was my first job, and I met some nice people in that town. I remain friends with many of them since I left. I always visited many of them when I am in the Gray area. Emery Lamar and his mother are some of the ones I always visited. Mrs. Hammock died in 2013, after a somewhat long illness. She was a person everyone loved. She had those "carrying ways" about her, always showing concern for those in need. They lived in one of the finest homes for Negroes in Gray at the time- they still did and do.

There were quite a few good Negro business people in Gray at the time, the Blacks, the Colliers with the funeral home, the Pitts, just to name a few I still remember. I knew James and Juanita Pitts from Fort Valley; Juanita was my classmate. A small world.

I did all the required things teaching Ag. We had the barbeque fundraiser, and I took the boys to the annual meeting at Camp John Hope, the same camp I was initiated into APA, the same camp John Hope the Dean took us when I was a senior at Fort Valley State College.

There was a class fund-raiser throughout the school, including elementary and high school classes. Mr. Crofford's wife's class had raised the most money, and he put $5 into another teacher's amount to keep his wife from winning. That was the type of person he was among other unmentionables.

Farming and the teaching of agriculture were going through some changes in 1958. To better prepare for the pending changes, I decided to go back to school and get my master's.

Michigan State College, here I come.

Michigan State College, June 1959

THE CLOSER IT CAME to the end of the school year, the more I prepared for graduate school. Had I stayed in agriculture, I would have gone to Michigan State College to do my master's in agriculture there.

While visiting Papa Hicks back and forth to Fort Valley on weekends, I told him of my plans and that I needed his help in selecting a major and a college. He said that there was but one major for me and that was counseling. I asked him what was that? He said you knew them as advisors. The new field is called guidance and counseling and that was the only place he saw me. Then I asked him to give me the five top schools which were offering this major; Michigan State was among them. Needless to say, that was one of the schools I had thought of for graduate work in agriculture.

Off with my effort to get into Michigan State College (MSC).

I spent that summer back in Miami, working with Daddy and enjoying the city until I took off for Michigan State.

I purchased a train ticket for Lansing, Michigan, with an overnight stop in Chicago, Illinois. I did not want to spend the night in the train station so I took a room at the YMCA which was nearby. That in itself was an experience; with all types and kinds of men coming and going all night, it was not a place for one to rest.

When I began emptying my pockets for bed, out came the car keys. In my excitement leaving for Michigan State, I put the car keys in my pocket rather than giving them to Daddy. Neither did he remember them at the time. They too were excited and happy about my leaving for Michigan State. I still do not know what they did to get home.

The next morning I boarded the train for Lansing. There were several other students in my train car going to MSC. We were all friends somewhat when we arrived. But one of the students, T. Ray Lawrence, coming from Mississippi with that red streak of hair, got his pants zipper stuck. Everyone took turns trying to get it working before we got to Lansing the next morning.

We arrived at the Lansing train depot about five or six o'clock in the morning, but we could not check into the dormitory at MSC before eight or nine. We were stuck in the potbelly train station until that time.

MSC is in East Lansing not too far away. When that time came, we checked into our rooms in Armstrong Hall—a new dorm quite different from Jeanes Hall at Fort Valley State. I was assigned a roommate from Memphis, Tennessee, Square Partee. Have you ever heard of such a name of anyone, especially a Negro man in the States? He was a math major and a chain smoker, a habit I had to get used to being around which was not easy, but I made it.

I was a veteran, thus I got the full GI Bill benefits to attend college. I had forty-eight months of the GI Bill. It paid my full room and board. Out-of-state tuition was just $100 at the time. I lived on campus and took advantage of all its benefits. This campus area housed the male students, graduate and undergraduate—the Brody Group as it was called. There was a central dining hall which accommodated six dorms; each dorm group had its own section in the dining hall.

Michigan State is larger than Miami with its farmland. It is a land grant college like the University of Georgia is. Each state has one, and in the South, there is one for Negroes and one for Whites in most states.

MSC had its own bus service for students to get around the campus. That in itself lets you know how large the campus is in size not to mention its student body. It was about eighty thousand at this time. It is a hilly campus and I lived on the northwest entrance side and the graduate counseling building was on the extreme southeast side. I could walk the distance faster than waiting on the bus which had to circle the campus. (This was like taking the bus around Cook County in Georgia.)

The first week I thought I was coming down with rheumatism. Every bone and muscle in my body was aching. I was going to the infirmary until my roommate told me what was happening to my body. My pains were from walking those hills, an exercise I was not used to doing. I drove everywhere I went before I went to MSC.

The next thing I remember was having to report for registration at a specific time—2:15 p.m. In spite of the thousands of students in the gym, I was in and out in about thirty minutes. I met with Dr. Costar, my advisor, who suggested I take only four courses, twelve quarter hours of credit rather that a full fifteen hours of credit. This meant I had to attend summer school to obtain the forty-five credit hours needed for the master's.

He told me what those courses were to be. I picked up the cards for the four courses, paid for the credits, and took some type of shot on the way out of the gym. I think it was a flu shot, but I'm not sure.

I then went to the bookstore and purchased the four books and other equipment I thought I might need.

My classes were scheduled for Tuesday and Thursday only. I could have taken eighteen or twenty credit hours with all of that time on my hands. Here I was, a full-time student, living in the dormitory with the GI Bill and eating in the cafeteria with nothing else to do but over study, which I did.

My major classes were somewhat like they were at Fort Valley. I was in the same classes with the same students. I had to take two courses in Counseling and Guidance and two in areas which I needed to meet the requirements for the degree. One of the courses was a sociology course in Human Relations, and the other one was Adolescent Psychology. Both were undergraduate courses of things, which I had not had at Fort Valley but needed for my master's in counseling and guidance at MSC.

When I began reading the books, they all were so simple until I had completed both counseling and guidance books before class had begun. I had the time to read all the other books listed on the reading list as well within a few weeks. I asked myself is this graduate school?

There was one other Negro student in my classes, Obrey Ratcliff from Ohio—a talker. I was quiet. No one hardly spoke to me in or out of class and I did likewise. My socialization was on campus, in the dorm, and with Cecil G. Smith from Bermuda. I became friends with most of the students on my dorm floor.

That first quarter I had only two papers to do. I chose to study the history of the Guidance and Counseling field—a very ambitious undertaking for a three-credit course. But I thought that was what graduate school was all about, and I had the time to do it. I was able to do this research with ease and with the help from my new friend from Atlanta, Georgia, James Mitchell. (We remained friends until his death. More about him later.)

It was James "Jim" Mitchell who told me about the State of Georgia paying Negro students to attend graduate school out of Georgia; any school they chose, they paid the difference. He gave me the information and I applied. Now the State of Georgia, working with Miss Harris from the State Department in Georgia, reimbursed me all the money I had spent thus far on everything—the out-of-state fee, room and board, and transportation money for me to travel three times during the year to and from Nashville.

I had to open a bank account because I had money coming in from everywhere it seemed.

Classes started. I felt that I was doing well without any reinforcement from the professors.

Charles and Russell were both living and working in the auto factories in Flint, Michigan. Charles invited Cecil and me to spend Thanksgiving with them. I was able to see and spend some time with Russell and Ella Mae. Charles's wife's name was Mae Ella. What a coincidence.

It began snowing. I thought I had seen snow in Japan, but it was not anything like that snow in Michigan. I had to buy myself some snow gear. It kept snowing on and off all winter; big piles of snow everywhere became hills of ice. There was a river (the Red Cedar) running through the campus, and it was something to see it frozen over until May of the next year.

The school quarter came to an end just before Christmas. James Mitchell told me that I could ride as far as Atlanta with him. This

I did. I had driven until we were in Cincinnati. I got tired and Jim took over. I got in the back and went to sleep. All of a sudden, Jim slammed on brakes. I woke up and asked him what was the matter? He said he was going blind and had lost his eyesight. I looked out of the car and said there is a river of water with fog out there. We both got out of the car and started to look around. We saw this small sign which said, "Stop, Ferry Crossing." We did not know what to do. I asked Jim did he take a wrong turn? He said no. Then we heard these bells on the river. Here comes a flat-bedded ferryboat. A few people got off with cars. I asked Jim if he were sure he wanted to put his car on that flimsy-looking ferry? He said he had no other choice and he did. We learned later that many a car had been driven into that river at night because of poor lighting and warning signs. The warning sign should have been larger and posted earlier.

We made it to Atlanta. I took a train to Miami. Daddy met me at the train station. I enjoyed being with the family again for Christmas. I had spent Christmas with them the year I worked in Gray. Mama gave me a thick sweater for Christmas to take back with me for that cold weather in East Lansing. I still have that sweater today, and when I wear it in New York, everyone asks me where did I get that sweater from? I just smile and think of Mama.

As planned, I met Jim in Atlanta after Christmas to come back to Michigan State. On the way back, he asked me what my grades were? I told him that I had not gotten my grades. He said I should have because he had received his.

I immediately went to see Dr. Costar when I got back on campus. He told me that my papers were rejected in both classes because they thought I had a ghostwriter. He went on to say that the papers were too extensive and too perfect for a beginning graduate student coming into a new field from agriculture, too. I told him I had nothing to do but read all those simple books, and I had an undergraduate degree and had done well in writing; thus, those two papers were nothing for me to do.

He said, before they could give me a grade for the two guidance courses, I had to critique an assigned book and the other professor would tell me what I was to do in his course to get a grade. Boy, was I pissed.

I went to see Jim Mitchell and told him what had happened. I told him I was leaving for another school. I was not going to take that crap from them when they had suggested I take only twelve credits in such a simple major. And I knew they thought that a Negro student could not be that good in English or any subject for that matter. Jim said, "No, you are not leaving. I will help you." Together we ripped that book apart with my criticisms.

When I started to do the research on the topic for the other course, I realized that the professor had given me his Ph.D. topic to research. I told him I was not going any further with that. He could do whatever he wanted. Then he said that was his graduate topic for his doctorate degree and he wanted to see just how good I really was.

I completed the review for the one course and turned it in to Dr. Costar. He wrote me a comment after he had read it stating that I had done an excellent job, and the faults that I found with the book were the reason they stopped using it as a text for the course. I got a B.

Already I had told the other professor that I was not going any further researching his topic. They got together and decided he too would give me a "B."

The next quarter I had a course in the Review of the Literature in Guidance and Counseling, taught by Dr. Costar. I sat in front, and whenever he misquoted any research or book, I would say, "Did not so and so say the same thing in his book?" Then he would say, "Oh, that is right." I gave him hell all quarter in that class. He gave me a "B" but did say later that he realized that I had to have read those books during the other courses and quarter because I could not have known what I knew about all of them so well so soon.

I did not agree with many of the studies on race and race relations in the undergraduate Human Relations class taught by a Jewish professor, Dr. Milton Rokeach. He said one would discriminate on the basis of one's religion before they would on race. I asked him did he really think that was true for Negroes? He said yes! I then said, "No one has ever asked my religion when they said I could not enter certain places or ride in the front of a bus."

He had a film of a Negro man fighting a White man and there was a knife in the scene. The question the students in the class was asked was, "Which one had the knife?" I was the only one who was able to see in a flash that the White man had the knife. The students were shocked when the film was played back slowly, and they saw that it was the White man with the knife.

There were several other quoted racial situations which I did not agree with and I told him so. Dr. Rokeach said that it was people like me who ruin experiments. I said, "No, it is professors like you who draw conclusions on experiments which were not proven based on fact."

Jim Mitchell took a course under Dr. Rokeach later and they used his book, *The Open and Close Mind*. Because of my experience, Jim decided to critique his book as his class project. We literally closed ourselves in one week end and pointed out everything we felt was wrong with the book. Students' papers had to be discussed and/or defended in class. Jim did not have to defend his paper in class because Dr. Rokeach brought two other professors to help him deal with Jim's arguments. The other two professors took Jim's points of view, and Jim had nothing to do but see the three professors go at each other. Jim told me after class that he would get an "A" or an "F." He got an "A."

(I was working at Brooklyn College during the eighties and I saw where Dr. Rokeach had revised that book. I did not spend any money to see how much he had changed his "racial mind." or how much he changed based on what Jim and I said was wrong with the book.)

At this time I knew my grade. But I really did not expect to get a "C." I got a "C" in the other undergraduate psychology class I had to take as well. Instead of teaching, the professor just ran his mouth about anything. And he had been giving that same old test for years.

The undergraduates would come in at the beginning of the quarter and come back at the end and take the test with the answers known from other students who had the test before. He did not print the test on new paper, the test was on the old faded paper. He had used it so many times before. I know this sounds like sour grapes. I would not want to take credit for something I did not know or earn. If I thought I did not know enough for more than a "C," I would be man enough to accept the C like I did in Freshman Orientation at Fort Valley State.

The third quarter I had a female professor, Dr. Norris, my only female professor at MSC. The first day of class she told me not to expect an "A" in her class because students generally don't know that much about this subject to get an "A." I asked her, "How does your subject differ from the others? I had not made an "A" in any of them either. How could you say this when you don't even know me?" I got the "B."

I needed a B average to graduate and I was now entering the third quarter with those two undergraduate Cs.

One of my courses was Counseling Lab. It was the course where one counsels high school students while being observed and evaluated behind a two way mirror; there would be about three or four professors and the same amount of graduate students listening in on how well you were doing.

Each Friday the class would meet to hear what they were doing wrong in their counseling lab.

My cases were never brought up for discussion. During the mid-term I went to Dr. Costar and asked him was he aware that I had never been discussed? He said, "Yes." Then I asked him how was I to know what to do to improve. He said, "Maybe you over explain test results to the counselees." I said that I could not take for granted that high school students understood the tests I gave them because they were not tests on academic subject, they were IQ tests and aptitude tests, not teacher made tests. He had no further comments for me.

My scheduled counseling scheduled time was 11:00 A.M. on Wednesday each week. We had been informed that should we miss a session our grades would be affected accordingly. I was told that my schedule for the week had been changed from Wednesday to Thursday the same time. One of the graduate assistants who was assigned to our class called me about 11:00 P.M. Wednesday and said he could not sleep because of me. I asked him what had I done to him and what this was about? All kinds of things started going through my mind until he went further as to why he was calling me.

Then he told me that they did not know what the deal is with me. They think that you have all of this before somewhere because you are too good at counseling. They are bringing in a student from some place where no counselor had ever been able to establish rapport with him. And he then said, "Should that happen with you, just terminate the session and leave." Now I am concerned.

It is Thursday at 11:30 A.M. and no one has come to get me to go into the counseling room with my new counselee. I asked Dr. Costar had they forgotten that I had been told to come in today instead of yesterday? He said, "No. In fact, you may leave because your counselee is not coming." I said it is Thursday and there is no way for me to have another session before the quarter ends. Dr. Costar said, "I said don't worry about it, didn't I?" Now I don't have my quota of counseling sessions and I have no time to make it up.

It is summer. It is time to meet with the committee to determine whether you will get certified or not to become a counselor. There were thirty five students in this counseling class. I was the only Negro at that point.

I went early to the session to see what was happening with the other students who were being evaluated. Students were kept in session for an hour or more. Some came out crying. They finally called me in. I sat down and they asked what I thought my weaknesses were. I said I did not know because no one had helped me, only you telling me that I overinterpreted test results to my clients.

In front of the committee and me, Dr. Costar tore up his notes and told me that I could leave. Startled, I asked, "What did I do wrong? I just got here and other students were here for more than an hour and you all did not help me during the class either, and now you are dismissing me this way?"

Then he said, "Why waste time when you see yourself as we do?" I was shocked by that statement and somewhat confused, too. I left.

A week had passed and no word about my grade? I remembered the graduate assistant who had called me about the client I was to see who did not show up. I got in touch with him and I asked him if he knew my grade. He said, "Saul, you know I am not to tell you this, but the way they have treated you this year is a disgrace. They think that the NAACP sent you here as a test to see how we were treating Negro students." Shock number two.

Then he said, "There were five As given and you got one of the As." Shock number three.

I looked for Jim Mitchell to tell him the good news.

When I got the official notice about my grade, I went to Dr. Costar concerning my average, two Cs and one A. I had taken more than the required number of credits, and he said they would drop one of those Cs and that would give me the required average. Now I would have all Bs, one C, and one A, as I understood it. And with the A in the evaluation, I would be certified with a master's in Guidance and Counseling from Michigan State College.

Now let's back up socially during the year. I did not know that there were but a few Negro students at MSC other than the athletes. The athletes had their own dorm and their own majors, as I was told later. Their only job was to win games. Their educational requirements came into question later. President John H. Hannah was the chairman of the Human Rights Commission of the United States of America.

One Saturday morning, I decided to visit the student union building. I was startled when I walked in and there sat about two hundred Negro boys and girls throughout the union. From my initial reaction, one would have thought that I was White.

Cecil and I took advantage of the out of class activities, separate or together. First of all, I did a lot of ice-skating. I swam a lot in the indoor swimming pool during the winter months and the outdoor pool during the summer. We attended all the musical concerts (Cecil was a music major). We attended all the home sports games and Cecil would fall asleep during the games. He said he did not understand any of that.

Michigan State had one of the best bands and sports teams. They filmed the football team during a game one Saturday for the movie *Spartacus*. The school mascot was Sparty.

During the quarters I would sometimes play Scrabble in the female dorm. One night I wanted to use the word "zax," and no one knew it or would go get a dictionary. They would not let me use it. I told the group before you go to sleep look up that word "zax," which is a cutting tool.

Cecil and I did not have any type of job or needed one at Michigan State. We had been working before MSC and we had our financial resources in place before we got there and we were not recent graduates from college as many of our dorm mates were. We were a little older than the average entering graduate student, too. In fact the eighteenth of January 1960, a deliveryman from a local bakery brought me a birthday cake from Daddy and Mama from Miami. We invited the men on the floor to have cake with us. The eighteenth was Cecil's birthday and the nineteenth was my birthday. On my birthday, the same bakery brought Cecil his cake from his parents in Bermuda. We invited the same group back for more cake. Two nights in a row.

It was later said that we had the bakery send us those cakes pretending that our parents had done so. The students were envious of us because we were always well dressed and we had our own money. I still had all those clothes I had made in Japan with me.

My roommate always had to borrow money from me until he got his work-aid check at the end of the month. I gave him a check each time and he later began paying me back with a check after having told the others that I did not keep cash on me and always had to give him a check when he borrowed money from me. I know he would have to deposit that little money he made to be able to write me that check.

During the spring, I went out on the golf range once with James Mitchell. The first and last time I have tried playing golf.

Cecil and I attended the graduation exercises that summer, but we did not participate with the other students, marching in cap and gown. Any student who was completing his requirements during the summer quarter could march in the June graduation. That was not important to me. I had marched at Fort Valley State, and nothing could match that graduation in 1954. President Harry S. Truman was the keynote speaker.

For the summer, Cecil and I got an apartment together right off campus—my first apartment. It was the first floor of a house which had the top floor rented out to students as well.

I cooked and Cecil kept the place spotless. The landlord told us that we were such good tenants that he hated to charge us rent.

We would invite some of the friends we had made in the dorm for some meals. Three guys from India were among the guests we would have over. T. Ray Lawrence would come by as well. He too stayed around that summer.

Cecil had this girlfriend from his undergraduate days in Ohio who was old enough to be his grandmother. He invited her by for dinner one night and she brought her girlfriend. I wish you could have seen us entertaining our "grandmothers" as they sat there over made up with their false eye lashes and dyed hair.

When Cecil and I would go to a bar in East Lansing, we had to show ID to get in, not required of the White boys much younger than we were. Really, this was my first face-to-face discrimination. I guess prior to this I had been avoiding this. I had never wanted to be or go anywhere I was not wanted or appreciated, especially in a bar in East Lansing among those White folks, and I didn't even drink.

McDonald's was new at the time and was just across the street from our apartment. We went there every now and then because that type of restaurant was new to us. It was a new type of place to get hamburgers. They would advertise by stating the number of burgers they had sold up to that time.

Somehow, I heard about the Dean of Students job at Edward Waters College in Jacksonville, Florida. I applied. I had to get a recommendation from Dr. Costar. He wrote to President Stuart, the president at Edward Waters College, that I had received the best master's MSC had ever awarded to a student in Guidance and Counseling. He wrote this knowing what my grades were.

Sight unseen, I was accepted to be the Dean of Students that September at Edward Waters College. Dean Bethay.

Edward Waters College, 1960–1961

DR. WILLIAM B. STEWART, the president of Edward Waters College, must have put in the placement office at Michigan State College the ad for the Dean of Students job; otherwise, I do not know how my Guardian Angels let me know about it. The position came with a "furnished apartment" on campus and eating arrangements in the dining hall. Edward Waters College is one of several schools related to or dominated by the African Methodist Episcopal Church.

Having just completed my master's and having been offered a job of this caliber in Jacksonville, Florida, seemed too good to be true. And it was.

I went home (Opa-Locka, Florida) and informed Daddy and Mama that I would be working in Jacksonville. They were just as excited as I was. Inasmuch as I would be living on campus, I saw no need for a car. I packed my Tokyo-made suits and other clothes and headed for Edward Waters College.

As it turned out, the apartment was a large room in the freshman, sophomore, and junior boys' old wooden dormitory; seniors lived on the top floor of the main building, Lee Hall. The head of Buildings and Grounds had the other apartment in this dormitory. It was not Armstrong Hall at Michigan State.

During the initial registration, I was attempting to cut the registration line to enter the Registrar's office when a student grabbed my arm and said, "Dog, where do you think you are going? You better get to the foot of this line." Another student who apparently had seen me somewhere on campus, grabbed him, and said, "Man, turn that man loose, that is our new Dean of Students!"

One of my first projects was to teach the boys how to live in a dorm. We did not have a dean of men, so I served in both capacities. We had dorm meetings about taking care of a room and room inspections, which I would be doing. I tried to let them know what they should do to help improve their rooms and the dormitory at large.

Working with the Buildings and Grounds man, we let the boys clean out all of that stored-up junk in the pigeon-dominated attic and paint it. We purchased a Ping-Pong table and a pool table for them to play on. The problem was, they thought that they would be able to play pool and Ping-Pong any and all times just because it was in the building in the attic. No. We had set times for the attic (rec room) to be open in the afternoon and in the evenings during the week and in special times also on the weekends.

They felt that it was theirs after they had done so much work to get it fixed up and painted the room in the school colors. They thought that they would be able to use it at will. I enforced those recreational rule hours along with the sportsman-like conduct rules, also.

They burned me in effigy because of those rules. Someone had just put the fire out when I got outside of my room. We did not have to call the fire department. It was a small bag of paper hanging from the ceiling near the front door that they had burned. I told someone to tell all the boys in the building if they were not down in the lobby within ten minutes to come later with their packed bags for home—suspension!

They all were there dressed in their underwear or pants, but they were there. I told them, "If this is all you care about and do not appreciate what is being done for you, burn the damn building down. I have some place to go and I know most of you do not. I am going back to bed." Things began to change for the better in our relationship from then on. So much about Hurst Hall for the moment.

I had office hours for counseling, but my teaching job was teaching Freshman Orientation. I soon realized that the other students needed some "orientation" too. I began having meetings with all students about things I felt they needed to do to improve student life on campus. We formed a student organization (SO), having a president, vice president, secretary, sergeant at arms, and class representatives—freshman, sophomore, junior, and senior, male and female. The Dean of Women was a member as well. The other students were automatically members, too. There was no money, so we did not have a need for a treasurer.

My office was in the Lee Building (the church and auditorium) on the second floor under the senior boys' dorm. I had to borrow a typewriter from the typing room each day for my secretary until one day the typing teacher said we could not do that anymore. I went down to the business office and told the business manager, Mr. Barnett, that if I did not have a typewriter in my office the next morning I am out of this place. His secretary, Geraldine, told him we better get a typewriter up there immediately because that man is crazy.

Now was the time to raise money for school. The next thing I knew students were all over the place interrupting everyone's class, selling boiled peanuts and God knows what else to raise this money. The fund-raiser was advertised to help purchase a new building; there was a picture of a proposed new building; I was told that this was done each year, but there was no new building yet. I felt that some of this money went to the Bishops.

I sent out a notice to everyone that there was to be no more selling of any kind during the school hours. I am sure President Stuart did not take well to that stoppage, but he did not say anything to me. Neither did anyone else, as I remember.

There were strict rules for girls. Women could not be out of the Dean of Women's sight, literally. Working with the Student Organization, I made arrangements for the girls to be able to visit for two hours in the boys' dorm/room after dinner (midday) on Sundays, but the doors must be kept open if they were inside the rooms. Some of the boys made extra effort to improve the appearance of their rooms. Some even brought cheap curtains for the windows. I got some of the female faculty to serve as chaperons. That became a big hit with the students. The administration, including the Dean of Women, did not take this idea too kindly either, but I had enough faculty support to make it happen.

Next, I arranged a one-hour study hall for the athletes after practice and dinner, Monday through Thursday. I got faculty members to help the athletes with their schoolwork. The athletes did not take kindly to this, and I don't think the coaches liked it at first either because I required that one of them be there each night and take attendance. The coaches finally cooperated with me because they saw how it was helping the student athletes academically.

We dealt with all students concerns in the Student Organization, and I included some of the things I felt would help Edward Waters College students become more proud of the school and themselves. We had written rules affecting everything students were involved in. Working with the academic dean, we reviewed the policies on class behavior, attendance, lateness, dress codes in the classroom and in the cafeteria on Sundays, etc.

I along with the students, faculty and administration began to relax some the second semester. We all seemed to be able to get alone and function better. I was proud of what I saw from everyone's cooperation. Edward Waters had a very good staff, and they too wanted the best for the students and the school.

There was one professor that I wish I had the means to make him Dean of Men. He helped me in so many ways. I relied on him in my understanding and in my working with the staff, administration, and the church folk. I could not have made it without his voluntary help and support. His name was Joseph C. Paige, a brilliant young man. He really cared for all students and showed it in so many ways. Joe, I thank you!

My time spent on weekends was visiting friends and relatives. I began dating, so some of my frustration was taken care of that way. I am sure it was seen in my relaxation on campus as well. One of the things my date and I looked forward to was the barbeque dinners sold on Kings Road, a corner not far from the college—in fact, on the same street as the college.

Now if I were going to stay in this position, I would need an advanced degree. I had been thinking about doing my doctorate at the University of Wisconsin, but I did not want to go that far during the summer.

I realized that I had not really seen New York and maybe I would spend the summer doing that. But I could not justify my spending the summer there as a tourist. I said why not take some classes, not planning on a degree. I ultimately wanted to go to the University of Wisconsin.

I made application at Teachers College, Columbia University. I sent for my transcript from MSC and I was told that I had not completed the requirements for the degree; I did not have a "B" average.

I called Dr. Costar and he told me to come back and take one course. I asked him if he were kidding me? I asked him what about that "C" you were to have removed from my record? He said that he had forgotten about doing that. I told him Columbia had accepted me without knowing about the transcript being a problem, I guess. He said that he would get in touch with Columbia University and work something out.

Arrangements were made for me to take any course at Columbia and they would give me credit at MSC. I was officially admitted under those terms. Have you ever heard of any nonsense like that? It could only happen to me, as most things did at Michigan State.

But since I was to be in school just for the summer and not as a tourist, I would need some place to stay.

Many a Sunday I would have dinner with one of my cousins and his family in Jacksonville. This was my cousin Ralph's brother in Adel, Alfred, and his wife, Rossie Williams. Rossie would prepare the best dinners each Sunday. I could bring my girlfriend at times when she was available. Rossie was an excellent cook and made certain that I had the best. Nothing was never too good for Dean Bethay in their sight. They were so proud of my being their cousin and Dean of Students at Edward Waters College, too. They let everybody know that.

In sharing my summer plans with them, Rossie said that she had a friend in the Bronx that I might be able to stay with during the summer. She gave me the name and address and I contacted Ethel and William Higgins on Briggs Avenue in the Bronx. Sight unseen, they said that they had an apartment that I could stay in for the summer.

Back to Miami briefly, I packed my suitcase for the train trip to New York. Now I had my friend from Fort Valley, Losey Keene, living in Washington, DC. I made arrangements to stop over a day there and see the sights I had never seen before. Washington, DC, was among one of the most beautiful cities I had ever seen, and it still is.

Based on what I told the Higginses I would be wearing, they met me at the train station. Papa Higgins drove from Manhattan to the Bronx. If I had the money, I would have told them to turn around and take me back to the train station for Miami. But I had gone this far in arrangements with Columbia until I had no choice. I had never seen such a place as the Bronx, and there were people everywhere you looked.

That same day, the family took me to Orchard Beach in the Bronx; it was not Hawaii or Miami, if you can imagine what I mean. I have never been back to that beach again.

I was immediately adopted as the Higgins's son. I became Mr. B, or Brother. I was a part of everything they did that summer and thereafter. They had cookouts every weekend, it seemed, and someone was always visiting. Papa Higgins painted somewhere all the time on weekends. He was a cook in one of the hotels in Manhattan.

It was a four-story house. I lived on the top floor in the attic room. A good room. Cecil Smith was in town that summer and he and a friend of his, Johnny Walker (a real person, not the alcohol), visited.

Like Rossie, Mama Higgins was (and still is) an excellent cook. She prepared all my meals while I lived with them.

Now it is Monday morning and I was told how to take the subway to Columbia University. I just knew I would never make it, but I had been given excellent directions.

I met with my advisor, Dr. Esther Lloyd Jones, one of the nicest White ladies I had ever known. I had not met too many White women before either. But this was New York. Apparently, Dr. Costar had made the arrangements with her because my master's did not come up in the discussion. She was so patient in explaining the requirements for the doctorate in Student Personnel Administration in Higher Education, the degree I needed to be certified as a Dean of Students.

She asked me what I had been doing, and I told her about Edward Waters College. I also told her that I wanted to continue being a dean. She seemed impressed. She told me the courses required and aided me in selecting the ones for the summer. This session with Dr. Lloyd Jones was not like anything I had had a MSC. How different two places could be. I should say two persons.

We agreed that I could handle three courses; I knew that nine credits would be easy based on my experience at Michigan State. But I forgot that these were summer courses and not quarter courses. One course was a three-week course, too.

Dr. Lloyd Jones taught one of the classes, Student Personnel in Higher Education. I had to work my butt off meeting her demands and requirements, but I made a deserving A.

Mental Hygiene is a graduate course in this field which I had not had in getting my master's. It was a simple course. On the first test, I got a C on the multiple choice test. I went to her and said, "Dr. Alma, there must be some mistake?" She said my choices were correct but they were not the answers I was supposed to know.

I then said, "Are you kidding me?"

She said, "Beginning students should not know those answers."

Then I said, "Why would they be among the choices?" I told her that I had a master's in Counseling and Guidance from Michigan State and had just completed my psychology requirements there, and all of this was covered in the books I had read. I did not tell her my grade in psychology, but I knew the subject matter from my reading.

Then she said, "I don't know how I am going to be able to test you."

Here we go again. I suggested I do a paper instead of the exams. She said, "Fine."

I reviewed one of the psychology professor's most popular books, *When Teachers Face Themselves*, by Thomas Jersild. She gave me an A for the paper and a B for the course. Fort Valley, the University of Hawaii, Michigan State, and now Columbia. It has to be me not the same story at each college. Sour grapes maybe!

I know that this sounds like the same story every time I get a grade which I feel I did not deserve based on the knowledge I got from the work I put into it. I have no reason to lie about something like this, which has no bearing on anything at this time. But it is an experience I will never forget unless I get Alzheimer's. I may not be an A student, but under any good teacher, I am better than a C student.

I made an A– and two B+s that first summer session. Later Michigan State sent me a copy of my transcript with Columbia University's three credits typed at the bottom of it without any explanation. What a story.

At some point during that summer, Dr. White, president of the Mississippi Valley State College (MVSC), Itta Bena, Mississippi, got in touch with me and asked me to come by and see them on my way back to Florida because he had a dean of students job I might like. He said they would pay my transportation. What did I have to lose?

Before I left New York, I saw a different movie each day and went to Radio City Music Hall, too.

But when I saw that campus at Mississippi Valley State, my answer was yes before he had promised me a house on the campus. What Edward Waters College did not have, Mississippi had it tenfold.

I let Dr. Stewart know that I would not be coming back. Now on to the MVSC, September 1961.

Mississippi Valley State College (MVSC), September 1961–1962

IF YOU REALLY WANT to see a beautiful campus you have to see "Valley State" as it is called. It was a new campus built in a former cotton field off High Way 82, between Greenwood and Greenville, located in the town of Itta Bena, the Delta.

The college has faculty housing; married couples had new homes, and single faculty shared apartments which were not bad at all either. There is a Dean of Students house which I should have been assigned, but because I had no family with me, I was told I had to live in an apartment and share with someone else. I could have held Dr. White to my living in that house but I was so impressed on sight until I got noting in writing; it was all verbal and I could not have won in court. But I was happy to have a job on such a well furnished campus with such a qualified staff. I would have taken this faculty to any college and known that they would do well. Most of them were working on their PhDs and many of them got their terminal degrees before they retired. I am not among that bunch. I might have had mine too had I staid. That story comes later.

The Dean of Men position was vacant and I was given permission to get my own dean of men if I knew someone I felt qualified. No problem. I immediately contacted a friend of mine from North Carolina that I had met while at Michigan State, and he also graduated from Michigan State with a degree in counseling and needed a job. My Guardian Angels at work.

I contacted Cleophus Williams and in two weeks he was there. He became my Dean of Men and my roommate. By sharing the apartment, we could discuss many of our concerns before we went to a formal meeting with the others.

This year the staff was fifty percent new; the new staff worked well with me, and together we got a lot of new needed things changed for the students' benefit. I give President White credit for "finding" this college and for the work which had been done before I got there. It was an educational institution, not one for just show. It held its own in doing that as well. What I did not like, later Dr. White had the Board of Regents on campus and gave them lunch. He could not eat with them on his own campus. What a shame.

The college had a reputation of suspending students for little or nothing. Many times without any kind of hearing. It seemed before I got there whatever the President said went without anyone taking the students' side or position. I do not know what the former Dean of Students saw his role to be. One of the biggest files in his office was the suspension files. You could not find any school which had the well-behaved student body as The Valley. Here students were afraid to breathe without thinking that it might be too loud and they would get suspended. The Dean of Women, Miss Ratcliffe, was with the initial group; thus, she was no help for the girls.

Other than teaching orientation to about two hundred and fifty freshmen, my new job in my new school was to organize the students. Within this new student organization, we formed a discipline committee made up of faculty and students, headed by the Dean of Men. We did not include the Dean of Women. My organizing the students wherever I worked was not to be antiadministration; it was needed for the students. It is the students who make the school. No student, no school.

There was a young man in my freshman class who had a junior and senior brother on campus. Billy, the youngest of the three, always wanted to miss lunch to help me organize the collected assignments whenever I gave one. They were known as the Darden brothers. They were excellent baseball players (T. Ray Lawrence had taught them in Amory, Mississippi.) They were popular among the students and were honor roll students. More about the Dardens later.

One day the president of the Student Organization was in the Student Union Building, and he and his girlfriend got into something and he slapped her. He himself came to me and said, "Dean, I will see you next quarter." The discipline committee did not have to meet. He helped make the rules and he was the first to obey them. Billy McKnight was his name.

MVSC had a new student union building which housed the book store. There was a director of the student union but had no counseling responsibilities, just managing the building. Student programs and small socials were held there. One big event we had on Sunday afternoon was the College Bowl game. The Shop Department build us a very nice set copied from the TV set.

I have never been in any place which was kept as clean as this college. Your office would be dusted during lunch if you did not tell then not to. One of the chemistry teachers did have to tell them not to wax his lab because he was always slipping and sliding. The lawn was kept manicured and one would never see any out of place garbage of any kind in any place. The custodial staff worked all the time; it was well staffed, and the place was just kept clean.

The President's wife, daughter, and son-in-law were employed there; the wife worked in the Bursar's office, processing applications for student loans, his daughter was the Registrar, and the son-in-law was the Superintendent of Building and Grounds. They were all good at what they were doing, but the wife acted at times as if she thought she were the President. It was only she I had to put in her place a few times because of her telling me what or how to do something. None of his family members who were working had a degree at that time.

I would give this faculty a top grade for performance; it was an excellent teaching staff, well qualified in their individual discipline. MVSC had an excellent music department. The band went to the Rose Bowl Parade in California one year and the choir could have performed at Radio City Music Hall in New York because they were that good.

Would you believe that a couple was teaching there at the time from Opa-Locka, Florida, who lived less than ten streets from where I lived in Opa-Locka. I was able to ride home with them one Christmas. How convenient.

A few Sundays after Christmas, I broke all my Sunday routines; I did not go to Sunday school, I did not attend the College Bowl game at the Student Union Building that afternoon, and about five thirty that Monday morning, the paperboy came knocking on my apartment door.

He said, "Dean, there is a phone call for you out in the washhouse."

I said, "You must be mistaken because no one would be calling me there."

Then he said, "But a lady asked for you."

I reluctantly put on some pants and went out to the wash house and picked up the telephone. It was Mama's voice. She asked, "Where were you all day yesterday? Everyone tried to find you and kept telling us you would be a certain place at a certain time and they would have you call home." I asked what was the matter? She said, "Your daddy is dead." Mama then gave me a brief report on what happened. I told her that I would be home as soon as I could get a flight out.

I got dressed and went to my office to make plans to be away for at least a week or more. When my secretary came in, I broke the news to her and asked her to inform everyone who needed to know and to tell Dean Lowe to get a substitute for my classes.

Dean Williams would be able to take care of the routine things until I got back. The next thirty minutes my office was flooded with everyone giving me condolences. I took as much as I could and I made the excuse that I had to leave and pack.

I made arrangements for someone to take me to Memphis, Tennessee, for a flight to Miami—one of the longest flights I have ever been on in feeling. It seemed longer than the flight from Miami via way of New York, California, Hawaii, and Mid Way to Tokyo.

The family was waiting on me to help make the final arrangements for Daddy's funeral. Everything went well. It was the car accident which killed Daddy in front of the house.

When I returned to the campus, I immediately began thinking about my summer plans. I decided that I was still not ready for the University of Wisconsin. Why not back to Columbia and New York for summer 1962?

I had met a person at Zipha's graduation in 1958 whose name was McKinley Smith. Everyone called him Smitty. He lived in Brooklyn. We had kept in contact since then. He asked me to stay with him and his roommate, Monroa B. Goutier, that summer. It was just what I needed. They had parties every weekend, an apartment full of people. That was the beginning of my getting to know people in New York and introduced to the social world.

Again, I took nine credits, three courses, that summer. I made mostly B+s (according to my transcript) without any feelings of having been under graded too much at the time. I was not going to become possessed with grades as long as I was meeting the requirements and learning a new field. I was going from "Guidance and Counseling to Student Personnel Administration in Higher Education.

I was in the library and caught a student hiding a book that she wanted to come back for without having to recheck it out. We laughed about the incident and began dating. That was Lucille Howell from Newport News, Virginia.

Columbia University was more what I expected graduate school to be like. I spoke to Dr. Lloyd Jones and told her about my plans to transfer to the University of Wisconsin. She was shocked. She said no one transferred with that many earned credits toward his doctorate. She convinced me to stay and complete my doctorate degree under her. That was not too hard to do because I knew she appreciated me, and I her.

(After summer school, I did my movie route with a big weekend party at Smitty and Monroa's.)

Now back to Mississippi Valley State College. Dean Williams for some reason took another job closer to his home in North Carolina, and when I returned to campus, we had a new dean of men. I had no say in the selection. But as my Guardian Angels would have it, he turned out to be an excellent choice, Dean David H. Wicks, formerly from Saints Junior College in Mississippi, where Dr. Arenia

C. Mallory was the president and a member of the Church of God in Christ, the church my mother and sister Alline were members in Miami.

Mama would raise the most money in Miami for the Emanuel Church of God in Christ and was crowned Queen for more than twenty-five years. She would say that crown was not hers, but she was not going to give it away; it had to be earned. I made certain that she had a new dress each year for the Crowning of the Queen Ceremony—Mother Bethay.

Mama and Alline attended the Church of God in Christ Convocation in Memphis, Tennessee, each year. I made the bulletin for the Emanuel Church of God in Christ annual fund-raiser in Miami, which featured Mama. I spoke a couple of times on that big day.

Everything was in place and all new staff seemed to fit in well. The students were doing well and I was happy with everything. What more could one ask for with one exception—I now had a new apartment mate. Somewhat younger than Dean Williams, and he had his own idea about housekeeping. I cooked for both of us as I usual did in the apartment when Dean Williams was with me, but the new apartment mate did not want to pay his share. Really, he should have been in my student groups at Edward Waters College; he was more like a typical college student than a grown man.

I got a student to begin cleaning the apartment on weekends and he did not want to help pay for that either. If I can live with a chain smoker, I can tolerate most anything else. Which I did for that year.

I had taken the flu shot that year, and one day I was coming across campus back to my apartment and could not move. A student saw me and asked what was the matter? I said, I did not know and asked him to help me to my apartment. There I stayed recuperating from the flu for ten days.

I applied for a leave of absence from Mississippi Valley State to do my residency toward the doctorate. Everything was accepted beginning in the fall of 1963, not the summer. T. Ray Lawrence was living in Brooklyn near Monroa and Smitty and he suggested I stay with him that summer. I did but I needed a job inasmuch as I was not to be in school that summer taking nine credits. Lucille Howell visited me that summer in Brooklyn. No food this time. We ate out.

I wore out two pairs of shoes, beating the sidewalks of New York City, looking for a part-time typing job with no success. I ended up at the Inter-Church Center in Manhattan. I told the lady what I was looking for and she said that I would never get a job the way I was going about it. She said, "If you do not plan to work but one day, apply for a full-time job." Then she said, "You are too honest about everything. Some things you just don't tell rather than tell the whole truth. No one would hire anyone with a master's degree looking for a clerical job part-time in New York."

I was still dating my Fort Valley State girlfriend, Gene, who was in summer school at New York University. While waiting for her to get out of class for our date that evening, I looked up above where I was sitting and saw that I was under the Employment Office of New York University. I went up and asked the lady if she had any typing positions? She said, "Yes, complete this application." I completed the application as follows with Hiram Culmer as my only employer since I left the Air Force in 1958:

> *Saul H. Bethay*
> *High School Graduate*
> *Four Years in the Air Force Typing*
> *Job—Assisting my brother-in-law after the Air Force with his gardening business in Miami*

(I knew I could write my own recommendation from Hiram Culmer if she wanted one.)

Then I was asked to take a typing test along with about five girls. The typewriters were singing when they were typing. I was pecking along. She met with the five girls and told them that they could leave. About thirty minutes had passed and I had this date with Gene. I went to the secretary's office and asked her had she forgotten about me? She said, "No, I thought you came for a job." I asked, "Do I have a job?" Then she said that the person I would be replacing did not leave work until 5:00 p.m. and I could not go to see the secretary there until she left. Lying does pay off in New York, it seems.

At 5:15 p.m. I went to the ninth floor of the Main Building to the Dean of the College's office. I walked in and the administrative assistant began telling me what I would be expected to do. The Dean was writing a book, and there would be a lot of correspondence I would be typing for him, and I should report to work tomorrow at 9:00 a.m. Whoa!

I met Gene. We had a hurried dinner and I went to Brooklyn to get ready for this job. I was there at eight thirty the next morning to make sure that I would not be late on the subway the first day. Five to nine I went in. She showed me a desk and gave me this disk. I told her that I had never used one of these on my other job; we only had a manual typewriter. She said, "I'll show you how it works." She handed me earplugs, which I placed in my ears. I put the disk in the machine and she helped me turn it on.

The Dean had gotten a letter from someone in Europe which he had dictated his answer for me to type. I still do not know how long it took me to do the draft, but when I finished it, I took it into the secretary. In a few minutes she came back and said, "The first thing one learns in this office is, no one corrects the Dean. Is that understood?" I said yes. She then said, "Now type this the way the Dean has dictated it without any changes."

I pecked the retyped letter and gave it to her. In ten minutes, she came back out and threw the last typed letter on my desk and said, "You have just got here and now the Dean wants you to correct his writing. If he wants you to correct him, correct him. Retype it the way you did it the first time."

I did not have any more problems correcting the Dean. Later on, he asked me to start proofreading some of his manuscripts. I had some questions about some of his quotes. Then he asked me to go to the New York Public Library to verify what I had questioned. My job turned from typing per se to going to the New York Public Library most days as a "research assistant."

I would finish what I had gone to the library to do by 11:00 AM. Then I would call the secretary and tell her that I was having some problems finding and completing some of the material. She said, "That is what you were sent there to do. Don't come back until you have what the Dean wanted." (Once you start lying, you have to keep on lying. I needed a job.) Off to the movies I would go. That became the routine for the summer.

Now it was time for me to become a full-time student at Columbia University. I came in one day and told the secretary that Columbia had accepted me for September. She said, "What! You do not have to go there, the Dean can get you into anything you want here at NYU and I am sure he can get you a full scholarship. This way you can still work with him and attend school."

I told her that I had waited too late to inform Columbia that I would not be coming and I had not done anything about getting my transcript from Adel for NYU. The principal may not be working in Adel this summer and I would lose this semester. Then she said, "Okay. Work with us part-time." I said, "I will try." I came in a few afternoons the first week and then I told her that Columbia was really hard, and those young people seem to be so far ahead of me until I felt I could not keep up with them working part-time. It was best if I gave the job up.

She said, "Keep the key to the office and any time I feel I could help the Dean with his work, come in. That is all you would have to do here." I took the keys and still have them some place. Now off to Whittier Hall, Teachers College, Columbia University.

Columbia University, September 1963

AGAIN A FULL-TIME STUDENT, living in a dorm, eating in the cafeteria, going to the Apollo Theater every Wednesday to see the new show, having dinner at the Red Rooster, attending weekend parties and studying my "A" off was my routine from September 1963 through the beginning of the summer 1964.

Alfred Hicks

While living in Whittier Hall at Columbia University, 1963–1964, my homeboy Smitty and his friend Monroa B. Goutier had a big party one Saturday evening and invited me along with another student from Tufts University in Boston, Alfred Hicks. We hardly noticed or said anything to each other all evening. The crowded party ended and everyone had left but this young man. Smitty had told me to spend the night rather than take the train back to Manhattan. Monroa had told Alfred the same thing.

They only had a let-out couch for us to sleep on. I had no intention sleeping in a bed with someone I did not know and had just met for the first time. Al felt the same way. I said that I was closer to Manhattan than he was to Boston, so I was leaving. Smitty and Monroa said neither one of us was leaving. It was about 4:00 a.m. Sunday and we somehow ended up staying that night together.

Somehow, before we left that morning, we exchanged phone numbers and agreed to stay in touch. When Al came to New York, we began meeting for lunch. That friendship lasted until his untimely death in 1984. More about Al later.

Now I am enrolled in five classes, fifteen credits, for the fall semester. Only one was hectic; it was a research course where one had to pick one word used in counseling and trace it from its beginning and show how it got into counseling and guidance.

I chose the word "role." I was spending most days in the library preparing this report to be able to share all my research findings in one and a half hours to the class the first week in December. Another student was assigned the other half of the three-hour class.

One day I realized that I could not show how the word "role" got into my field of counseling because my field as it became known did not exist.

I had a homeboy from Miami working in the library, Tony Grant. I went to him and said how sick I was to realize after all this time that my research was in vain. He said, "I am sick, too. I can't believe this happened." I asked him what was he talking about because I am talking about all the research I have been doing all semester can't be used? He then said, "Don't you know the president is dead?" I thought he was talking about the president at Columbia University. I did not even know him, and if I did, I don't think his death would be affecting me the way it was affecting Tony. Then Tony said, "Saul, President John F. Kennedy has been shot and he is dead!"

Then the lights in the library became dim and an announcement was made that the library was closing and we all had to leave.

Jim Mitchell was now living in Harlem on 141st Street, I was on 120th Street. I went to his apartment and sat at the TV all weekend. But while we saw the story of President Kennedy's shooting and all that which took place thereafter, I told Jim about my predicament. Jim never got upset about anything. As he said at Michigan State, "We can fix it."

He read through all of that research, more than a hundred five-by-eight cards with the quotes from the authors written. About four days of all of this, the president's death, and my notes, Jim said, "I have it." He said, "All the world is a stage, and we are all actors, and from time to time we all play many roles. Shakespeare."

The word changed its spelling many times. It was "rolle," "roll," and finally "role," as we know it today. (I could go upstairs and look it up because I still have all of those cards because I cannot bring myself to throw them out. I will never go back to school or even try to give another speech on them.)

Thanksgiving came and went and I was still at Mitchell's, revising my research and preparing for my presentation. School finally reopened the beginning of December and I went in knowing that I had to give my presentation soon. Dr. Westervelt, our professor, told the class because of the library closing, everything was pushed back a week. So my time now would be after Christmas. My Guardian Angels at work again.

I had all the Christmas holidays to work on my presentation, I thought. That Christmas, Lucille Howell and Al both decided that I should not spend Christmas alone. Unbeknownst to each other, they both came. Al stayed with me and I got Lucille a room in the girls' dorm at Barnard College, near Whittier Hall. Lucille brought a complete Christmas dinner with all its trimmings on the train. Al kept the room filled with Chinese food. It snowed all Christmas. I would spend some time with Lucille and the other time trying to study with Al there in the small room with me.

Be careful what you wish for. This was the time I wish I were alone for Christmas. I had too much schoolwork to think about to have all these visitors. Christmas came and went, so did they.

Now back to reality.

When my time came for me to present, I went first. As I went through each card, I noticed the time and began rushing. Dr. Westervelt told me to slow down. I showed her the stack of cards I had to go through in my hour and a half, then she said, "Take the whole period." The period was three hours with a break. When I finished, the class gave me a standing ovation. I knew I had an A then.

During the spring semester, I had another research course where I had to compare and contrast the differences among a two-year private and a two-year public college and a four-year private and a four-year public college's student personnel programs. I went to Dr. Klop and told him I needed more time because I had to visit one of each of these colleges after I had been given an appointment to interview the staff in each of these areas for my data. I had to ask for an incomplete because I did not have my own transportation to get to and from these places. He gave an incomplete and a B- for the course later.

This assignment should have been my dissertation from the amount of work I put into it. When I got my grade, Dr. Klop said the reason he did not give me an A was because I did not tell about their business office operation, which had nothing to do with personnel services or counseling and guidance.

I enjoyed all my classes at Columbia. I had good professors. I learned a lot in each of their classes. At Michigan State, my classes were on Tuesday and Thursday; at Columbia they were all at night, so I had all day to spend in the library.

Summer came. I moved out of the dorm and stayed with Tony Grant, who had an apartment in Brooklyn. At this time, I had begun looking for an apartment for Alfred Hicks and me and a job for me for the fall.

Al was moving to New York to teach in the public schools. He had just completed his master's at Tufts University in Boston. I was staying to write my dissertation for my doctorate. Al said to try to get an apartment so when I went back to Mississippi, he would be able to keep it on his salary.

I took three more courses that summer while I was looking for a job and an apartment.

In one of those classes was a familiar student, but he said he did not know me. I said, "But I know that I had met you some place before." He became annoyed. I left it alone for a couple of days and then I asked him where was he from?

He said angrily, "Florida."

I said, "So am I." I asked, "Where?" He gave me the name of a town I had never heard of. I said, "That is not it."

Then when I asked him where he attended college, he said, "Florida A&M."

Then I said, "Do you remember your freshman year, you shared your bunk with someone?"

He said a bad word using the Lord's name in vain. But he remembered me then. That began a friendship. Later for George Mims.

Tony Grant introduced me to another young man from Eaton, North Carolina. There were not that many Negro students in graduate school at the time and Tony made it his business for us to get to know each other. His name was John Wesley Jordan. More about him later too.

One day Tony told me that they were looking for a guidance counselor in Englewood, New Jersey, in their junior high school. Remembering what the lady told me, they did not need to know immediately that I was studying to be Dr. Bethay. I had the qualification with my master's in Guidance and Counseling from Michigan State, so that was enough to get the job.

I asked Tony how I would get there? He called the secretary of the student services office, and she told me how to take a bus from Port Authority on 42nd Street through the Lincoln Tunnel. If I knew how to get back from halfway there, I would have done so because I knew I would not be doing this each day, trying to get to work.

Finally, I got there. I went to the Englewood Junior High School and met Mr. Davis, the principal, and Dr. Jess Barker, the Director of Student Services. Shortly thereafter, they said I had to meet with the superintendent, Dr. Mark Shead. He asked me what was I doing and I told him about my work at Columbia and some of my research projects. He became so impressed by my knowing so many Harvard (his school) professors' work that we talked for more than an hour while Dr. Barker and Mr. Davis sat outside.

The job was mine, but I had one problem. I told one of them about the traveling which I felt that I could not do each day. I was asked how did I get there and I told them. They said no; I should just take the bus near the school, and it would take me across the George Washington Bridge and I could take the A train to Brooklyn.

I took the job that day. I took the A train that day, and when I got back to Tony's place, I had a notice that I had the apartment at 232 Rutland Road in Brooklyn, all on the same day, August 1, 1964.

I called Al Hicks, who was cooking at a camp in Vermont, and gave him the good news.

Now Englewood school system for the next thirty years.

Englewood Junior High School (EJHS), 1964

It is September 1964. This is my real beginning being on my own. A long way from Cook County, Adel, Georgia, 1934. I have my first apartment. I am paying rent. I am paying light bills. I am paying telephone bills. I bought a television. I bought a let out couch. I purchased curtains for my windows. I had cushions made for the window seats. I have Sears and Macy's credit cards. I made $7,000 in ten months. Where do I go from here?

Dr. Claude Saint-Come, Ph.D.

For nine years, I rode the subway train to the George Washington Bridge where I would take a bus to Englewood. Most times I would be the first one there after the custodians.

I saw some very interesting happenings while riding that subway for nine years. One day a little child was fooling around, doing something, and the mother kept telling him to stop. He kept ignoring his mother. Finally, a lady went over to the child, slapped him, and said, "Now, mind your mother." Everyone gasped, including the mother. The child stopped. The mother said nothing. And the subway car was quiet the remainder of my ride.

(In the meantime, Al and I purchased a house with an apartment in August 1969, which I will tell you more about later.)

One afternoon, a man sat down beside me as we were leaving the George Washington Bridge subway station. He began talking to me like the lady did on the bus from Miami to Jacksonville, Florida. He started telling me about his wife leaving him in full detail, the whole story. He would cry at times when he would tell about some of the good times. I finally told him that I was sure it would not be as bad if she had not left him for another woman. He said, "I never said that. Where did you come up with that bullshit?" and started crying harder and louder. He quieted down and said, "I am sorry, man, but that is the truth."

A young man used to get on the subway every afternoon when the train reached midtown. He would get off at my station. We began talking. He was from Haiti. He lived with his grandparents, an aunt, and a female first cousin. He was enrolled in one of those schools at the time which took advantage of foreigners. He told me also that he could not study at night because of his cousin and times he had to babysit. Fast-forwarding.

One of my neighbors, Ethel Wright, had a husband who could not be left alone and she would often ask me to babysit him. One Saturday morning Ethel wanted something from a specific store and made me promise that I would not get it from any other store. This store was crowded, but I went anyway to please Ethel. Who else was standing in the checkout line but Claude Saint-Come, the young man from the subway train. By the time we reached the clerk, he had told me his life story, which was not a good one. That is a book in itself. But I will try the brief version of it.

I thought of Claude the next time Ethel wanted me to sit with her husband. I got in touch with him and told him that he could study while he babysat because the husband was no problem at all.

That became a habit. Finally, one day Ethel told me that Claude was not going home at night but would sleep on that old couch she had in an off room in the cold basement. I spoke to Claude and he said things were getting worse at home and he hated to go there. I spoke to Ethel about renting that room to him and I would pay her $100 for utilities and Claude could eat with me down the street.

She thought that would work out fine. Then she went to the extreme fixing up the whole basement. She had the floors redone. She had the walls painted. She got an electric heater for the room. She purchased a couch and bed linen. She was happy. I was happy. Claude was ecstatic.

Years went by and things were going well with everyone. Ethel was writing a book, I had several jobs, and Claude was doing fine. Things were going too well to be true.

I never knew Ethel had any relatives in New York, but they began coming out of the woodwork, and one of her great nephews wanted to set up a lab in the other room in the basement at Ethel's expense. Then Ethel began complaining about one thing after the other about what Claude was or was not doing, including keeping the lights on too long. I said to her, "I told you, if you wanted more money for the utility bills, just let me know." But it was these jealous grand relatives, not the bills.

The complaints got so bad until one day I asked Al if he minded Claude living in our apartment downstairs? He said no.

Before I go further, let me tell you a little more about Claude, my son, the most brilliant person I have ever known. He knew about three foreign languages, including knowing English better than any Americans. He was studying German when he died (more about that later too). He built a computer in my basement. He was an excellent writer; there was not anything I felt he could not do well.

Claude was born in Haiti, Port-Au-Prince, with the full name Claude Marc Mary Saint-Come.

During this time, Claude finished Manhattan Medical Assistants' School with a Medical Laboratory Technician Technology Certificate, but he could not get anyone anyplace to let him complete the required onsite training he needed for his license.

One day I was telling Jim Mitchell about Claude's problem with school. He said Fordham University had a program that Claude probably could get in. Fordham had a new campus in Manhattan, not the main campus in the Bronx. Claude was accepted. He did so well until his advisor felt that Claude was too smart to be at that campus and he needed more competition with those students in the Bronx. He transferred to the Bronx Campus.

The first problem came from a chemistry experiment which he could not get the results recorded after he had completed it. This should not be the case because it should record whether it was correct or not.

There was an expert upstate and Claude took his results to him. He too said that it was something they were doing to keep this from recording. It had nothing to do with Claude's work. Claude would not let me put on my blue suit and go speak to them.

Another situation took place at Fordham. Claude got a B in French when he could have been teaching the subject. The professor said he could not be given an A because that was his native language and he had an advantage over the other students. Then I said I was going up there and tell them to give all the Americans Bs in English if that was the way they grade students.

Anyway, Claude graduated with honors. Now the real problem. He began applying for medical schools. We spent a fortunate in application fees to be rejected by all medical schools he applied. When Maharry and Howard, two Black medical schools said no, I knew it was a losing battle. With Claude having an A average in the sciences from Fordham University and being rejected, I knew we were fighting against all odds.

I said, "Claude, give up on being a doctor. Become a teacher." Something I knew he would be good at as well.

Long Island University had just opened a campus downtown Brooklyn. He was accepted to do a master's in biology. He took care of the rats in the lab. This was not a paying job; he just did this on his own inasmuch as he spent a lot of time there running experiments. Then something came up and they wanted Claude to take care of all the animals, including cleaning their cages.

I put on my blue suit and went to talk to the professor. I said no, he was not on a scholarship at LIU and he was not going to do their work; I was paying his full tuition.

Simultaneously Claude began taking courses at New York University (NYU) while he wrote his master's thesis at Long Island University.

He needed his transcript from LIU to complete his application for a full-time student at NYU. He had completed his thesis, which was not accepted. The reason was I had typed one word wrong and they would not approve it until that word was corrected. I did not go to work that day. I put on my blue suit and went to LIU. I told that professor if that thesis was not approved today and his transcript in our hands before 5:00 p.m. every newspaper reporter and TV station newsman would be on this campus to see the worst demonstration New York has ever had. I knew that a PhD dissertation can be approved with outstanding corrections, and I knew that a little old master's thesis could be accepted pending the correction as well.

The secretary in LIU's registrar's office had left something off the transcript, which she said was not necessary. I told her this was my area of expertise—put it on! Reluctantly she did. I said "Thanks!" and got the heck out of there.

When Claude went to his advisor at NYU with his application for the Ph.D. program, she said that she thought he was already admitted because she had taught him two courses already.

He was accepted. He did well in all his classes and got $40,000 to test some peptides for some foreign company. Also, he worked in the lab at NYU for good pay and he was my assistant at Medgar Evers. He would work during the day until I came in. We had no money problem.

This money paid for Claude's Ph.D. Any problem Claude might have had at any of the other schools, NYU made up for them. A happy experience all the way through.

Claude finished his course work for the Ph.D. in biology and completed his dissertation, which was accepted on the spot with a wine party given in his honor for having earned one of the best degrees in biology anyone had ever been awarded. There was a typing error in his dissertation, which I found later.

I believe there were ten thousand graduates with Claude. It was the most organized graduation I had ever seen; that many students could come in and be seated in thirty minutes or less without any confusion or delay. Guests were seated according to their relative degree; thus, we could reach out and touch Claude as he passed. Needless to say, "proud" pictures I took in Washington Square Park in the Village at that graduation speak for themselves.

Claude graduated from the same school (NYC) where I had my first job. I could look over my shoulders at my first office on the ninth floor of the Main Building. Graduation was held in the park I ate lunch in every day during that summer job in 1963. At this same park, I saw many a concert, artist, show, and all other forms of entertainment throughout my stay in New York City.

Now let us get back to my new job. Englewood is a small town a few miles from the George Washington Bridge in New Jersey. I took the position as guidance counselor at the Englewood

Junior high school to stay just one year. I needed the job to help with my expenses because the Southern states only pay if one is in school full-time. I was not a student at this time, only researching for my dissertation

This school served seventh-, eighth-, and ninth-grade students of all races about a fifty-fifty make up race-wise. Englewood had a private school which pooled off many of the White students. Englewood was trying to cope and adjust to integration.

I was brought in because I filled more than one role. I was a male. I was a Negro. I was a trained guidance counselor with a degree in counseling and guidance. I dressed to look like a role model for male Negro students. Yet it took the state Department of Education in Trenton five years before I was certified because they could not find two courses in guidance and counseling which I had not had. Most counselors of that day were excellent teachers and went back to school and took fifteen credits in counseling and were certified. They could not see that I came in with more than one hundred credits in guidance and counseling. All new employees were required to take six additional credits regardless of the number of credits they came in with. They could not fire me because of that. I finally went to Jersey City State and took two courses I had had, which they had under a different name.

Take a look at my resume.

Personal Data Sheet

Former Resume

Permanent Address:
Saul Henry Bethay
220 Rutland Road
Brooklyn, NY 11225

Full Time Position:
Guidance Counselor: Janis E. Dismus Middle School, Englewood, NJ, 07631
(1964-1994)

Responsibilities:
Counseling: Individual and group - academic, social, personal and career;
Testing: select, supervise, administer and interpret group tests;
Scheduling: Planning master schedules, teachers' schedules and student schedules (individualized programs); participating in curriculum development and implementation; participating in teachers' team meetings; arranging and participating in conferences - student, teacher, parent and interested others; conducting orientation programs: students, professional staff and other interested persons.

Education:

Undergraduate: Fort Valley State College, Fort Valley, Georgia, B. S. 1954.
Major: Vocational Agriculture
Minor: General Science and Functional English

SAUL HENRY BETHAY

Graduate: Michigan State University, East Lansing, Michigan, M. A. 1961
Major: Guidance and Counseling - Elementary and Secondary
Minor: Student Personnel Administration
Teachers College, Columbia University, New York, NY, doctoral level, summers and one school year, 1961-1968
Major: Student Personnel Administration in Higher Education
Minor: Special Education.

Additional Studies:
Armed Forces Institute, Tokyo, Japan, 1956
University of Hawaii, 1957
Jersey City State College, New Jersey, 1969
In-Service Training, Englewood School System: Sensitivity, Drugs, Sex Education, Computer Programming, Word Processing, and Writing.

Positions:
Teacher, Vocational Agriculture: Maggie Califf High School, Gray, Georgia, 1958-1959
Dean of Students: Edward Waters College, Jacksonville, Florida. 1960-1961

Responsibilities:
Organize, direct and coordinate the Student Personnel Program; Counseling - academic, personal, social, and vocational; Testing- select, supervise and administer tests for admission, educational and vocational placement; Housing; Orientation and Teaching.

Personnel Supervised: Dean of women, teacher-counselors, dormitory directors and their assistants, and two secretaries.

Consultant: To the counseling staff of the Duval Medical School for Nurses. Jacksonville, Florida.

Dean of Student Personnel: Mississippi Valley State (College) University, Itta Bena, Mississippi, 1961- 1963
Responsibilities: The administration of the student personnel program: counseling, financial aid, placement, testing, health services, religious activities, student activities, orientation and student housing.

Additional Part-Time Positions:

Administrative Assistant: New York University, Summer 1963
Responsibilities: Research, editing manuscripts and typing

Staff Writer: Howard University, Washington, D.C., Spring 1964
Responsibilities: Research and writing drafts of research projects.

Research Assistant: Bernard Baruch College, New York, N. Y., Summer, 1970
Responsibilities: Analyzing and editing data and typing

Field Analyst: Greenleigh Associate, Inc., New York, N. Y., Summers, 1971, 1972 and 1973
Responsibilities: Evaluating Title I Summer Programs and Report Writing

Consultant: Medgar Evers College, Brooklyn, NY, 1972
Responsibilities: Assist with the accreditation in Curriculum, Counseling, Testing, Programming, Staffing, Recruitment, Retention, Promotions and Orientation.

Coordinator: Adult Continuing Education Programs, Medgar Evers College, Brooklyn, N.Y., 1973-1975
Responsibilities: Administration and Supervision of the Adult Continuing Education Programs

Coordinator: Mobil Academy, Medgar Evers College, Brooklyn, NY Summer 1985

Responsibilities: Select and supervise staff; plan and supervise the academic program; select books and equipment and assist in writing the final report.

Adjunct Professor: Medgar Evers College, 1975 -1985
Responsibilities: Teaching: Basic Communications Skills
English and Grammar Usage
Reading in the Content Area
Math for Basic Education Students

Counselor: Medgar Evers College, Brooklyn, NY. 1977-1980
Responsibilities: Counseling adult continuing education students and students in special programs and funded projects.

Coordinator: After School homework-Study Program, Englewood, New Jersey, 1985.
Responsibilities: Supervise teachers and work with discipline

Counselor and Assistant to Program Director: Brooklyn College, 1986 - 2008
Responsibilities: Recruit, test, screen, counsel, and schedule adult students for the Adult Degree Programs: Special Baccalaureate Degree, Small College and Week-End College.

Counselor: William Paterson College, Spring 2009
Responsibilities: Counsel grandparents rearing grandchildren in Paterson, New Jersey

Awards and Plaques:
1958 - National Defense Medal
1958 - Good Conduct Medal
1958 - Good Conduct Medal
1958 - Honorable Discharge
1983 - The Emanuel Church of God in Christ Plaque
1990 - The Janis E. Dismus Middle School Award
1995 - The NAACP Award

1995 - The Fort Valley State University National Alumni Association Award
1998 - The Holy Ghost Training Center Award
2012 - The Bethay-Inman Family Reunion Plaque

Publications (Contributing Author/Editor):
ELEMENTARY SCIENCE PROJECT FOR DISADVANTAGED CHILDREN, K–6 AND THEIR PARENTS, Howard University, Washington, DC, 1964.
ENGLEWOOD SCHOOL DEVELOPMENT PROGRAM: OUR INTERCULTURAL HERITAGE, Englewood Board of Education, 1966.
AN EVALUATION OF THE ELEMENTARY AND SECONDARY EDUCATION ACT TITLE ACT I SUMMER PROGRAMS FOR COMMUNITY SCHOOL DISTRICT 18, "Junior High School Program," Greenleigh Associates, Inc., New York, September l971.

Professional Associations:
American Personnel and Guidance Association
New Jersey Guidance Association (State Committee Member)
Bergen County Guidance Association (Executive Committee)
Englewood Counselor Association
American College Personnel Association
Association for Non-White Concerns in Personnel and Guidance
American School Counselor Association
Association for Counselor Education and Supervision
National Education Association
New Jersey Education Association
Bergen County Teachers Association
Englewood Teachers Association
New York School Counselor Association

Now you have a snapshot of what I have done in general. Now let me highlight some of the people and things I have been involved with during this time.

The Englewood Junior High School had the traditional subjects English, math/algebra, social studies, science, and reading/foreign language, with an excellent wood shop, metal shop, and print shop. It also had homemaking for the girls. All students took gym, art, and music. We had a band.

Seventh-grade students came from a central sixth grade school to the junior high school. The Lincoln, Roosevelt, and Quarles elementary schools sent their graduating fifth graders to the Engle Street school for one year, then they came to the junior high school as seventh graders.

I was the counselor for the eighth- and ninth-grade boys and I had a coworker for the eighth-and ninth-grade girls. A female served as the seventh-grade counselor for both boys and girls.

Students were grouped in their classes according to IQ tests and aptitude tests results. (I had to change that fast.) We would have as many as twelve different groups in one grade. The junior high had nine hundred students when I first got there. I got to know my students by having group counseling and guidance meetings with them all. The principal and my coworkers wanted to know why I needed to meet with all students, especially the good students, you know who. I told them I was their counselor and not a disciplinarian. I was not going to confuse my students with that double role.

All students had the opportunity to tell me how well things were going before there was a problem. When a student had a problem, they had no fear about seeing me. Teachers and parents began coming to see me as well.

If a student were referred to me for counseling, not discipline, we would try to solve the problem between us. (The vice principal was the disciplinarian.) Next, we would include the referring teacher. Then the parents had to meet with me and the student. If this did not work, the parents had to meet with all of us together—the teacher, the student, and me. Each of us was given an assignment to help the student. A follow-up meeting was held to keep abreast of the student's improvement.

If the student seemed not to be able to make it after all of this, he was put on a daily progress report where every one of his teachers had to complete the report on his progress in subject matter, homework, and classroom behavior (discipline).

The student had to return that signed progress report by his parents to me each morning and I would take a quick check and give him a new one for the day. Everyone involved had a running account of the student's daily progress.

I became an overnight success with the students, teachers, and parents. I became known as that new counselor the junior high school had. With this backing from everyone, the administrators let me do most things I wanted my way for thirty years. I was never selfish. I was always open to new ideas, which made sense to what we were doing. I gathered different opinions; I was not a know-it-all person.

We had a Negro cleaning lady for our offices, Mrs. Sarah Valentine. In our first evening parent-teacher conference, I was sitting in my office after school. The cleaning lady came to me and asked me what was I doing for dinner? I told her, "Nothing."

She said, "Come to my house and have dinner with us."

I said, "No, that would be okay."

She insisted by saying that it would not be a problem. Because "I figured you would not have any place to go and I have dinner almost ready. You come to my house after work."

During my tenure, I got few other invitations of this sort from any of the staff, and there were Negroes on the staff, too. It took the cleaning lady to show some concern for me.

Mrs. Sarah Valentine adopted me. The family adopted me. She had two daughters in Hampton Institute at the time and a married son in Englewood. They adopted me: Celeste Valentine (Finney) and Carol Valentine (Drakeford Lee); a married daughter, Vivian Valentine Davis, in Wilmington, Delaware; and a brother, Buster Valentine. I became their brother and Uncle Saul to the nephews and nieces. Her church members adopted me as well. That was my home away from home when I had to stay over for an evening meeting.

I always went home no matter how late it was when I left school. Riding the buses and subways at that time was never a problem or concern day or night. I am glad I do not have to do that today.

My one-year stay turned into thirty years, from September 1964 to June 1994.

1964–2017

Ernesto Vanterpool,* My Barber

ONE WEEKEND I WAS walking down Nostrand Avenue in Brooklyn when a young man and I became engaged in a conversation. I was looking for a barber. He said, "I cut hair."

I asked, "Do you have a shop?"

He said, "No, I cut out of my house on Saturdays." He was originally from the Dominican Republic (DR).

I said, "I'll see you next Saturday."

I kept the appointment along with all those other men from the DR. He had a wife, Lillith, a daughter, Ruth, and two sons, Leo and Robert Vanterpool. That could not be done that way today. More about them later, too.

Getting your haircut at Ernesto's was like attending a party. One could eat all the time he was getting his haircut. That was how I was introduced to West Indian food. When you would ask him how much you owe, he would say "Whatever you give me." Could you believe that? He was my barber until he left New York to follow his Getty's job in Oklahoma. They became my other family, Uncle Saul.

Before Ernesto left, he and Lillith always came to our rowdy parties. It was the thing during the early sixties to have house parties every weekend. You gave one or you were invited to one. We would get about fifty people in that little apartment, 232 Rutland Road, before we purchased the house in 1969. We were known as the partying guys; everyone wanted to come—a reputation I kept until about 2012.

Leo was having trouble with algebra at Erasmus High School here in Brooklyn. Ernesto asked me to see if I could help him. Of all the subjects I did not have in school, algebra was one of them. But I was able to take his book and help him do well. I too learned a little something. Leo was able to graduate and ended up at Fisk University in Nashville, Tennessee.

Al Hicks, my apartment mate, worked each summer at the Farm and Wilderness Camp in Rutland, Vermont, lived on Rutland Road in Brooklyn, and worked in Rutland, Vermont, for thirty years.

This was a Quaker camp and boys and girls came from all over the country. It was ahead of its time in integration. Rev. Abernathy's and Mr. Andrew Young's children attended this camp. (One summer, I had to help Rev. Abernathy's children transfer buses at Port Authority for Rutland, Vermont.) The boys and girls; they slept in three-sided cabinets, and they socialized without any racial tension. I would go there a weekend during the summers when they had Family Day, and a few times I went up to bring meats back to our freezers.

Let me tell you first about those swinging couples who were counselors there. They swapped partners and finally two of them wanted a full-time different mate. They divorced and married with children. I still visit one of these couples when I am in Miami. They have been my guests in Brooklyn a few times as well.

One day, I was at camp and went swimming. There was a young man who worked in the kitchen who wanted to go swimming with me. I asked him if he could swim? He said yes. I swam out to the barge and back and back to the barge and lay down. This young man got halfway and ran into trouble. I was tired but swam out to him and held on to him and told him how to tread the water until I could swim ashore and get the lifesaver, which I was able to do and pulled him in.

He could have drowned. I would have been blamed and guilty the rest of my life because I was known as a good swimmer and everyone would have wanted to know how did I let this happen.

Al began taking Leo Vanterpool to camp with him to work in the kitchen. The first summer Leo was there, Ernesto asked to go up with me to see Leo. When we got there, Leo ran by and said "Hi,

Dad" and kept running with the others. Ernesto said, "I have come all this way to see this boy and this is all I get."

We had to buy a small freezer, which I kept until July 2011, to store the meat we purchased in Vermont during the summers. Later we had to get a full-size freezer and a second refrigerator to accommodate our meats all year. More about Vermont later.

The Reids and the Rivers

I have never been without a family even here in New York. I met Clara Reid and we dated until her untimely death. Her mother, Mrs. Ruth Reid, adopted me as her son; I not only dated her daughter, she invited me to have dinner with them many a time. I was introduced to Clara's married sister and her husband, Sue and Harry Rivers, who became my family and best friends as well.

Clara worked at her alma mater, Hunter College, until her untimely death in St. Vincent Hospital in the village of Manhattan. Clara seemed to be so excited to see me on this visit, and immediately after my arrival in her hospital room, her heart began failing her, and the nurse told her mother, sister, brother-in-law, and me to leave her room immediately. The nurse came out later with blood all over her uniform and said that they were not able to save her. She was dead. What a shock this was to us. It took a long time for us to leave the hospital and prepare for this sad funeral.

Sue and Harry were expecting their first and only child, Pamela Sue Rivers, who was born soon after Clara's death. Alfred Hicks and I were asked to be Pamela Sue Rivers's godfathers after she was born—a title I still hold with great respect. Now it is only Pamela Sue Rivers and I alive out of this group. Mrs. Ruth Reid is dead. Alfred Hicks is dead. Harry Rivers is dead. Susan Rivers is dead.

It was Sue and Harry who came over with new clothes on the night Al and I informed them that we had been house-robbed of everything, including our car, and a carload of our personal stuff was taken. I still have the trench coat they brought for me that night to have something to wear out in the cold thereafter. The robbery was not as bad as we had it sound in our excitement in telling them about the four-hour robbery by the two men, which had been set up and planned with the young man lying down on the floor next to us, tied up as well—a young man who had lived with Al and me and his cousin, John Jordan. Someone once said, "Your enemy cannot harm you, but watch your close friend."

Sue and Harry were excellent parents. They made sure that their daughter received the best education which they could afford—elementary, high school, and college. There was not anything Pamela wanted she was not able to get when her parents were alive. Her parents moved out of New York until her father died. Then she and her mother moved to the Bronx for a while, then they moved near Pamela's cousins in Maryland, where they were living when her mother died.

Pamela came to live with me for a while after her mother's death to try to get used to being without an immediate blood member—no grandmother, no father, no mother. Now it is just she and I trying to help her get back on her feet in work and living. Only if you have been there at such a young age when you lose both parents in death will you know how painful that must be. Pamela Sue Rivers is a strong young lady. Pamela knows I love her and will always carry my role as godfather to the utmost. I see the same respect coming from her as she did when her parents were alive. I got my own house pool table given by them. I got my long leather coat given by then. I got my first big flat-screen TV given by then. If there were anything they thought I did not have, including clothes, I either got it on Christmas or on my birthday in January. Mama Reid, Harry, and Sue are gone; now Pamela Sue Rivers and I are left to carry on. We will survive!

Mama and Papa Hicks

Mama and Papa Hicks had come to New York for vacation and to see some Broadway plays. Naturally, they would visit us. We told them how to take the subway back and forth, but they began talking to someone and they told them where they were going. Then they said, "I do not know why they told you to take that train when this one stops at Rutland Road." We were expecting them about five or six o'clock for dinner when about nine they came in tired. They walked about forty blocks.

During the visit Mama Hicks said she had a childhood friend who lives somewhere on Rutland Road. We looked up the address, and it turned out that she and Ethel Wright had gone to school together in Vicksburg, Mississippi. Ethel Wright lived at 130 and I lived at 232 Rutland Road—six degrees of separation, or what a small world.

Joseph Paige, 1964–1965, and 232 Rutland Road

Joe Paige contacted me somehow and told me that he was working at Howard University and had this research project and needed a staff writer. Tuesdays and Thursdays I would take Eastern Airlines to and from Washington to work with them on writing their results for reporting their findings. The project was about Ghetto families taking advantages of all that the Government had to offer them.

They met with families and told them about food, medical, and educational services, which they were entitled to and how to go about getting them.

(I began collecting those small bottles of alcohol they gave out on each flight. I ended up with over one hundred of them—quite a display in my dining room.)

Joe Paige was the young man I had worked with at Edward Waters College in Jacksonville.

When I went to Washington each week, I stayed with Cleophus Williams, who now was a counselor in one of the high schools in DC. Transportation was $35 each way and I had no room or board to pay while in Washington.

Again, I took that flu shot, and again I was laid up for ten days. It was Thanksgiving and we had guests for dinner. I got up from the table feeling fine, I thought, and went to the bathroom. On the way back, I ended up on the bed for ten days. I said then that if I am going to be this sick from the flu shot, I rather deal with the flu. That was and will be my last flu shot.

Still in the apartment, during one of those bad winters in the midsixties, we had a card party. Someone looked out of the window and said someone has stole all of our cars. Excitingly we all looked out and discovered that the cars were not stolen just buried under all that snow. Some of the guests were from Washington and Philadelphia and had to come back for their cars two weeks later. That could not happen today. The cars would be towed away as soon as some of the snow was removed.

Al was an excellent cook and entertainer. We converted the living room into a dinner room when we had sit-down dinners, which was quite often. We used real china and glassware for formal dinners.

Purchasing the House

It was the winter of 1968 when the landlord came in with his overcoat on talking about how warm it was in there and asking for a rent increase. We said that we would increase our rent $50 more. After the landlord left, I said to Al, "Let me talk to our neighbors to see if they were still interested in selling their house."

They said, "Yes!"

I said, "How much do you want for it?"

They said, "$35,000."

I said, "No, I will give you $30,000.

They said, "We'll take it!" I told Al what I had done when he came in.

I was making about $8,000 or $9,000 in Englewood at the time, and Al was making about the same. I had committed us to purchasing this house without any money. I got on the telephone and called everyone I knew who had a nickel or two and that Friday when I got home, I had $9,000. The closing was $5,000. We closed August 1, 1969 five years from the day we moved into the apartment.

The owners left the beds which I still use, chest of drawers, record player, cabinets, and piano. They came back later and asked if they could have the piano back for some relative who was taking music. Neither one of us played which was not a problem. We wanted the house. Monroa and Smitty helped us move all our accumulations across the road from 232 to 220 Rutland Road. Our stuff made the house look so empty, moving from a small three-room apartment to a huge nine-room Brownstone House.

What came with the house was a three-car garage, and neither Al nor I had a car. We kept the tenants in the garage for $30 each per month. They were keeping a young man in the apartment who had mild mental problems. The State was paying them $800 per month to keep him. They asked us if we wanted to keep him. I worked in Englewood and Al in Manhattan, and we did not want to take on the responsibility when we would be away all day during the week.

John W. Jordan, the young man I met at Columbia University in the summer of 1964, wanted the basement apartment. We rented it to him for $150 per month and we paid $296 per month mortgage. This house is called a Brownstone. We have garages but no backyard. We can get over one hundred people on top of the garage entertaining. Al wanted the large back room overlooking the garage; I wanted the large front room overlooking the front corner. There is a small room in between. There is plenty closet space everywhere in the house as well as in the apartment, each has two large rooms and one small one. The apartment has its own entrance from the side. One could enter from the garage or from the kitchen if they so choose but things were changing in the streets.

Once we were somewhat settled in, we had a house warming party. We were shocked at the things the guests brought us. One group gave us a full set of dishes, which can only be used with a special group. They would scratch too easily. We got other things for the kitchen and dining room, towels for the bathroom, and sheets and blankets for the bed.

Helen Russell gave us a six-eye gas-burner stove, which I still have. For those who had given us money to purchase the house, we had the following plaque made and cited during the housewarming:

**OUR SINCERE GRATITUDE
AND APPRECIATION
WITH SPECIAL RECOGNITION**

**MR. BILL COLE
BROOKLYN, N.Y.**

**MR. & MRS. HIRAM CULMER
MIAMI, FLORIDA**

SAUL HENRY BETHAY

DR. & MRS. O. E. HICKS
FORT VALLEY, GEORGIA

MISS LUCILLE HOWELL
NEWPORT NEWS, VIRGINIA

MRS. ANNIE MAE JACKSON
MIAMI, FLORIDA

MR. JOHN WESLEY JORDAN
BROOKLYN, N.Y.

MR. CORNELIUS PAGE
BROOKLYN, N.Y.

MRS. RUTH E. REID
BROOKLYN, N.Y.

MISS HELEN RUSSELL
BRONX, N.Y.

HONORABLE MENTION

THE BETHAYS
MIAMI, FLORIDA

MR. MELVIN GADSON
BROOKLYN, N.Y.

MR. MONROA B. GOUTIER
BROOKLYN, N.Y.

THE HICKSES
BIRMINGHAM, ALA. – BOSTON, MASS.

WHY I HAVE SO MANY NAMES

**HARRY, SUE AND PAMELA RIVERS
BROOKLYN, N.Y.**

**MR. McKINLEY SMITH
BROOKLYN, N.Y.**

**ALL OF OUR DEAR FRIENDS
INTERNATIONAL**

**SAUL H. BETHAY - ALFRED HICKS
220 RUTLAND ROAD
BOOOKLYN, N.Y.
AUGUST 1, 1969**

JOHN WESLEY JORDAN*

ONCE WE HAD GOTTEN settled, John let one of his cousins (Eric) stay with him for a while without any problems while he lived with us. John taught English in the New York school system during this time. A group of the teachers and John would each buy a bottle of alcohol on Friday evenings and spend the night seeing who could drink the most. This went on for years. John became an alcoholic. Later, he was missing for a week and no one knew where he was. He told me some time later that he was in jail during that time; he had been arrested for being drunk.

I was a collector of the two small bottles of alcohol airlines once gave you on each flight. I had over one hundred small bottles of all kinds. I was cleaning one day and I noticed that one of the small bottles had been opened. I check it and found it to be filed with water. I checked the others and they too were filled with water, all of them. I am not sure if some of my regular whiskey had not been contaminated with water, too. I am not a drinker, so I would normally never have any other reason to check the bottles other than cleaning them. I then took all my other regular bottles of whiskey and put them in the closet in the small room upstairs and put a padlock on the door. We kept all brands of whiskey in our house for our parties. Al could get it cheaper in Vermont and we would buy it by the case. We were always ready for a good party.

Fed up with the school system's program of teaching English, John got some help with his drinking; He married, had a son, and joined the Army with a master's degree in English; the degree he earned at Columbia, where I met him. While in the Army, he became saved. Every word was "God," "Praise the Lord," "Thank You, Jesus," from that time on, even today, everywhere he goes. The next thing I knew, John was a preacher while a member of the US Army. He too did a tour of duty in Hawaii. Everybody seemed to have followed me everywhere I went

John was discharged from the military and found his own church upstate New York. The Holy Ghost Refuge Church; it had a mission to help people like he once was with their drinking problems. A few of them visited me once from upstate and John told me what could not happen while they were visiting, especially the drinking. Would you believe that?

One evening, Claude and I were working at Medgar Evers and it looked like it was going to snow. I told him, "Let's go home, no one would be coming out in this weather."

Al had just come home from an operation at one of the hospitals in Boston. About 9:00 p.m., the front door bell rang. I went to the door, and who was standing there in all that snow but Eric. I said, "Boy, what are you doing out there in all of this snow?" He said he was just passing by and thought he would stop in and see how Al and I were doing. I offered him something to eat, but he said no. He asked about Al and where he was. I told him about Al's operation and that he was upstairs in his room in bed. Eric wanted to know if anyone else was living there. I said no. (This was before Claude moved in with us.)

Then he said that he needed some cigarettes and was going out to get some. I told him nothing would be open in this area during this snow and that Al would let him have some of his. He said that he could not smoke Pall Mall and he would find some place open and be back. In about ten minutes, he was back without cigarettes. Later on he said, "I got to find some Cigarettes." And I let him out of the house again, looking for cigarettes in all that snow. He comes back again without cigarettes.

Sitting there talking, the next thing I knew, someone had knocked me on the floor and the other person had run upstairs and was dragging Al down the stairs with his recent operation, which I was most concerned about. The one downstairs made Eric get on the floor, too. He tied us up with our hands behind our backs, face down on that cold hardwood floor, and covered us up with our scattered rugs.

They kept asking where did we keep our money. We kept telling them that we had no money. They searched our wallets, but Eric did not have a wallet, so they kept kicking him, saying, "Boy, where is your wallet?" I would tell them to stop kicking him; he did not live here. Then they began going through the house putting everything they could find in pillowcases while we lay tied, head covered on the floor.

When they had filled up as much as they could carry, they came across a set of car keys and asked whose were they? (Al had bought a Volkswagen van at this time and it was in the garage.) Al said, "Mine." They asked about the car and where it was. Al told them. All Al wanted was for them to leave. One of them went out and open the garage door and started all over again filling the van with everything they could put in the car. (They went through everything again for about four hours.) When they had filled the station wagon, they took a gallon of whiskey and poured it all around us on the floor and said if we move, they were going to set the damn house on fire.

I had gotten loose but I did not want to do anything because of Al's condition, so I lay still. One of them went outside and the other kept creeping toward the kitchen door. This one kept sticking the butcher knife into the hardwood floor stating that he should stab us. Bit by bit, he too left and I heard them drive off in all that snow.

I untied Al and Eric and immediately Eric said he had to go, too. I told him that he should not go out in that weather, stay here with us. Eric said he had to get of here. He could not take any more of this. He left. In about fifteen minutes after I made sure Al was okay, I said to Al, Eric was a part of this. I gave him all the information he needed and let him come and go twice without thinking anything like that. He was going out telling them everything they needed to know when they came it. They had to take the glass panel out of the door in order to get in and that was what was taking so long, and Eric kept checking on them to see why.

We called the police and they finally came. They kept complimenting us on our art and how well we kept the house. I told them to concentrate on what they had taken from us including the Volkswagen. They finally made a report.

Afterward, we filed a claim with the insurance company and an agent had to come out to go over the claim.

Sue and Harry came out with new coats and the like to replace some of the clothes. Later on, I kept missing pillow cases without knowing why. Then it dawned upon me that they took them when we were robbed.

A week later, Claude came in from the subway and said the car was on Flatbush in the middle of the road. What would happen if someone was seated in the passenger seat, it would not crank unless they raise up. I used to jokingly tell someone sitting there that they were too fat; that's why the car would not crank and they had to get up. We got the car and brought it home. We had to have repair work done on it.

Years later, John and I were talking about the robbery and he said the moment I told him about what happened, he knew Eric was a part of it. John said later that Eric ended up back in Edenton, North Carolina, in the streets on drugs. I am sure that was his problem when he was here. I said as long as he was not near me, it was okay.

John is now retired and moved back to Edenton, North Carolina continuing his missionary work and preaching. He has been here twice; once when he was still living upstate and once here for a funeral.

Mama and Victor Bryant Sr. Visit and the Bikes

Mama and one of my nephews came to visit us soon after we moved to the house from the apartment. I had just purchased a new bicycle and Victor wanted to ride it up the street and back, then he wanted to ride around the block. The next thing I knew was someone coming to my door telling me that someone had taken your nephew's bike and he tried to chase them to no avail. Victor came in crying. I asked if he were hurt? he convinced me that he was okay. Then I said we could always get another bike. I believe that was my second one to be stolen. That was the period when bikes were being stolen from lock and key. No matter what you locked them with, they had cutters and would have them and gone in less than five minutes.

It was the World's Fair and we went about three times. I would go as far as the first exhibit and let them spend the day seeing all they wanted. I was amazed how much walking and climbing Mama could do at this fair. As long as she was enjoying herself, so was I.

Many years later, I bought Claude a bike like the one I had at the moment. This one was stolen, too. I got him another one that he kept until he got his master's, and then he sold it without asking me if I wanted to keep it. It did not matter because I did not need a bike anymore.

I once was leaving my barber, Ernesto, when a taxi almost ran me down. I stopped riding in the streets and would push my bike to the park and only ride over in the park. As of this writing, I have five bikes in the garage; only one of them I bought.

CARS

AL PURCHASED A VOLKSWAGEN, and it was that car the robbers used to clean us out. I brought me a Volkswagen, also. Coming from an End-of The Year School Party in New Jersey, it caught fire and burned up. And I later brought my first Dodge. Then I bought a Plymouth. Then I was given a beautiful black-and-white Cadillac. I took Monroa and his housekeeper to church one Sunday morning and on my way back, two kids stole a lady's rented car, which she left running while she went shopping. I stopped them when their car knocked my car across the road against a tree. The passenger side was completely destroyed. Had Monroa and Authur been in their seats, they would have been killed. No one understand how I was able to walk. My side of the car was not scratched. The ambulance came and the medics insisted I go to the hospital for examination. I had a little bang on the head, which they treated, and I was required to take outside treatments for a month or more.

Engle Street School

THE GUIDANCE DEPARTMENT AT the Englewood Junior High School was "together." They had to find some way to break us up. We did our job too well. We could schedule 900 students by hand during the summer in six weeks and everyone would have an individual, handwritten schedule in September.

Alan Brodsky was a high school guidance counselor; De Benedetto was an elementary guidance counselor, and I was certified elementary and high school. The Board of Education of the school district wanted to change everything around. The principal at the sixth-grade school was taking a leave of absence to complete his doctorate, a social studies teacher from the junior high was to be the new principal at the sixth-grade school that year; the sixth grade school's guidance counselor was being transferred to the new middle school, and the high school trained counselor, Alan Brodsky, was being transferred to the sixth-grade school.

I put on my blue suit that night to attend the Board of Education meeting. I was to tell the Board of Education about the mistake they were making reassigning everyone to positions outside of their certification. Claude came over to go to the meeting with me. I had gotten an agenda earlier to know what point on the program I would be speaking.

We got to the meeting earlier. They passed out agendas to everyone. A few minutes after Claude had received his, he said, "Saul, I thought you said that Alan was being transferred?" I said that he was. Then Claude said, "You better look at this agenda."

I said, "Claude, please leave me alone, I am going over my speech."

He said, "This agenda has your name, not Alan Brodsky's."

I reluctantly took a quick look and could not believe what I was seeing. Since 4:00 p.m. they had substituted my name for Alan's.

Now the meeting got started. When my time came to speak, I said, "This is like my speaking at my own funeral, trying to convince God why I was not the one who should be going." They all thought I was making a joke when I would say Alan should not be transferred—no, I mean why I should not be transferred. It was I who was to become the new guidance counselor at the Engle Street School. I would be coming in working with a staff who had been working with another counselor for many a year. And now a male working with young boys and girls.

One teacher made a referral for me to see a student's parent. I made the appointment and gave it to the teacher. She said, "I cannot attend. I have something to do after school."

I said, "How am I to meet with this parent without you?"

She said, "I will give you ten minutes and I must leave."

I said that would work. I could take it from the introduction of the problem.

The parent and child met me in my office. Then the teacher came in. I told the parent the teacher's time restraints. I asked the teacher to state the problem. Then I asked the student to respond. Then I explained to the parent and students what had to change and how we were going to work together to make the change happen. Then I said, "The teacher has to leave now."

Then the teacher said, "No, I have a little more time."

I explained what each of us was to do to help the student along with what would be expected from the student and that we would have a follow-up meeting in one month to check on our progress. I said it would be my responsibility to keep everyone abreast of day-to-day transactions during the month.

Everyone agreed with his/her assignment and the timetable set. Now thirty minutes or more had gone by and the teacher was still there. I said, "Mrs. B, what happened with you having to leave?"

She said, "Mr. Bethay, I have been teaching for more than twenty years, and this is the first time I have ever felt so supported by a counselor or principal. I have never experienced anything like this before in my career."

Need I say more? She told everyone about the conference with the parent. The other teachers could not wait to have a need for a conference with me or a parent and student.

I could not see all students who wanted to see me. I had worked with the principal in the junior high school when he was a social science teacher and there was not anything to convince him about me. He knew me because we had worked together for many a year with both students and parents.

I got me a tape recorder. I met with the teachers first and told them my plans. They agreed, and then I met with the students and told them what they were to do. First, a student had to get permission from his/her teacher for a schedule to get scheduled to record what they wanted to if I were not available. I would play the tape and send for the student later if I felt the need warranted it.

I had a blank form for students to complete:

Name: _____
Homeroom Teacher: _____
Why you need to see me: _____
_____
_____
_____
_____
_____

The student would get so fascinated with the tape recorder that he would tell or talk about things he/she had not intended to tell me. The students and teachers got caught up with this counseling technique, and it got back to the parents. They wanted to know more about it. We scheduled a guidance night with just parents and let them hear some of the edited tapes of their children. I explain the confidentiality of the tapes and how and when I would erase them.

One father came up to me after the meeting and congratulated me on the procedure. Then he said, "I knew that one of those boys was mine. He has never talked to or with me that much in ten years.

He is a changed boy since he has come to this school. I want to thank you for what you are doing. Where were you when I was in the sixth grade?"

My replacement moved back to the central fifth-grade school, and I followed this class to the middle school the next year; thus, I was their counselor for two years. Now the middle school is a sixth-, seventh-, and eighth-grade school with all this reorganization.

I remained the sixth-grade counselor until I retired in 1994. It became my responsibility to orientate and prepare the fifth graders for the middle school with the help of my two colleagues.

I would take a group of sixth graders each May to the Engle Street fifth-grade school, and they would demonstrate for them everything awaiting their arrival, a student for each subject and activity. That too was a very successful orientation for the new students. It was good for the students because they came knowing what to expect in terms of homework, supplies, procedures, and overall schedule.

Janis E. Dismus Middle School and Mrs. Sarah Cheatham

There were a lot of interesting developments in the Englewood Junior High before it was changed to the Englewood Middle School and later to the Janis E. Dismus Middle School

The junior high had an education curriculum at that time which prepared students well for high school in all areas. As mentioned before, we junior high school counselors prepared the schedules for the students entering the tenth grade, and when the school was changed to a middle school, we prepared the schedules for the eighth graders entering the Dwight Morrow High School. We worked six weeks each summer, preparing students' schedules for their next grade.

Let me do a few name-dropping before I go much further. I had the opportunity to be the guidance counselor for Bruce Hopper, Billy (William) Willoughby, Ernest and Marvin Isley of the Isley Brothers, Bernard Belle, who wrote for Michael Jackson, and John Travolta. Among the girls whom I worked with were Regina Belle, Tracy Ross Lang, and Sister Souljah.

An Afro-American woman was on the board of education in Englewood during the early part of my tenure. After her untimely death, they renamed the Englewood Middle School to Janis E. Dismus Middle School, which was formally the Englewood Junior High School when I began in 1964. Confused?

We developed one of the best guidance programs of its day anywhere. We were so impressed with ourselves until we were going to present our program at one of the guidance and counseling national conventions one year. (When I accepted the job in Englewood, I made Dr. Shedd include in my permanent contract that I would be able to attend the national guidance and counseling convention each year at the board's expense. One director of pupil services wanted to renege, but I made her stick to the agreement.) We based our opinion of the program on the approval we were getting from the administration, faculty, students, and parents. Also, we too were pleased with our work!

Our guidance team included the psychologist, social worker, learning disability specialist, nurse, disciplinarian, and counselors. Initially when a student had any kind of problem, he/she ended up in special education, it seemed. That became a big department once Federal money became available for special education.

We improved our referral procedure, which the team had to adhere to before any student could be placed in special education. Each member of the team had a role to play in processing (making) a referral. If testing were done, the results had to come before the team for a final decision (acceptance) or placement. No one person could have a student placed into any program without the total team's approval.

It was the counselor's duty to prepare the referral form for his/her counselee and coordinate the efforts of each team member. The counselor also convened the group for final actions/decisions based on the final recommendations received from each member of the team. I have never been so impressed with a group as I was with that team.

The psychologist would never meet with the team before he ran his report by me to see if I agreed with his findings. I must say that was somewhat true with the other members as well. My opinion was always respected.

The team's recommendations had to have the parents' acceptance before any final action could be taken, especially a placement change into special education.

I feel the team worked well together and we socialized well together. (I held the end of year Engle Street School party at my house in Brooklyn. They came all the way from New Jersey.) Through the years, many of the faculty and staff have partied in Brooklyn with me—Christmas, weddings, fund-raisers, cookouts, etc.

Many changes began to take place due to the different superintendents, principals, and student personnel directors we began to get. Each one came in with his/her ideas/agenda. That was not a problem if their ideas would fit Englewood School System's. We did not resist change, but we were not going to change just for change's sake no matter who was in charge. We stood firm as long as we could.

Another major staff change took place later; another middle school guidance counselor was transferred to the high school. After the one year at the Engle Street School, I remained at the Janis E. Dismus School until my retirement in June 1994.

When Dr. Henry J. Pruitt became principal at the Middle School, one saw an all-student principal. Each year the freshman class, sixth graders, had a class trip to either the Benjamin Franklin Museum in Philadelphia, Williamsburg in Virginia, or Washington, DC's historical sites. There would be as many as three buses of eleven- and twelve-year-olds on a three-night trip away from home. I remember this boy coming to me before we left on one of those trips (who had never been away from his parents over night) and said, "Mr. Bethay, will you take care of me?" I had never been so touched.

In those days, one chaperon could easily take care of ten students without any concern anyplace we visited; staying overnight was never a problem either. Could you imagine trying to do something like that today? Dr. Pruitt also arrange local trips and annual picnics for the students.

Now let me tell you about a few of my other memorable happenings during those thirty years in Englewood.

One day a girl had been excused to go the gym's restroom. I saw her on the second floor in her gym shorts. I took her back to the gym class and told the teacher where she was. She went home and told her mother that I would not let her use the restroom. The mother called me the next day and said, "Mr. Bethay, if my daughter s——s on herself, I'm coming up to that school and smear that damn s—— in your face."

I said, "Lady, I really don't know you, and I know that you don't know me. I work in Englewood, but I live in Brooklyn where we are the kings of smearing s——. So anytime you are ready, I shall be waiting."

We had locker inspections at school. One day a bottle of wine was found in this girl's locker. We called the parent for a conference. He had to leave work. He started off by telling us what he was going to have done to us for accusing his daughter of having alcohol in school. Mrs. Cheatham, our disciplinarian, none better, told him, "Ask your daughter." He asked his daughter and she admitted having it in her locker. Then he asked her where she got it from. She said, "On top of the cabinet in the dining room." The embarrassed father took his daughter home to serve her three-day suspension.

This took place before we had begun the in-school suspension room.

One afternoon I stopped at a gas station to get gas. When I went to pay, I had no wallet. The station attendant let me go with the promise of coming back to pay later. Mrs. Cheatham always stayed late after school in some type of after-school program. I went back to school and told her what had happened. She asked me to give her the names of all the students who were in my office that afternoon. I mentioned three students' names. She said, "Mr. Bethay, let's go get in your car and go to so-and-so's house."

I said, "Are you sure we should do this? I do not know for certain that a student had taken it."

She said again, "Let's go!"

We went to this lady's house who took in foster children. Mrs. Cheatham asked where this boy was. Of all days, he had not come home and it was after 4:00 p.m. Mrs. Cheatham said that we were not going anyplace until this boy comes home. About 5:00 p.m. he comes in. Before anyone could say anything, Mrs. Chatham said, "Where is Mr. Bethay's wallet?"

"I don't know anything about a wallet," he said.

Mrs. Cheatham said again, "Where is Mr. Bethay's wallet?"

He said, "I don't have Mr. Bethay's wallet!" More forceful this time, she asked the boy. He began crying and said, "He should not have left it in his coat pocket."

Mrs. Cheatham then said, "Where is it?" He said he threw it away and did not know where.

Mrs. Cheatham gave me money for gas and toll to get across the George Washington Bridge. Now I had no license or money.

I had to be at school the next morning for a meeting with the superintendent, principal, and some other people about some school matter. During the meeting, the principal's secretary came to the door and told Dr. Pruitt that a little girl was there who said her daddy told her to see Mr. Bethay the first thing this morning before she went to class. She was let in. She said, "Mr. Bethay, Daddy said you might need these." They were my street number slips. I do not remember anything else about my wallet. I did not win either.

Even today, Dr. Pruitt teases me about those number slips during that meeting. We had an Afro-American superintendent at the time, so everyone present knew what those slips were. At least they saw that I was not being paid enough and I had to supplement my income.

Mrs. Cheatham was the best detective any school could ask for. She made the school run smoothly and my job easy because she took care of any discipline problem. If a student had done anything which warranted punishment of any sort, it was Mrs. Cheatham who did that. I then would see the student to help him/her not do it again.

We began an in-school suspension program where a student came to school but had to stay with Mrs. Cheatham during his/her suspension time, completing work the teachers had sent to Mrs. Cheatham for him/her; thus, the students never missed school or schoolwork because of suspension.

My group guidance sessions were ongoing throughout the year. I was not just an office counselor; I visited classrooms and observed students in classes. It was never a problem for me to walk into a class and stay without previously announcing my coming. I had that kind of rapport with teachers; thus, I knew my teachers and they knew what they could expect from me.

There were times, however, I would have a parent meet with me to rehearse him/her as to what to ask the teacher about his/her child's schoolwork in and out of school and what were they expected to do at home to help improve the situation. From many of these parent-teacher conferences, the child may be put on a daily progress report.

We kept students abreast of the rules and regulations, so not knowing was never an excuse.

I always got to school early and there was this student whose mother had to drop him off before she went to work. So I began letting him come into my office before school. I would go over his homework with him, and we had developed a good student-counselor relationship. One morning I was asked to cover the homeroom he was in. Just before the bell rang for the first period, he asked if he could go to his locker to get his books, which he should have done before homeroom. I said, "Yes, but go on to your class when you leave the locker." He was back before the bell rang. I said, "I told you that you did not have to come back." He tried to push by me to come into the classroom. I picked him up by the seat of his pants and the other hand on the back of his neck and dragged him to my colleague's office, Mrs. Washington, on the second floor. I angrily flung him into it. Every time he tried to get up off the floor, I would knock him back down. I had beaten him up so badly until I called his mother and told her what I had done. She came up to the school crying, telling the principal that she did not want we to ever have any dealing with her son again; thus, he could not be in my group guidance sessions anymore either.

Later on, the student asked if he could attend the group guidance sessions again. I told him, "I never took you out. Your mother took you out, and only she could get you back in." The mother called me and asked me if I would let him back into my guidance and counseling program. I knew he had learned his lesson. That could not be done today either. I would be suspended at least.

One morning Mrs. Eason, a teacher, came into the office and closed my door and said, "Mr. Bethay, I have something to tell you, but I do not want you to tell anyone else." Before I could respond, she said, "Who am I talking to, I have known you for over twenty years and you have never told me anything about anyone, and each time anyone tells you something, you act as if you are hearing it for the first time."

Now how did I really meet Mrs. Cheatham. One morning I was in the nurse's office, Mrs. Gadsden, when these two boys got into something between them. I told them to stop. I looked around and they were at it again. I slapped one of the boys on his head and said, "Didn't I tell you to stop!"

This lady was in the office and said, "Who are you?"

I said, "I am Mr. Bethay!"

Then she said, "I am his mother!"

The rest is history. I became Brother Saul and Uncle Saul to this day. I was adopted into this family as well. Mrs. Cheatham's other son and her mother and sister would not do anything without including me. Her mother loved me as a son all the rest of her living days. I flew to Chicago to attend Grandma Sarah Floyd's funeral. And there is not a month that would go by without Brian Cheatham and I being in touch with each other—the boy I hit on the head in the nurse's office.

I had not made any plans for retiring, but the notice came out that anyone who had thirty or more years could retire with thirty-five years instead of thirty. I called downtown and asked if this could be the same if one worked another year. I was told that this was a one-time deal. I made the school mail person wait until I completed my retirement application, which went in that day.

Honestly, I can say, the sendoff which I was given was the biggest one that school system has ever had for any one person. This may have been "good riddance," but it was an occasion I shall never forget. I do believe the entire Englewood school system was involved.

Every thing or organization I have ever been a part of in those thirty years participated either in the planning, helping execute, or participating directly or indirectly in that wonderful retirement party, not to mention everyone presented me with an invaluable, lifelong gift of some kind—Mrs. Cheatham, the guidance staff, the PTA, the Teachers' Association, the Middle School, Fort Valley State Alumni Association, the Mississippi Valley State Alumni Association, Medgar Evers College, Brooklyn College, New York University, my adopted families, and new friends I made during my tenure.

Luckily, I had come in a van; otherwise, I would not have been able to take home as many of the gifts as I did that night. New Orleans, Itta Bena, Miami, Chicago, Newport News, Philadelphia, Washington, Baltimore, Wellington, Birmingham, Boston, Atlanta, New Jersey, New York State, and New York City—the five boroughs—were represented with their good wishes and gifts. Dr. Pruitt did film a portion of the retirement party. A larger place would have been the only suggestion one could have made, but they made this restaurant accommodate close to two-hundred-plus people, it seemed. The menu in itself was awesome.

Highlights in Englewood

ENGLEWOOD WAS MORE THAN work. Let me go back to my first friend, my mother, Mrs. Sarah Valentine. The name in itself is love. That was she.

After I had gotten to know Mama Valentine and was introduced into the whole family, especially the cousin she lived with before she remarried, Kate Brinkley, we became family. Any entertainment they had, Claude and I were expected to be there. They adopted him, too.

Mama Valentine made sure that everyone knew what I was doing for Claude. She had her Church do a fund-raiser for him; they all liked his accent and loved to hear him talk and enjoyed dancing with him. It was the Ebenezer Baptist Church of Englewood, New Jersey.

For three Christmases, Mama Valentine gave me the same gift. The third Christmas, I said, "Mama, do you realize that you give me the same thing each Christmas?"

She held up his and her paper cup and said, "You would not know it by this plastic cup."

I got about three dozen of her glasses and had them washed. I got someone to go around the room and have everyone put their paper cup in the garbage. I never used plastic again; I can serve two hundred people without using paper or plastic, thanks to Mama Valentine. I could serve over two hundred guests with china, too.

Mama Valentine was dating this deacon from church, and they later married. He became my father, Father Saunders. Mama Saunders moved into his apartment. One morning, before I went to school, I made them this special breakfast. But I did not know he was not an early riser. I disturbed his sleep, fixing this breakfast which he did not enjoy because I woke him up too early, messing around in the kitchen. One learns.

Father Saunders died after a long sickness. Mama Sanders moved in with her oldest daughter and her family in Wilmington, Delaware. I became Uncle Saul to that group. They too are a part of all my family affairs even today.

Before Mama Saunders moved, she gave me priority of everything she had in her apartment. I have her crystal tier candleholders which are worth a fortune today.

I always visited her and the family often in Wilmington once she moved there. She was always that kind, caring, concerned person who first invited me to dinner in 1964 in Englewood. I shall never forget her. How could I? I have thousands of pictures of her and that family. I am still close to my three sisters, Vivian, Carole, and Celeste. I do not hear from or see their brother Buster.

Mrs. Mary Eason* (Just Died September 15, 2017.)

Mr. Eddie and Mrs. Mary Eason had three boys. The middle boy was shot and killed by another boy in Englewood. That family was never the same. The youngest boy had a nervous breakdown as a result of this shooting. Mrs. Eason became too protective of them and would not let them grow up on their own.

They too became my family. We visited each other often, participating in all our social affairs on special occasions and especially Christmas.

Mrs. Eason was in an art store in Bergenfield, New Jersey, and the owner had this wooden candy/nut rack in the window to attract customers. She saw it and went into the store and told the owner that she has a friend who had to have that. He said it was not for sale.

She said, "Yes, it is. I must have it." It sits today in my living room on a marble round table, which I have been keeping for a friend since 1990.

Mrs. Eason taught English in the Englewood Middle School. She produced this play called, *Englewood Goes Broadway*. It was a production worthy of Broadway. My friend T. Ray Lawrence, the problem with his zipper on the train, via way of Michigan State, sang in that production.

After Eddie died, Mary came to me and said, "Mr. Bethay, Eddie has this special pistol and I do not want to keep it in the house with the other two boys. I want you to have it." I could not bring myself to having a gun, so I said no. Then she said, "I had just brought Eddie this full-length mink overcoat, and I don't have a son who would ever wear it. I want you to have it." That I have. (At one of my Christmas parties, I had a fashion show entitled "Men Over Sixty." I modeled that coat. My goddaughter's family had given me a full-length leather coat, and I modeled it as well. I had on a leather-brimmed hat, pinstripe suit, and sunglasses. I walked throughout the guests as my attire was being explained. I took off the coat and began dragging it through the room. Just as I started up the stairs dragging the leather coat, I dropped it on the first rung of the stairs and kept walking. The crowd screamed.)

Car Burning and Mr. Samuel Wynn

On my way home from one of our Englewood School System's end-of-the-year faculty school parties, my car caught fire and burned up. I had to spend the night with my friend, Mr. Samuel Wynn, who now teaches in the elementary school.

A little about Mr. Wynn. When I first got to Englewood in 1965, I met one of my students' uncles who came up to visit them each year from North Carolina. We became friends and he would visit me at school during the time I worked there. I kept telling him about working in Englewood where he would make more money. He was reluctant, I think, because he doubted himself teaching up north.

I finally convinced him to apply, and he finished his career as one of the best math teachers the elementary school had ever had. Instead of always going to Mama Saunders, later on I would stay at Sam's house before an evening meeting, and he would cook that special dinner for me. An excellent cook he was. We became good friends and he introduced me to all his relatives who lived in Englewood. This was the family Sam stayed with during the summers he would visit Englewood when we first met in 1965.

I became friends with this family, who was Sam's brother-in-law.

The Wallet on the Top of the Car

One pay day, I had cashed my check during lunch in preparation for our spring vacation. I took some things home from my office inasmuch as I would be away for a week. I put things in the back seat of the car. Every time I would be meeting another car, they would wave at me and I would wave back. Their wave was always a pointing one. This went on until I got out of Englewood and made my turn for Route 4, heading for the George Washington Bridge. Luckily, I stopped at the first gas station to get gas and went to pay and my pouch with my wallet was missing. Then I knew what everyone was trying to tell me as they passed. I remembered the last person who had done so. It was just before I got onto Route 4. I left my car and ran back to that spot, and on the side of the road against the curb was my pouch with $800 in cash. My Guardian Angels at work again.

Picking Up Teachers in Manhattan

Once I got a car, over the remainder of my tenure, I would pick up at least one teacher who lived in Manhattan. First, it was Miss Barbara Stroud, who lived at the foot of the Manhattan Bridge just as one got into Manhattan. I did this as long as she worked at the Middle School. Later she ended up in Atlanta and worked as a hostess at one of the famous restaurants there. Later she moved to California and began another successful teaching career, one she did until she retired recently. We always kept in touch, even she and her two sisters, who still live in Manhattan. One did recently die. Barbara puts together jazz CD's and sends me one or two each Christmas. I have a large collection, thanks to her. She visits me whenever she is in New York.

During the time she lived in Atlanta, she met Leo Vanterpool. It may have been due to my introduction on one of my annual summer visits. They remain good friends even to this day. Leo even visits Barbara when he goes to California, which is quite often.

Later on, I began picking up one of the music teachers in Manhattan and take him to work each morning. He was one of the band instructors, a very good one. He worked with the Steel Drum teacher, Mr. Hubert Ashley. We had an excellent music department during that time.

I need to mention the choral teacher for a specific reason. For some unknown reason, one morning, I said, "That is a song from *A Little Night Music*." (This was a Broadway musical I had seen some time ago.) "Send in the Clowns" was the title of the song.

My secretary said, "Oh no, Saul, that is not from that *A Little Night Music*. I saw that play, too." In walked my colleague, Ruth Grupper and said that one of her sons was in *A Little Night Music* on Broadway. If that was not enough, in came Mr. Murphy with the album with the recording. Eileen, even to this day, thinks I got all of them to come by that morning. I said to Eileen that no one else knew that we were having this discussion before they came in. What a coincidence. That guidance staff still meets most months for lunch or celebrate our birthdays; Ruth's and mine are in January, Eileen Cohen's is in April, and Alan Brodsky's is in July. (Eileen died in March and Alan died in June 2017, the month before their birthdays. They both are missed!)

One afternoon, Eileen asked me to drop her off at Fifth Avenue and Fifty-Ninth Street. I said you want to go to Grand Army Plaza. She said, "No, I want to go to Manhattan, not Brooklyn."

I said, "Eileen, there is Grand Army Plaza at Fifty-Ninth and Fifth." She said no because she once lived in Manhattan and knew all the different sections.

When we got there, I told her I would not leave until she went and read that street sign.

She came to school the next day and told everyone never to argue with Mr. Bethay about anything you don't agree. He is always right. We laugh about that at some of our luncheons even today. (I only argue about things I know I am sure of. I am not a know-it-all.)

Other Riders to Englewood- Stan Greenburg and Bea Maldonado

Later, I began picking Stan Greenburg up in Manhattan and take him to his band job at the Dwight Morrow High School in Englewood. It was Bea Maldonado next to be picked up. Bea and I are good friends even to this day.

When Bea Maldonado began teaching at the Middle School, we became friends. She too rode with me each morning along with Stan as long as he lived in New York. Some days Bea came back to the city with me if she were ready to leave when I was. I could not wait because I always had another job either at Medgar Evers or Brooklyn College.

One morning, I was low on gas and was to get some when I got in Jersey. As it would have it, the traffic was at a standstill on the George Washington Bridge. I had to keep turning the car on and off in an attempt to save gas. Finally, we got across the bridge and I kept passing gas stations, and Bea would say, "Saul, why are you passing these stations and you are low on gas?"

I told her, "I do not use those brands."

One afternoon, I was letting Bea off on the East Side Highway and she needed bus fare. She was standing outside of the car when I gave the money to her. When I was handing her the money, I told her the people who saw us knew I was paying my trick for the day. Bea never forgets that either and still laugh about it.

Bea and I socialized together; we attended many plays and visited each other's homes. Bea and some of her friends attended many of my parties in Brooklyn. Bea was present at my retirement party, and I was at hers years later. I met Bea's family from San Antonio, Texas. I visited hers in San Antonio. And her mother cooked me an excellent, enjoyable Mexican meal when she was visiting Bea and her sister in Manhattan. I had Mola for the first time, and I still stop by to see Bea for McDonald's occasionally when I am in the Village so we can catch up on our gossip.

Bea has shown her true friendship many a time when I have had family problems and/or concerns—sickness, death, etc. She treats me as if I am her best friend.

Administrators I worked with in Englewood, New Jersey- 1964—1994

    Mrs. Janis E. Dismus, President, Board of Education
    Dr. Mark Shead, Superintendent of Schools
    Dr. Larry Leverett. Superintendent of Schools
    Dr. Henry Oliver, Assistant Superintendent of Schools
    Mrs. Ruth Johnson, Superintendent of Schools
    Dr. Jess Barker, Director of Pupil Services
    Mr. Davis, Principal
    Mr. William Johnson, Principal
    Mr. Zeug, Assistant Principal
    Mr. Savage, Assistant Principal
    Mr. James Young, Assistant Principal
    Dr. Henry J. Pruitt, Principal
    Mr. Jerry Weiner, Principal
    Mr. Donald Huggett, Assistant Principal

Brooklyn College, 1985

My phone kept ringing and someone would say, "Saul, I have a job for you at Brooklyn College."

I would say, "Who are you?"

He would say, "I am Lee Stokes."

I would ask, "Do I know you?"

He said, "I am that person you worked with on that committee last summer when the Guidance and Counseling Convention was held here in New York.

I then said that I hardly remember you and now you are offering me a job. But I don't want a job. My son has finished college now and I am going to try and make it on one salary for a change. I am tired working two to three jobs at the same time.

A couple of weeks would pass and he would call again. This went on and off from October to the first of December. He finally said that he had fired his five counselors and needed someone with my background and skills in this program at Brooklyn College.

I asked him why did he think I would be the person for the job? He said that he was so impressed working with me on the committee this past summer that he had no doubt. "I am desperate Saul, please come!" He said.

I asked him his position at Brooklyn College. He said, "I am the new Evening Dean of the School of General Studies (SGS) and the program that you would be working would be with adults only; no one younger than twenty-five - Brooklyn at that time had a day program and an evening program with the week-end program being a part of the evening division.

To try to stop the phone calls, I told him that I would see what I could do within a six month period and after that, do not include me in your staff.

It turned out to be one of the most unique college programs I had ever seen or heard of or worked in; I saw it as a challenge, too. I could keep my job in Englewood and work after school, arriving whatever time I got there. It could not be done today with the traffic.

This was the initial staff:

>Dr. Leland Stokes, Dean of School of General Studies (SGS)
>Mrs. Frances Sullivan, Secretary
>John Pavona, Week-End College Director
>Dee Catarina, Director of Special Baccalaureate
>Richard Smith, Director of Small College
>Patricia McCarrack, Secretary
>Phyllis Gross, Secretary
>Edna Gross
>Judy White, Secretary
>Brenda Watts, New Guidance Counselor
>Saul H. Bethay, New Temporary Guidance Counselor

What makes this staff worth mentioning is its uniqueness. We were a team in everything we had to do. Among the three programs, we scheduled the student by hand individually. We would work as late as 1:00 a.m. "We" meaning the entire team—no one went home at 5:00 p.m. when we were scheduling.

When I came aboard, they were scheduling students for the spring semester for the three programs: Special Baccalaureate Degree, Small College, and Weekend College. Not only did I not know what I was doing with scheduling college students, I did not understand the three different programs either. (In Englewood, at least I knew what I was doing when I was scheduling middle school students, but being here at a college with a program I had never heard of was a nightmare.)

Let me share some of the highlights and/or incidents I experienced during my tenure.

An Afro-American student went to Dean Stokes for something and he told him to go down the hall and see Saul. He did not go. Sometime later, he went back to Dean Stokes with the same concern. Dean Stokes asked him did he see Saul? He said no. Dean Stokes told him, "You leave my office now and don't come back unless Saul tells you to see me. Okay?"

Confused, he left and said to himself, "I can't believe that Black man is sending me to talk to a Jew about my problem."

I saw this student who kept coming pass my office, looking in, and keeping going away. Finally, I became concerned as to why and what was he up to. I went out in the hall and asked him, "May I help you?"

He said, "No, I am looking for Saul."

I said, "I am he, come into to my office."

He came in and we dealt with whatever he had come for to his satisfaction. Then he began laughing. I asked him if he cared to share the joke? Then he said, "I am not quite sure because it is about you." My temper rose a little, but being the counselor I am, I gave him a chance to explain himself. Then he told me about Dean Stokes telling him to see a Jew about his problems. He said he had never been so shock and embarrassed when I told him that I was Saul. This student's name was Nastley Thomas, who lived two blocks from where I live, and we became good friends and neighbors.

Brooklyn College was known as the Jewish school unofficially among the City Universities of New York.

Nastley later told another student about his experience with me and advised the student to see me about any of his school-related concerns. This student's name was Therone O. Evans; Peedy was his nickname. He was attending Brooklyn College only to collect the GI Bill money. After meeting with me, I helped him to see that he was wasting good youth time and he needed a degree for the future.

I got him matriculated into Brooklyn College's degree-bearing program because he was too young at the time to be in any one of my programs, but he became my counselee unofficially and my friend even at the time of this writing. I could counsel and enroll him into his classes from my office which I did.

Peedy told other students about my counseling and my qualities in listening. He gave me the name Big Ears. He got interested in earning a degree. He also realized that he could be a good student and went on to finish his bachelor's and master's degrees at Brooklyn College.

Peedy was working at the post office while he was in school and could not find another job after graduation which paid him as much. He always said how he hated the post office.

When my friend Monara died, I was able to help Peedy get Monroa's apartment—a large apartment with two bedrooms, living room dining room and a bath. This apartment is only two blocks from where I live. When Nastley was alive, he lived only two blocks away in the other direction. What a small world, including Brooklyn, with its four million or more people.

Nastley Thomas, our mutual friend now, ended up with some type of chronic illness and died as a result. We miss him very much.

Dean Stokes left this job in about three years thereafter. Brenda Watts lasted only one year. When I learned that Dean Stokes was not returning, I did not come back either. John Pavona was assigned as temporary director of our division. He called me at home and asked why I didn't return to work? I told him that I thought since Dean Stokes brought me in, I had to go when he left. He said, "That is not true, your job is still intact."

I stayed at Brooklyn College for twenty-two years working under new deans, directors, and coworkers. (Later John Pavona died, and more recently at the time of this writing, Dean Stokes died as well.) More about their departure later, too.

Only adults over twenty-five years of age could get into these adult degree-bearing programs. Students all had to apply first by taking the CUNY exam (I will try to explain that later). Only full-time students could be in the Special Baccalaureate Program. Small College students were part-timers, attending with less than twelve credits per semester. Most of them carried only six credits, not more than nine at a time. Weekend students could carry a full load, depending on their background and how well they did on the CUNY test. Student who did not pass the CUNY exam could take remediation courses until they could pass the test.

Students who had trouble passing the exam could be placed in a program called 05D non-degree-bearing program. More about this group later.

The SB program was for those students who qualified on the CUNY test and the SB test; the SB test was harder than the CUNY test. This was the SB students' program:

>   Special Baccalaureate, twelve credits per semester
>   English
>   Literature
>   Art
>   Music

One professor was responsible for teaching twenty-five to thirty students their listed liberal arts courses the first year—twenty-four of the required credits for graduation.

The second year, that same group would be taught the social sciences by one professor, receiving six credits each semester (twelve credits for the second year).

Those same SB students took their sciences—chemistry, physics, biology—in their third year.

Students would earn 42 of their 128 credits (128 credits were the required number of credits a student needed to graduate when I began at Brooklyn College). They had a language requirement and a major to complete for their degree.

Dr. Dee Catarina

Dr. Dee Catarina received her doctorate degree from Fordham University while she was still working at Brooklyn College; she was a graduate of Brooklyn College herself. Dee became the director of the program after John Pavona's death. We worked closely in everything we did as long as she was there. Some nights we would work past midnight, like during registration, and I would have her spend the night at my house rather than drive to New Jersey by herself.

The new administration did not appreciate Dr. Catarina's successful programs with adult students—many who outshone the other college students. She took this administrative disrespect as long as she could and finally left for William Paterson College in New Jersey. We remained friends even to this day. She supports or attends all my functions—weddings, birthdays (we both were born in January), Christmases, dances, fund-raisers, and at times bereavements—Al Hicks's, my mother's, Claude's, Lionel's, Papa Saunders's, Mama Saunders's, Smitty's, Monroa's, Helen Russell's, and John Blanding's.

I have always been special guest at Dee's parties. I am a member of that family as well. I am Uncle Saul to her grandchildren, Sam and John.

My first visit at Dee's in New Jersey, she had the best Southern, Black dinner one could ever have. Boy, was I pleasantly surprised. These were just some of her main menu which tasted better than any Southern cooking one could find anyplace:

>Barbeque beef ribs with special seasoning
>Ham hocks with vegetables (I won't cook mine after this)
>Rice
>String beans
>Potato salad
>Salad
>Rolls

They liked my deviled eggs and fried chicken, so when I would attend Sam's parties, including her graduation parties, I was expected to bring that.

I was a special weekend guest at Sam's wedding in 2013. I had my own two-bedroom apartment at the motel, I was given a tour of the Catskills, and I was royally dined throughout the weekend. I participated in all the wedding activities the entire weekend. I only had to drive my car to Dee's and Rick's. I rode with them the rest of the weekend.

If that were not enough, on the way home from Sam's wedding, we went to this special restaurant in Newark. I could not eat because I ate three breakfasts because I had planned on going directly to play pool once I got back into the city that afternoon. I was still too full from breakfast. I had to take that delicious meal home, which lasted the remainder of the week. Had they told me at breakfast that we would be having dinner on the way home, I would not have eaten so much at breakfast, something I normally do not do. Why this time, I still do not know. They did not tell me about the dinner we would be having on the way home. That too was a planned part of my special weekend with them.

Dee and I tried to have lunch once each month in Paterson at this famous Italian restaurant. I eat the same thing each meal—beef tripe—because it was better than any I had when I was on the farm in Berrien County in Nashville, Georgia.

Dee was at my retirement celebration in 1994 and told the guests that she spent more time with me when we worked together at Brooklyn than she did with her Sweetie, Rick. More about Dee later.

Small College (SC) student had to meet the same requirements as any other Brooklyn College student; the difference was that they could do it in the evenings, taking one or two classes each semester. We had our own small college English class and professor. SC students had to satisfy the *CORE* requirement, the language requirement, and a major to qualify for graduation with the initial one hundred twenty-eight credits required. The required numbers of credits changed before I left. Brooklyn College was requiring more credits to graduate than any other CUNY schools at the time.

Dr. Richard Smith

Richard Smith (the director of small college) told me one day after Dean Stokes left that he told Dean Stokes that he must be crazy bringing an Afro-American into that type of setting as a counselor, my being from Fort Valley State in Georgia with a major in agriculture.

Richard was Afro-American himself and from Atlanta too and knew of Fort Valley. But he did not know me. Later on, he told me just how wrong he was. He said he had never worked with anyone whose skills and abilities working with adult students he respected as he did mine. What a comeback from his initial opinion/impression of me. But he was man enough to tell me.

When Richard was working on his Ph.D., he came to me and asked me to help him with his outline and general approach. I took about ten minutes and gave an outline. He looked at it and said, "No, that is not the way they want it done at The Graduate Center of the City University of New York." I told him I did not realize that they would want it any different than Columbia, where I had submitted my outline; Claude had gotten his Ph.D. from New York University, and I had helped Ila Wells get hers from Illinois University.

Much later, he came into my office, slammed the door shut, and threw his research on my desk. It frightened me. He said, "What in the hell are you doing working here at Brooklyn College? Why in the hell aren't you teaching how to write dissertations at the Graduate Center or some other university?"

Once I realized that he was not really angry at me, I asked what was the matter? He said, "Saul, I came in here a year ago and asked you to help me with my outline for my research, and you in five minutes gave me one, which I rejected. Now I took a look at what they are telling me and what I must do, and it is verbatim to what you did in five minutes. What in the hell are you doing here?" he said again.

"Richard, just relax," I said. "All we have to do is put the research in its proper place and the other parts of the required material will not be that much trouble either."

I worked with Richard on completing his dissertation. He got his Ph.D. When it comes to PhDs, I am like the "Brides Maid, never the bride."

Richard worked well with the Small College students and his colleagues. At times, he taught the math class if he could not find a teacher he felt qualified to do the job with the adult students he wanted. All our students were special to all of us working with them. That was seen in the students' performance as well.

Richard too left Brooklyn College after he got his doctorate, but we kept in touch as well. He and I were never as close friends as Dee and I. Richard has been to many of my affairs. A good person. My last account of his whereabouts was at a college in the Bronx.

The Week End College students could take as many courses as they could qualify or handle, coming only on weekends. For some majors, they had to take classes during the week as well.

The Weekend College Students

I LEARNED AFTER I began working there that some of the 05D students had over one hundred credits leading nowhere. One of my first jobs was to get rid of the 05D part of the weekend program. It was a program taking students' money without qualifying them for a degree ever. I began requiring that all students must fit into one of the three programs to be accepted. No more non-degree students in our programs.

I was a full-time counselor! Students came to see me on their own, but I met with each student, planning his/her schedule for the next semester or summer. That is how I spent my time between semesters, meeting with students, planning their degree requirements.

After a student met with me and we agreed on what he/she was to register for, I would register that student the first day of registration from my office. At this time we did not hand-register students as we did the first three years when I was there staying up after midnight with the entire staff working.

Later we got computers and I was given permission to register my students from my office. If a student needed permission, I could call that department and get it without any trouble ever. I got equal, if not more, cooperation at Brooklyn College from a group of people I did not really work with; we just happened to be in the same college, and my students had to take classes in their departments. Our programs were well respected, and our SB students were among the top students on campus. Most of them graduated with honors and went on to graduate school where I submitted recommendations from Brooklyn College. I am still in touch with many of these students from all our programs; some are neighbors and friends and attend my fund-raisers and house parties.

It was my job to recruit, test, and register all students for our programs. I gave both the CUNY and the Special Baccalaureate Degree program tests. The tests were prepared and scored in the testing department. The results were sent back to me directly and immediately.

We were a school within a school. We had our own completion programs each year for those students receiving their degrees and who were receiving special honors and recognition from us. Our graduates also participated in the regular graduation, too. Our students would invite their significant others to these affairs. The president, dean, and faculty who worked with our students were invited also. As time went on, I worked with new and different presidents, deans, directors, secretaries, and staff members.

I had a good relationship with them all. I got nothing but the best cooperation from everyone. I could walk into most of their offices without an appointment. They knew I came on duty just before it was time for them to leave, yet they helped me with whatever I needed to make certain that I got through the night or weekend when their offices would be closed.

They all had respect for what I was trying to do for the adult students and the way I was doing it. I could not have asked for better cooperation from anyone whom I had to rely on to complete my job.

Because of the cooperation I received from everyone, I was able to stay as long as I did. It was only when they began to look at the total budget and decided to phase out the special adult degree programs I decided I had enough. I should have stayed two more years because the City University had just begun three years earlier to offer retirement pay for part-timers. But I did not see myself doing anything different at Brooklyn College than what I originally came in to do. So I left. Hindsight is 20/20, but I left with nothing but good memories. What a part-time career I had at Brooklyn College. I went to stay six months and stayed twenty-two-plus years.

Highlights at Brooklyn College

The President's Birthday Party

I WORKED UNDER THREE different presidents while at Brooklyn College. The first one died soon after I was there. The Faculty Circle had receptions/parties at the President's house every so often. I would attend. They were always well done. The college staff helped with the preparation and serving. Dee Catarina was a top member, and she made sure that I was a part of anything I could be in, including the Faculty Circle, even though I was not a faculty.

My second president, Dr. Vernon Lattin's birthday party was celebrated at 220 Rutland Road with the Faculty Circle and a few friends I included from Brooklyn College. I know we had a house full. It was not a sit down dinner; everyone held his/her plates and drinks. A little awkward but we managed.

The reason I am mentioning this is because with all those "new" White people in my home for the first time, it began to rain. Raining not the problems. My roof began leaking at the foot of the staircase in the living room; a house full of people and a bucket in the middle of the living room catching rainwater. What an impression for an Afro-American man to make to his new president and new White guests.

The leak did not dampen the party. (The tin top roof at Side Camp in Georgia did not leak it made noise from the rain, but you would not get wet on the inside.) Now I am here in the great city of Brooklyn with a leaking roof. Picture that! (I am now waiting for the weather to change so that I can get a new roof at the writing of this draft. Not the same leak, however.) I have patched that room several times since then; I thought I had it tarred over, but the last winter, it came through.

I now have all new roof everywhere.

Luncheons

After Dee left Brooklyn College, the five of us kept in touch. Dee, Frances, Pat, Phyllis, and I would have a Christmas luncheon at 220 for many a year. One Christmas I took Tony Hardie to the airport while I left them at the house. I got stuck in the snow and traffic and got back just before everyone was getting ready to leave. We exchanged Christmas gifts, and they made their way outside themselves. I do not know why I did not let Tony get a taxi to the airport. Hindsight is 20/20.

At other times, I would have my Brooklyn College staff (at the time) over for lunch each year. Those two things became somewhat a tradition—Christmas parties and luncheons at 220 Rutland Road.

Years later, Pat's father died and she moved to another apartment. She gave me a twelve set of dishes from her apartment. Why am I mentioning this? What was more surprising was the set itself. It matched a set I already had. We all were pleasantly surprised.

One should see all the gifts they have given me over the years: caps, hats, shirts, sweaters, jackets, etc., things which will never wear out. They are all top quality. They have kept me in style and well dressed. More about this, too.

Retirement Parties

We had Frances Sullivan's retirement party at 220. Another new group of guests, one that had not been to a Black man's house for a party before, I am quite sure. There were about forty of them, mostly White. One man asked if he could look around. Another guest was impressed with my art collection. One wanted to know if I lived alone. One of Frances's grandson said, "I thought that I was coming to an old dinky apartment, this is a nice house." Another guest asked one of my Black neighbors who was in attendance if she were one of the workers. Sylvia Waters told her, "Oh no, my dear, I live across the street."

I had a full staff taking coats, serving the party and bar, about six people full-time throughout the evening.

Another of the guest told Frances later on how her evening was ruined. I had drinks and hors d'oeuvres from six to seven in the living room. She said that she kept eating the hors d'oeuvre after she went into the dining room and saw no other food. She had not eaten, thinking that she was coming to dinner.

At seven o'clock, I asked everyone to leave his/her glass in the dining room and go outside. She said to herself that she did not come dressed for the outside. But when she got on the covered garage top and saw those tableclothed tables, linen napkins, silverware, new glasses for water, liquor/beer and champagne, and all of that food (with her full stomach), she did not know what to do. She had filled up on the hors d'oeuvres. She said she had never been so embarrassed and outdone with herself.

Persons who had never spoken to me before would wave to me from afar after that retirement party. As I said, I had a full staff working as if it were a five-star restaurant. It was impressive, if I must say so myself.

Many years later, Dee retired from William Paterson College in New Jersey. I had her retirement party here as well. Why is this worth mentioning other than she is one of my best friends? It was the thirtieth of October and my friend Tony came in to help me get set for the guests. He said, "Saul, you better shovel that snow before your guests arrive."

I said, "Please don't come in with that bullshit when I have so much work left to do."

He said, "Go look outside!"

Reluctantly I went to the front door and the steps and ground were covered. The phone began ringing with cancellations because of the weather. Persons who were somewhat nearby came but left in the snow. Dee did not get home until about four in the morning after dropping someone off in Manhattan. We ended up with about thirty or more guests. Everyone seemed to have enjoyed him-/herself. It was a swell party, too. We did not let the weather dampen it either. It would only happen to me, but my Guardian Angels always come in for me every time.

In Honor of our Brother,
SAUL H. BETHAY.
Brother, you could take the easy route,
but you choose the upward path.
You could look out for number one,
but you choose to reach out to others.
You could drop out, tune out, run the other way,
but you choose to stand firm and be a man.
You choose honor, strength, and dignity,
knowing that along with all that responsibility
comes the joy of living life fully,
the pride of making a difference,
and the love of your family and friends.
Today in our absence, Brother Saul, Billy, we celebrate you!

Annie Mae Jackson, Miami, Florida
Alline Culmer, Miami, Florida
Charles Ludie Bethay, Valdosta, Georgia
Russell Bethay Sr., Miami, Florida
Zipha Lee Goins, Miami, Florida
Marian Marle Wilson, Miami, Florida
Robert D. Bethay, Chicago, Illinois

Dr. Steven B. Carswell, Ph.D.

Steve is one of two sons of my adopted sister Carolyn Hicks Carswell; the Carolyn Hicks whom I babysat when I was in college at Fort Valley. Steve has a brother, Billy, and a sister, Lisa.

When he was ten years of age his grandfather, Dr. O. E. Hicks, died and his grandmother and he came to stay with me for a while in Brooklyn.

Later that summer, Mama Hicks visited one of her sisters in the Midwest and asked me if Steve could live with me the remainder of that summer. I gladly said, "That would be just fine, I would enjoy having him with me."

Steve was a sponge for knowledge. He wanted to know everything he could about everything he saw or we did that summer here in New York. I made certain that we saw and did all the educational things available—The Empire State Building, the Statue of Liberty, New York Museums, Central Park, and Prospect Park here in Manhattan and Brooklyn. He collected shells on Riis Beach, and we visited Coney Island Recreational Park several times.

Steve finished high school and went to college.

Steve's life is a book in itself and I will wait and let him write that book.

Steve was the Valedictorian of his class at Wionia State University and gave the graduation speech. I flew out to his graduation and met the college administration, who was very pleased with Steve's academic performance. Steve introduced me as his father. I was asked to sit with the faculty during the commencement exercises. I sat in the front row in front of the podium where Steve spoke as my heart was bursting out of my shirt. He gave a brilliant speech. As I look at President Obama, Steve reminds me of him even in making a speech.

Now I have two sons—Claude Saint-Come and Steve Carswell.

Like Claude, Steve got summer jobs; like Claude, Steve got his master's; like Claude, Steve got his Ph.D., and like Claude, Steve got married.

Claude got married in Brooklyn and we had his reception here at 220 Rutland Road on the day New York had its first earthquake while I was on a ladder decorating.

Steve got married in Baltimore, where he had received his master's. Steve received his Ph.D. from American University in Washington, D.C.

I attended both boys' graduations when they received their doctorates—two brilliant young men. I got my Ph.D. vicariously through them. They both made me a happy father. I can say I am a proud grandfather of Steve's two boys even though they call me Uncle Bethay—Ryan Carswell and Aidan Carswell.

Helen Russell

I was sitting next to this only Black female student taking an exam in a class at Teachers College, Columbia University, when the professor asked me to move. I moved without any thought given. But when the exam was over, Helen asked the professor why she asked me to move. The professor told her that I was looking at her paper. Helen told her I should have been looking at his paper if anyone of us needed to. Anyway, why would I be trying to look at someone's essay test paper while they were writing it? Essay testing has always been one of my best skills once I left Fort Valley State College.

Helen was a nurse and a professor of nursing with two master's. She taught at Queensborough Community College. She wrote a book which I typed—*Pediatric Drugs and Nursing Intervention*. She was well read and traveled throughout the world. She wanted for nothing or lacked for nothing. She was not a "show off." One would never have known her worth from her behavior and her dress; she did not wear expensive clothes and/or jewelry; she owned both.

Like most of you who know me, Helen fully trusted me and knew that I would never try to take advantage of her or anything she had. The many things Helen did for me and wanted to do for me were always above board.

We always had and maintained an excellent friendship/relationship: the opera, concerts, theater, dances, parties, etc. I taught Helen to drive before she purchased her first of four cars, but I always used my car for dates and taking her places she needed me, including chauffeuring her family when they visited the areas. The family mostly stayed with me when they visited; thanks to Helen, I had the space.

Helen's housewarming gift was a six-eye gas-burning stove, which will last my lifetime. She loaned me $1,000, along with the many others, to help with the down payment on my house, and thank God, all of it was paid back in a reasonable amount of time—acknowledged in this book.

I could always expect $200 donations from Helen for the many fund-raisers I would have or participate in over the many years, regardless where they would be held and/or by whom.

All my family and friends loved, respected, and appreciated Helen. This was mutual.

My Guardian Angels will not allow me to hate or disrespect anyone regardless of their lack of understanding and/or knowing as to whom I am or who I was to Helen. There is peace in my "valley." Again, thanks to my Guardian Angels!

DISSERTATIONS

Dr. Ila Wells's "A Survey of the Negro Problem in the United States as Seen by British Travelers to America—1800–1861," Northern Illinois University, Dekalb, Illinois, April 1969.

Note: Ila stayed with me to do research in the New York libraries while completing her dissertation.

Saul H. Bethay—"With best wishes and love to a very 'special' person."

Dr. Claude Saint-Come's "Effects of ACTH Peptides on Recovery of Neuromuscular Function Following Crushing of the Peroneal Nerve of the Rat," New York University, New York, New York, June 1985.

Note: I helped type this dissertation, and Claude dedicated it to me:

Dedication

This dissertation is dedicated to Saul H. Bethay, a man of great vision, who knew that I came into this world to learn patience, discipline and independence. He was brave enough to teach an old and stubborn soul. Today "I AM" because of "HIM."

Dr. Stephen B. Carswell's "Pathways to Delinquency: The Role of Parental Attachment, Family Socioeconomic Status, and Deviant Peer Relationships in Risk Behavior and Delinquency among Urban

African American Middle School Students." American University, Washington, DC, May 2005.

Acknowledgment

Special thanks go out the members of my family, including my Mother Carolyn, Father Peyton, Sister Lisa, Brother Billy, Aunt Marian, Uncle Saul, late Grandmother Murlenun.

Highlights of My Part-Time Jobs

Staff Writer, Howard University, Washington, DC, Spring 1964

Twice each week I would meet with the research staff to discuss their documents. It was my job to prepare a report of their work to be submitted for funding.

Research Assistant, Bernard Baruch College, Summer 1970

I do not know how I heard about this job, but again an economics professor (this time) was writing a book and needed someone to type for him. I took this full-time job knowing that I would be available for eight weeks at the most.

I knew nothing about economic; thus, I could not look up things I did not understand or know. It was still the time one dictated his material for recording in a disk, and you had to put those earplugs on to hear what had been dictated for you to type. I had so many blank spaces with a question marks—economics has its own language I was not familiar with.

The maximum number of pages I would ever get typed in any one day was eight pages. I had a key to the office, and I could go and come anytime I wanted to, day or night. This would not happen today due to security.

I would type and leave the pages, and he would correct and fill in the blanks for me to redo. After about six weeks, I became concerned as to why he had not fired me. I left a note asking to see him. He made an appointment to see me. He asked what was the matter? When I told him my concerns, he said, "Don't you think if I felt like you, I would have been in touch with you, not the other way around? You are the best typist I have ever had."

Now it is almost time for me to return to my September full-time job, so I told him I was not pleased with the work I was doing, especially since he was paying me so well. He said, "You are too smart to be typing anyway. You probably would be happier working with the research team in the lab." I told him I knew nothing about economics and I did not want to take up anyone else's time teaching me. I think I want to leave. Also, I had a sister coming to visit for a week, and I would not be available anyway during the workday. He regrettably accepted the key.

Field Analyst, Greenleigh Associate Inc., Summers 1971, 1972, and 1973.

It must have been George Mims from Columbia University who got in touch with me about this field analyst job. I was happy to see him again, especially under these circumstances. Six degrees of separation again.

For three summers, I had a car to drive to some upstate camps to evaluate a Title I program. I was the evaluator for the education component of the program. I would drive up, get me a room in a motel nearby, and spend twenty-four hours there.

During this time the director, the counselor, and the middle school boys and girls would tell me all their like and dislikes. By the time I had heard from everyone and observed what I wanted to see, I had everything I needed to make my reports.

Only the groups changed each two weeks, not the problems or situations. Everyone called me Mr. Evaluator. They thought by telling me their concerns, I was in a position to make changes. That was not my job. I ended up with a good relationship with everyone and every new group of students.

I did have to make a report to the main office each week.

I could go to my main job in the mornings in Englewood to schedule my students for the incoming school year. I would leave there and come back to Medgar Evers College to work with my adult students and faculty; if I were not going upstate to visit the camp, I would go to Riis Beach.

One day I decided to drive up to the camps in Vermont. Just as I crossed the state line into Vermont, the patrol officer stopped me for speeding. Here I was out of state with a company car, getting a traffic ticket. Before he could write the ticket, another patrol officer came up and told the other officer that he had stopped the wrong car. My Guardian Angels at work again.

My evaluation reports were well accepted each summer. I was not required to be so detailed. The writers had very little left to do once I had completed my findings and recommendations.

There was a Black girl in the office who should have gotten a director's job, which was given to a White person who should not have even been considered. Several of us in protest did not return the next summer. I am not sure how long that program was in session or who did not come back to work. I know I did not. One of my best-paying part-time jobs thus far.

George Mims and I kept in touch after that. He became a principal in Long Island. He and Rudy Cain, who also worked in the office, both got their doctorates. Rudy became director of Empire State College branch near me in Brooklyn. This was a state-funded college where a student did not attend classes. The student would be assigned a mentor in his area of interest, and he would meet for assignments, and when the student finished an assignment, he would bring it to the mentor for evaluation and get another one. I believe colleges later on started having online courses as well for those who were interested. None of this type of "educating" would have been for me.

Consultant, Medgar Evers College, 1972

My friend Monroa B. Goutier was the administrative assistant to the president at Medgar Evers College here in Brooklyn. He told me about their need for someone with my background to help them with their accreditation. I had been through that before at my previous jobs, which were successful. This was the time when the key evaluator asked me why did I look so familiar? "Do I know you?"

I said, "First how did Medgar Evers do with its evaluation?"

He said, "They got accredited."

Then I told him that I was one of his son's guidance counselors in Englewood.

It was at this time I began working evenings and weekends at Medgar Evers College. I became coordinator of its Adult and Continuing Education Program. Adult students could take course for their General Education Development (GED). Some could take courses in English as a second language. I would teach off and on during my tenure.

One of the most rewarding courses I taught at the time was employees from the major stores throughout the city who took a class with me to help them prepare to become store managers. We met on Sunday from ten to one. We role-played the different situations a manager might find him-/herself in—making reports, interviewing, hiring and firing, public speaking, and writing memos. I would get to work about 9:00 a.m. on Sundays to get ready for the day and find most students there already. I changed the time from 9:00 a.m. to 1:00 p.m. and had trouble getting out of there by 2:00 p.m., if that was possible. I would dismiss the class and stay for anyone who had a personal need to see me.

Claude got his degree and I felt that I would make it on one salary. That did not last too long. With a new college administration and a new staff for the Adult Continuing Education, I was asked to direct a new summer program sponsored by the Mobil Oil Company. The students were in the park three days a week, and in one of the four days, they came to the Mobil Academy. They first had a Motivational

/ Career Readiness class. This was followed by reading, writing, and computer lab in the afternoon.

Students had to dress for school. Teachers had to sign the student's attendance card each period.

One day the team from Mobil was there and asked why were these kids using those computers? I said, "Those are ours students."

He said, "Dressed like that and so self-directed."

I said, "What you see is what you get."

They were so impressed, he asked what I needed? I told him I needed the staff's salary doubled to compensate for the hour they had to wait between classes, morning and evening. And I needed an ongoing evaluator to help with the final report. I got both.

Mobil team told Mayor Kotch about what we were doing, and he invited the whole staff down to his office to receive a Mayor Trophy. We all went down. President Dr. Jay Carrington Chunn II accepted the trophy and did not even mention any of our presence there. His acceptance speech was as if he and he alone did the entire program. He asked me to come back the next summer to coordinate the program. I asked him if he were kidding? That was it for me and Medgar Evers College and having to work two or more jobs at the same time. Or so I thought!

Vicarious Education

As early as my beginning coming to New York, during the summers, attending the weekly concerts in the park was something I looked forward to each year. The artists I did not see at the Apollo Theater in Harlem each week, I could see many of them in the parks or on Broadway or at the opera years later—Leontyne Price, Marilyn Horne, Joan Sutherland, Birgit Nilsson, Renata Tebaldi, Johnny Mathis, the O'Jays, Diana Ross, Gloria Gaynor, Jackie Wilson, Gladys Knight, Ray Charles, Nina Simone, Sydney Poitier, Nat King Cole, Spike Lee, Dr. Betty Shabazz, Lena Horne, Aretha Franklin, Claudia McNeil, Natalie Wood, Rita Moreno, Leslie Uggams, Robert Hooks, Ossie and Ruby Davis, and Dick Gregory, just to name a few. Those I missed during the summers I saw once I decided to live here in 1964.

Al Hicks first and then Helen Russell kept me in the operas, seeing *Madam Butterfly*, *Carmen*, *Media*, *Il Trovatore*, *Aida*, *Othello*, *La Forza del Destino*, etc.

I saw all the major plays on Broadway over the past fifty years. September 2014 is my golden anniversary living in this great city as a taxpayer.

The Philharmonic Orchestra and Leonard Bernstein Orchestra are two that I shall never forget seeing in concert at Lincoln Center in Manhattan.

I had the pleasure of meeting Adam Clayton Powell Jr., Dr. Martin Luther King Jr., Rev. Jesse Jackson, Shirley Chisholm, President Jimmy Carter, Hillary and William Clinton, and Andrew Young (as mentioned, my guest here once).

Venus and Serena Williams and Tiger Wood are my sport heroes and I have met them. I saw many of the US Open tennis matches here at the Arthur Ashe Stadium and many of the tennis players of the time, but I have never seen a golf match played live.

That which I did not learn from Side Camp Elementary School, the Cook County Training School, Fort Valley State, the Armed Forces Institute, Michigan State, Columbia, University of Hawaii, the In-Service Training Program, and Jersey City State, I learned on the streets of New York. That is my PhD!

Believe it or not, I once spent a lot of my summers on Riis Beach. I met a man from the Adult Nursing Home near the beach who always came on the beach and begged for beer and food. I would bring him some of each when I would go to the beach. I began bringing him to my house on some weekends. He begged me to take him out of that nursing home and let him live with me in Brooklyn.

I could not take that chance because he drank a lot and I had to be at work in Englewood. The nursing home moved from the beach area near downtown Brooklyn, and I did not see him that much then.

One day I got a call from the nursing home telling me that he had been dead for over a month, and my name was the only name they could associate with him from my signing him out some weekends. They told me also that he had $1,500 in his account, which I could have if I claimed the body. A friend of mine owned an undertaker business (Cooks Funeral Home), and they prepared and buried the body in New Jersey, where Lionel King and his mother are buried.

They gave me his wallet, ring, and watch, which I still have.

I served as a lawyer twice representing Ethel Wright and Monroa B. Goutier. I won both cases. I presented their cases before a judge and their lawyers. I still have the paperwork from each of these cases. I cannot remember what Ethel's case was about.

Monroa case was against a nursing home. They wanted him to pay for the time living there when he had no money to barely live. They wanted me to pay about $50,000 for his keep. Somehow and some way, that nursing home tied up Russell Bethay's account in Miami because I was listed as his heir. When I told them that Russell, my brother, who lived in Miami, did not even know Monroa and

I was just a friend who visited him at the nursing home, the judge threw the case out.

We had to have several court hearings because each time the nursing home lawyers and witnesses were not prepared. I had my account, Russell's account, and Monroa's account ready, and once I told the court our relationship and what the nursing home was trying to do, that ended that. The judge told the nursing home lawyers that Russell's account had to be freed in two days; I had no money to be freed. Can you believe this?

This reminds me that Social Security would not give me Monroa's $250 to bury him. Maybe I should submit this case to them and tell them how much money I spent in defending Monroa.

One Year in the Life of Saul Henry Bethay, 2003

It was the best of times, and it was the worst of times. The best of times first.

The New Year came in as usual, celebrating its arrival with Helen and friends at the Community Room on Linden Boulevard. Late that day, I attended an annual New Year's Day party at the home of one of my friends who had sold his dwelling for over a million dollars, and he wanted all his friends to be there one last time on that New Year's Day. The party as usual was successful and enjoyable—always a nice group of people to socialize with.

Leading up to January 19, the marathon of invitations began—luncheons, dinners, movie, gifts, and visitors throughout the month. Becoming sixty-nine was more like being a child at Christmastime than a birthday. February came and went without too much fanfare, just the recognition of the February birthdays—there are quite a few. Some of my best friends were born in February as is the case of January.

My youngest sister, Marian, turned sixty-five in March and wanted that to be her big celebration with all the family there. As my angels would have it, I was able to get a fare within my budget and still give a gift.

To me it was more than a birthday celebration; it was a family reunion of Marie and Ludie's children—only the youngest could not make it. The decoration was breathtaking; the outdoor setting was on the canal with tables with umbrellas throughout the backyard. As the Bethays would do, she had too much of all kinds of delicious foods and desserts for us to gain weight. I even got a chance to beat up on one of her neighbors on his own pool table. There was nothing like the beach in March coming from a cold climate.

I got my taxes done before the fifteenth of April and celebrated my friend Johnny's birthday with a fish fry for some of our friends. He was happy at eighty-one. Monroa needed some new bed linens, and I went shopping and decided to take the things to him before I went to work at three, which is quite unusual for me. But when I arrived at his apartment, I was told that Monroa had not awakened from the night, and it was about 2:30 p.m. The night before, I had tried to call Monroa on and off for more than an hour. Without success, I decided to stop by. He was not quite himself, a little confused in his speech, and he had left his medicine out, which was unlike him.

I called Helen, the nurse, to see if his insulin was still okay. I also let him talk to Helen to see if he was mentally alert. She assured me that the insulin was good after telling her what type. I kept asking Monroa if he were okay; he said he would be if I stopped asking him all those same damn questions over and over. On that note, I knew he was himself. I left about 10:30 p.m. to return the next afternoon with the things I bought and then found him unconscious.

When I was not able to arouse Monroa from his sleep, I called 911. Monroa being nearly four hundred pounds in weight, it took the fire department to get him off the bed onto a sheet and then to the stretcher in the living room. One week in intensive care at Kings County Hospital and another week and a half in Downstate, where I had him transferred after I came in after discovering that they had taken him out of ICU and had not given him any water all day.

I was informed by the medical team at Downstate that Monroa probably would not make it and I had better prepare for the worst. I called Smitty in Valdosta, Georgia, and gave him the update and asked that he join me in making final arrangements; we notified Monroa's mother and ultimately cleaned out his apartment. There was a breakthrough in Monroa's health, and they moved him to a semiprivate room, but all types of complications still existed—even his mental status was in question, not to mention the possibility that he had symptoms of having a stroke in his right arm. Smitty informed me that since there was this minute improvement, he would return home and get his situation in order to return. Day by day, there was some improvement in Monroa's health with the prognosis of having the need for rehabilitation. An acceptable rehab place was found with him having a private room at the beginning of June.

One of my former students and his wife, Jim and Julia Leonard, from New Hampshire, came down for the Fourth of July weekend and to attend a wedding. It was the hottest day we had had all summer. On their return home on the subway, the lights all over the northeast went out. They were fortunate enough to enter a station near the house. They walked through the car to the opening, got out, and was told how to walk the fifteen to twenty blocks to Rutland Road. I had come home from work to make sure they got in okay and was there when the lights came on. Now I am anxious thinking they would be on the train at the time of the blackout. Happily, they showed up hot and exhausted about an hour after the lights had gone out. As my angels would have it, I had cooked enough food for us to have for dinner on the stoop; it was too hot to stay or eat inside. Even during the night, we stayed on the roof of the garage to keep as cool as we could until about 1:00 a.m. They missed the wedding dinner and left for the weeding the next day in all of that heat. About 5:15 p.m., the lights came on and I attended my neighbor's daughter's graduation celebration in their backyard. It was a lovely affair, and the weather had cooled off considerably. Now back to Monroa.

From June to the time Monroa signed himself out November 17, he was in the Prospect Park Care Center on Coney Island Avenue, about twenty minutes from here.

Monroa said he could do at home what they were doing in the nursing home with just a little help. He had proven this to be true. But in the meantime, we applied for Medicare but did not accept what they had to offer—nothing for all his income and still be left with all his household bills and rent, not to mention his medicine. This too would not have included any custodial care. Monroa came home on the seventeenth of November and Smitty died on the eighteenth. I got Monroa situated at home and left, only telling him someone had died in the South and I had to attend the funeral and would be away from Thursday through Tuesday—no itinerary. (I met Monroa through Smitty. I lived with them one summer when I worked at New York University, on summer 1962.)

Monroa came home, and one of the ladies from the nursing home said she could give four hours, three days per week, and Robert Tadlock, who never stopped coming to see him, three to four times each week while in the nursing home, said he would continue his service. And I would fix dinner on Sunday.

Summer came and went, one of my best Englewood, New Jersey, friends died, and the Crab Feast (September 13) was a success. My friend Robert White from Maryland brought the crabs and helped with the final preparation. My dear friends from Hampton, Virginia, visited with me that week and offered a tremendous amount of help, including cash.

Patricia and Robert Harden from Sumter, South Carolina, called and asked if I would be in town for Thanksgiving; if so, they would like to come. They came and we had an excellent, quiet Thanksgiving. Now it was time for the Christmas party, December 13. My friends from Maryland returned and took over—barbequing ribs, cooking turkeys, making dressing, three bean salad, and a beet salad, and helping get dishes all set up for about seventy-five guests.

December began with my attending the Alvin Ailey's Gala on the third, followed by the supper on the sixteenth. Evelyn McKenzie, Larry Roberts, and Lucille Hagwood celebrated their birthday. I did not attend either. But instead, I invited two of my sisters and one brother to spend Christmas with me. They accepted and we had one of my best Christmases in New York. The highlight was keeping our youngest brother's arrival Christmas Eve a secret. Christmas Day was the usual breakfast, exchanging of gifts, and dinner. Helen and I attended an annual formal ball on the twenty-sixth. One of my sisters celebrated her sixty-seventh birthday on the twenty-seventh with a fish-fry party and peach cobbler for the birthday cake. On a scale of 1–10, I would give my Christmas a 20—Radio City Music Hall, Alvin Ailey, formal dance, parties at work, and the New Year's Eve celebration at Linden Boulevard ended the year.

Some of the Worst of Times

The garage leaks had to be fixed
Two refrigerators went on the blank within months apart
The washing machine began leaking oil and water and had to be replaced as well
Visiting the hospital three to four times daily in the month of April
Calling Monroa's mother, telling her that he was dying
Visiting the rehab/nursing home four to five times each week, between June and November 17
Writing to all of Monroa's friends and giving them a progress report
Keeping in touch with the medical team at the nursing home
Taking over the handling of Monroa's total finances, including paying his bills
Checking expenses for the cremation (the way he wants to go)
Smitty announced his illness
Smitty's death
Smitty's funeral
The death of Julia Bethay, my first cousin's wife, and my not being able to return to Valdosta for the funeral
Receiving the notice that Monroa's mother was critical ill and may not survive. At the time of this writing, she is holding on but eating very little. We are on a day-to-day watch here. She could not come here, and Monroa could not go there—no other relatives to my knowledge.

How Do I Cope?

I have ten full-time Guardian Angels looking out and taking care of me.

I am in relative good health, according to my doctors and dentist. I try to stay stress-free and worry less.

I have the best supportive family in the world.

I have the best group of close friends.

I have the best supportive group of friends.

I have no material needs or wants. My cup runneth over.

I have a part-time job made in heaven.

I attend the best New York has to offer—dances, concerts, opera, theater, and parties.

And two to three nights each week, I am able to unwind by playing pool with the best groups one could ask for and watching the stage shows the nights they are on.

Yes, in 2003, I saw the best of times and the worst of times, but I am off and running, looking forward to the year 2004 with great anticipation of all the good things life has in store for me. My motto: Think positive thoughts and positive things will come your way—including positive people.

May you too have a good year; mine has already begun with one birthday celebration, two more scheduled before the fifteenth, and I am off to Puerto Rico and St. Thomas on the fifteenth of January—continuing celebrating my seventieth birthday on the nineteenth.

Adios y buena suerte!

Saul (John*)

*My pool name along with Pops

Awards Committee at Fort Valley State University, July 31, 2006

It was a sad day when it was learned that Saul H. Bethay would no longer be at Brooklyn College after 21 rewarding years. The thousands of students whom he counseled and the professional colleagues with whom he worked are better persons with having had the experience and opportunity to work with him.

If ever a counselor was born, it was Saul H. Bethay. He brings a rare uniqueness to the role of counseling and guidance in a college setting. His appointment book was always full, which speaks for the quality and respect for his guidance. I do not know of any problem he felt too big for him to "tackle" and in the Adult Degree Program, there were many and of all kinds—academic, personal and social. Students always left his office feeling better than when they arrived. The office was known as a one stop office for counseling and advisement.

His work ethics were beyond reproach. He had a high respect for time and was not a clock watcher. Yes, I know this recommendation is for an honor or award, not a job, but whatever you are recognizing Saul for you could not have picked a more deserving alumni.

He always made Fort Valley State University look good here in the New York Area and at Brooklyn College.

Joan Alongi
Director

Our Responsibility to Our Youth

(A speech I gave to a church group in Miami in 1987)
Saul Henry Bethay

I. We have lost two generations of young Black people!
   A. Ages 12 – 29
   B. In all cities of any size
   C. To the street corners
   D. To the Video Game Rooms
   E. To the parks

II. Description - They are Angry, Confused, Frustrated, Poorly Educated, and Unemployed.
   A. Angry at
      1. Themselves
      2. Their Families
      3. Their Schools
      4. Their Government(s)
      5. Their Churches
   B. Confused
      1. No sense of direction
      2. Don't know where they are going
      3. They have no idea what they want out of life
   C. Frustrated
      1. Trying to find themselves
      2. Torn inside
      3. Unskilled

D. Poorly Educated - In and Out of School
   1. They lack . . .
      a. Common Sense
      b. Mother Wit
      c. Skill in
         (1) Reading
         (2) Writing
         (3) Arithmetic
         (4) Speaking
      d. The ability to make sound judgment and rational decisions
   2. In essence, they don't know how to use their "heads"
E. The Tragedy of this Description of our Youths
   1. They are the highest of the unemployed group in the Nation - more than 75% if not more.
   2. To control or dominate a person just keep him or her unemployed.
   3. Unemployment will strip one of his or her manhood or woman hood if allowed to persist faster than any other one thing I know.
   4. Work is like any other skill, training should begin early
   5. We cannot wait until our young people reach 21 to begin introducing them to the world of work. Actually they need a full time job.

III. How did our youth get to this . . .
   a. Angry
   b. Confused
   c. Frustrated
   d. Poorly Educated
   e. and Unemployed State?

IV. They had a lot of help . . .
   1. Their Families

2. Their Schools
3. Their Government
4. and Their Churches

V. The Family - Compare Family Life today with Family Life 50 Years Ago
   a. Time to get up in the morning
   b. When and how meals were prepared and served
   c. By whom
   d. How chores were assigned and who ended up doing them
      (1) Washing Dishes
      (2) Cleaning the House
      (3) Taking out the Garbage
   e. The lack of family
      (1) Talks
      (2) Planning
      (3) Recreation
      (4) and Family worshipping
   f. Knowing where family members were at all times - day or night. This change in family structure and routine has led to or contributed to this
      1. Anger
      2. Confusion
      3. Frustration
      4. Poor education
      5. and Unemployment

VI. Our Schools . . .

VII. Our schools are a mess. If business executives had to evaluate our schools today most of them would be closed before the next day. Why? Because the quality of the product our schools are producing - a product which is unmarketable; thus, what good is a product if it cannot be used or sold.
   a. The Superintendents
      (a) Experimentation

      (b) New Curriculums
      (c) Different Organizational Patterns and Structures
          1. Ability grouping
          2. Open classrooms
          3. Non graded classrooms
          4. Testing
  b. The Principals
     (1) Reports, Reports, Reports, etc.
     (2) New Math
     (3) The Computer Age vs. The Traditional Age
  c. The Teachers - Order, Discipline, and more forms and paper work
     (1) The Good Teachers lack parental and administrative support
     (2) The Poor Teachers have stopped trying; have given up. They show little or no concern for the children's lack of learning - Not getting in touch with parents before report cards. Waiting on Pay check!!!!
  d. Last but not least, our Poor lost, Angry, Confused, Frustrated, Poorly Educated and Unemployed Youths are preoccupied with "driving" everyone else in the school Crazy:
     (1) Late to School and to Class
     (2) No books, homework, pen or paper
     (3) Constantly bullying other students, teachers, and administrators

These conditions in our schools have made our youths . . .
a. Angry
b. Confused
c. Frustrated
d. Poorly Educated
e. and Unemployed and unemployable

VIII. Our Governments: Local, State and National
IX. What happens to a people in any society is greatly influenced by its government.
   a. Our youths are not even on the agenda of our governments today.
   b. Our governments are too busy building more jails and prisons, enlarging our courts, and employing more policemen, judges, and the lack for our youths - keeping themselves employed at our youths' expense!
   c. Too little time is spent on WHY we need any of these institutions in a great society such as ours; a society which is supposed to be for our youths.
      1. If this country wanted good schools, we would have good schools.
      2. If our governments wanted well educated Black youngsters, we would have well educated Black youngsters.
      3. If our governments wanted good teachers for our Black youths, we would have good teachers.
      4. If our governments wanted less Violence, Drugs, and Stealing, we would have less Violence, Drugs, and Stealing among our Youths.
      5. If our governments wanted less unemployment, we would have less unemployment. Example: Japan.

X. Poor People, Uneducated people, Unemployed People, make jobs for others.
   A. This tragedy in our Community, City, State and Country makes for segregation without laws or force.
   B. Whether you are aware or not, in this country, Money makes the difference!
   C. Money will not buy all the happiness we want, but it will surely pay for the miseries we all enjoy.

XI. Our Churches - How did the church help our youths get where they are today?
  A. The absence of total families in . . .
      1. Sunday Morning Sunday School
      2. Sunday Morning Worship Service
      3. Afternoon Worship Service
      4. Revival Services
      5. Easter Program
      6. Children Day
      7. Halloween
      8. Thanksgiving
      9. Christmas
      10. Bringing in the New Year Service
  B. Today, On Sunday, many of our youths are doing his or her own thing:
      1. They need Drugs and Alcohol to Function.
          a. To get started
          b. To keep going
          c. And even to try and stop.
      2. Yet they don't seem to be going any where.
  C. Too many of our young people are growing up without any church influence or affiliation.
  D. Churches do not have enough youth programs.
  E. They do not have enough youth participation in Service, Planning and Leadership Training in church affiliations.
 Yes, this too has led to our youths'
  1. Anger
  2. Confusion
  3. Frustration
  4. Poor Education
  5. and Unemployment

XII. Recommendations . . .
   1. The Family

a. Families need to go back to some basic family routines and activities.
   (1) Have a set time and place for doing everything.
   (2) Begin from day one doing those things together and consistently.
   (3) Don't wait until you take your children to a restaurant before you begin teaching table manners.
b. Know what is always going on in your children's education in and out of school.
   (1) Visit the school and meet with your children's teachers and administrators: Counselor, Supervisor and Principal. And you too can meet the superintendent to let him or her know that you are a tax payer and want to know what his or her plans are.
   (2) Attend all parent-teacher conferences, activities and/or functions.
   (3) Don't assume that the school is doing what it is supposed to be doing toward educating your child - make certain. If not, you might have to raise Hell even as a child of God.
   (4) The squeaking wheel gets the Grease. Squeak loudly!
   (5) Have some input in what is allowed in the dress code in your child's school. Families should have their own dress code.
   (6) Families must be aware of the political forces which affect their daily lives.
   (7) Families must participate in political elections - local, state and national.
   (8) Families must Vote!
2. The Schools
   a. Schools must be made to realize what their purpose for existing is - To prepare students to survive in a competitive society.

b. Schools must return to teaching our youths how to:
    (1) Read Well
    (2) Write Well
    (3) Speak Well
    (4) Respect themselves
    (5) Respect others
    (6) Respect an Authority above all others - GOD! We must return to praying and giving thanks to God in our schools. Jews still do!
c. Our Schools must stop tolerating teachers and administrators who are only in the schools to collect a pay check.
d. Schools must be run as schools and not a place where . . .
    (1) Lateness
    (2) Absenteeism
    (3) Fighting
    (4) Stealing
    (5) or drugs
    . . . Are permitted!
e. Schools must have a well-defined curriculum or educational plan for our youths; not one which changes every time a new superintendent comes into the system.
f. Our schools must graduate students who can compete on all levels - Pass tests with comparable marks as anyone else - other racial students.
g. There are a few schools which are trying to do the job as it should be done with a concerned staff. Why not all of our schools? You can make the difference!

3. Our Government
    a. Governments must be committed to good sound education for all of their citizenry - not for a select few

    b. Governments must give help to those schools which need the greatest support in personnel, materials, and money.

    c. Governments must supervise schools properly and make certain that money allocated for educational programs to help educate children is spent for that purpose only. No money should be made available to provide jobs for a select few and mis-education permitted to go on as usual.

    d. How to make governments work for you and your youths:

        (1) You must get politically involved.

        (2) You must know who has your children's interest at heart and vote for them; those who do not, vote them out of office.

        (3) Attend political meetings before and after political elections - get to know those persons who make decisions about your young people.

        (4) You must demand that you have a voice in how your tax dollars are spent.

        (5) Those you know who are not voting, encourage them to vote, too.

4. Our Churches

    a. Churches must set standards for the FAMILY, THE SCHOOL AND THE GOVERMENTS. Any Black person who is surviving today, got his or her influences through the church:

        (1) Singers

        (2) Speakers

        (3) Teachers

        (4) and yes, preachers

    b. Churches must bring the young people into their programs and activities. You must insist that they participate in your . . .

        (1) Sunday School

(2) Your Worship Service
(3) and any other activity of the church
c. Churches must return to providing the environment for our youths to:
(1) Practice their reading by reading the Bible in Church.
(2) Practice their singing by singing in the Church choir.
(3) Practice their public speaking by reviewing the Sunday School lessons and reading the scriptures to the congregation.
(4) Practice their self-respect, respect for others, and respect for God!

XIII. Working together, The Family, the Schools, The Government, and the Churches can help our youths get out of their . . .
A. Angry
B. Confused
C. Frustrated
D. Poorly Educated
E. and Unemployed state.

XIV. We all must . . .
A. Truly love our youths
B. Respect our youths
C. Believe in our youths
D. Encourage our youths
E. Listen to our youths
F. Talk to and with our youths
G. Work with our youths
H. and Worship with our youths

XV. Conclusion

Each of us has a role to play in this process. Tonight, you must examine your life to see what you are doing to help our youths in helping them solve their problem(s).

If you find that you are not a part of their Solutions, then you are a bigger part of their problem(s) than you realize!

Thank you!

I Sang for My Father

by Saul Henry Bethay

Now that I am living in the fourth chapter of my life, I have time to reflect. In so doing, everything goes back to my father, Ludie Bethay. Daddy died from my car falling off a jack on his body in front of our house one Sunday morning in Opa-locka, Florida.

I was always told by aunts and uncles and some siblings that I was just like my daddy. At first, I resented that statement and comparison out of not knowing him well and with some trepidation and fear. Daddy was firm but fair. Today, I know that no other man could have reared me better. Now I feel he saw himself in me. He let me have the freedom and opportunities he wished could have been available to him—opportunities and experiences separate us, not just knowledge or money. I chose a high school in a different county. I rode a bike to get to and from high school daily. I went to college with a sharecropper's income. I joined the Air Force after college. All of this was done with Daddy's support and in silence, without questioning me or trying to stop me at any point. Today I feel these experiences he was vicariously having through me until his death in 1962 and still looking down today. He lived to see me graduate from high school and came to my college graduation with proud. I became a teacher and a dean of students at two different colleges (Edward Waters College, Jacksonville, Florida; and Mississippi Valley State College, Itta Bena, Mississippi) before he was killed.

To say this, I must say that I have always felt free as early as five years old—free in the sense of the things I was permitted to do without asking or being questioned after I had done them. But the three times I was out of my permitted limits, he let me know who the man was.

Two examples of my childhood freedoms: I could go places locally without asking. I began driving a car at eight, backed in the ditch, towed out, and drove to the store and back by myself. I parked at the store so I could make a U-turn without having to reverse again.

Before I was twelve years of age, I was permitted to work for other people for adult wages—$3 or $5 a day—pulling vegetable plants or cropping tobacco. I even work in the fields with the World War II German prisoners on a farm. The prisoners would not let me work and let me sit in the shade all day—in their minds I was too young to even be in the fields. They shared their excellent lunches with me, all done without verbal communication or fear on my part.

Even today, it seems like a dream. I do not know how the guards permitted my being there, mingling with the prisoners. But I had worked for this farmer before they began using prisoners from Moody Air Force Base in Valdosta, Georgia. But also, I have always been accepted, respected, and trusted far beyond my chronological years among all people, Black and White, especially the older ones.

Until I was thirty and older, most of my association, verbal or otherwise, was with people ten or twenty years older than I was. They too like to have me in their presence and shared their most personal experiences.

Thus, as I became a man, I too began seeing some of Daddy's qualities in me or his qualities I wanted to acquire and copy—honesty, fairness, care, reliability, dependability, the need to know, ambition, hard work, friendliness, people seeking my advice, people trusting me with personal information, people wanting to be my friend.

I cannot image what Daddy could have become with the proper schooling and opportunities. With just three or four years of part-time schooling, he was able to be the man he was—a family man who, through hard work, knew how to take care of his eight children and at times grandchildren, at the same time caring for his parents, who always lived nearby.

Daddy could do almost anything when it came to building, fixing, or farming. When he needed a truck he could not afford, he chopped off the back of a car and made himself one using cross tires (part of trees as used on railroads) for the floor for the truck. What if he had had an engineer's schooling and experiences?

Of all the things I try to do or have tried, singing is not one of them. But through my actions, I feel I sang for my father and feel he is still watching and praising everything I do and have done. So that life Daddy did not get a chance to experience, I feel that I have helped complete it.

Daddy and my ten Guarding Angels are with me every day, all the time! I feel like a millionaire with everything except their money. I know I am blessed!

The Fort Valley State College (University) Alumni Association

Why this title? The school was a college when I was a student; so was Michigan State and Mississippi Valley State when I was a dean. A true university is made up of a group of complete independent colleges within the university system. California and New York are two systems which I know are true university systems. That is why I worked at Medgar Evers College and Brooklyn College.

It was my best way to give back to Fort Valley State when I learned that there was an alumni association here in New York. I immediately joined and became active in all its fund-raisers since.

There were the many dances, the cookouts, and the conferences here in New York as well as the annual Fort Valley State Alumni Association meetings held each year in Georgia.

I attended as many of them as I could and as often as I could, but I never forgot to give back through my financial membership and annual donations.

Soon after I became a member, I was made vice president of the New York Area Chapter; a position I took very seriously, and I have held it for more than twenty years.

I felt that we were spending too much money paying a hotel or other types of facilities to host a dance or an affair. I began having the fund-raiser at 220 Rutland Road, following the example Gladys Haugabook set while she was the president—one of the best.

Gladys began having fund-raisers at her home in Queens each year. In fact, Gladys and her husband, Jerry, were on their way to 220 Rutland

Road to an alumni affair when he became sick. Jerry was a hard fundraiser (worker) for the alumni association. We still miss Jerry very much.

We have our Beer and Crab Feast each September for our fundraiser and our Thank-You Christmas Party each December. The Crab Feast is held on my garage top and in front of it on the street. The Christmas party is held throughout the house—sit-down tables with Christmas napkins, silverware, and glasses on each table in each room, including two bedrooms and the apartment downstairs. I take out all the furniture in the living room for the dining tables and chairs. Yes, we have a Christmas tree filled with gifts donated by Robert and Su Bethay from Chicago. Santa comes all dressed up in his Christmas outfit.

Menu for our Beer and Crab Feast: Deviled Eggs, Hog Head Cheese, Crackers, Fried Fish, Bar-be-Que Pork Ribs, Baked Turkey, Fried Chicken, Roast Pork, Baked Ham, Pig Feet, Collard Greens, String Beans, Corn Bread, Potato Salad, Dirty Rice, Red Rice, White Rice, Cabbages, three Bean Salad, Cole Slaw, Pickled Beets, Butter Beans and Okra, Tossed Salad, Water Melon, Peach Cobbler, Pound Cake, Pineapple/Coconut Cake, Chocolate Cake, Fruit Cocktail, Mixed Drinks, Beer, Wine, Soft Drinks, Punch, Orange Juice, Cranberry Juice, and water.

I was in Miami on 9/11 and had to rent a car—no public transportation—and get my brother-in-law, Robert Goins, and my nephew, Victor Bryant, Jr., to drive me back to New York to get ready for the Crab Feast by Saturday the fifteenth that year.

I realized that I needed to shop in Miami and I filled the rented car trunk with groceries purchased (food) for the Crab Feast; forgetting that I had two suitcases of clothes in Opa-locka (Miami Gardens.) I had to take my clothes, along with Robert's and Victor's, and put them loose on the back seat of the car with space left for only one person to sit. I had to leave my suitcases and a few other things in Miami.

I called Gladys Haugabook in Jacksonville and she fixed dinner for us as we passed through Jacksonville that Thursday night. All of Gladys's meals are like Sunday meals.

It was my friend from Bermuda at my house who called me and asked if I were watching TV at 8:15 a.m. (9/11). I said, "Cecil, why would I be watching TV in Miami this time of morning?"

He said, "You better take a look!"

I was in Miami along with most of my immediate family attending one of my sister's birthday – Alline Culmer's celebration when this happened.

From Miami I made arrangements for peach cobblers to be made by Carol Pearson and picked up in Newark as we passed through; Robert White to get my alcohol and beer and crabs and fish in Baltimore for the first time, and one of my neighbors, Ruby Coleman, to make cakes for me. When I finally arrived in Brooklyn, Friday afternoon, after a three hours of delay trying to cross one of the bridges in Staten Island, I had my butcher to stop everything and cut up twenty chickens for frying, and I had no money to pay him. I purchased the eggs for the potato salad and deviled eggs.

Cecil from Bermuda, the four of us, had the place ready, including food for guests by 2:00 p.m. that Saturday.

The Christmas menu does not have foods which have to be cooked on the spot, such as barbeque, fish, and some of the summer dishes. Christmas is a sit-down dinner. Thanks to Mama Saunders, we have glasses and china.

We have some of the best programs and entertainment at the Christmas parties: professional Broadway singers, actors, and musicians. T. Ray Lawrence, Melvin Greenwich, Carlos Baptiste, George Nesbitt, and other artists who wanted to entertain us each Christmas—entertainment worthy of $75 per ticket.

One Christmas, Bill Broadnax and I did a fashion show entitled "Men Over Sixty." I brought the house down when I dragged my leather coat across and through the rooms and drop it on the stairs as I was going up. I went from hat, to shades, to coat, to shirt, to pants, to swimsuit in my original outfit, undressing. Bill changed outfits each act, including shoes. I kept saying, "The same shoes." Everyone would scream when I would get down to that in my different outfits.

I surprised my sister Zipha with a celebration for her birthday at one of these Alumni Christmas parties. She still tells everyone that it was one of her best birthday celebrations to date.

As previously mentioned, each guest is always given a wrapped/bagged Christmas Thank-You gift, compliments from Robert and Su

Bethay of Chicago—watches, rings, earrings, gloves, hats, scarves, wallets, purses, etc.—the best. Thank You, Robert and Su!

Our special guests and honorary associate members are/were always two Tuskegee Airmen, Alton Burton and George Bing. George Bing is deceased and he was at Brooklyn College working on another degree at the time we met. Mr. George and his wife, Ann Bing, and I became good friends, also Mr. Alton and Dr. Vashtih Burton, MD.

When Mr. George Bing died, we had his repast at 220 Rutland Road. Imagine having twenty Tuskegee airmen in your home with some of their relatives and friends. One of them was from Washington, and I offered him my apartment for the night. He gladly accepted, but we did not get any sleep because he told me the history of the Tuskegee Airman and gave me a video of the Red Tail Squadron. I donate each year to the Red Tail Squadron Foundation. What an experience.

The Burtons and Ann Bing are always my special guests whenever the Alumni Association is having anything social or I am entertaining. Because of their ages, one of the Burtons' sons brings them to my affairs even at the time of this writing.

I participated in my fiftieth anniversary at Fort Valley in May 2004. What a reunion that was, seeing so many of my classmates who are still around (alive). Daniel Williams was our main speaker. It was he who spoke for us when I was in the Sphinx Club of Alpha Phi Alpha in 1951. I gave some reflections of our fifty years since graduation.

After all those year after graduation, I had never been to the Classics held in Columbus, Georgia, each year. I took my social security money and purchased an airline ticket and rented a car when I got in Atlanta to go to my hotel room in Columbus. Why am I telling this? There was a formal dance that Saturday night, and only the queens and their courts from Fort Valley and Albany and the top alumni and college presidents from each school were permitted to attend. I from Brooklyn on a Saturday night in Columbus, Georgia, had nothing to do, and hearing the music from a dance which I could not attend was too much for me.

Another alumni member saw that I was upset about something and made me tell her. I finally broke down and told her how disappointed I was with this treatment about the dance. She made me go to my room and put on my darkest suit and go to this formal dance which I knew nothing about before I left Brooklyn. She took me to a table among the group. Everyone was looking at me, dressed as I was.

I soon left and as I was leaving, someone told me about a party the Zackerys (Clarence and Shirley Zackery) were having at their rented house; their entire family was housed in this large beautiful rented house. I went and had the time of my life with the best of food and meeting other guests.

That party saved the weekend for me, but it placed a damper on my going back even to Fort Valley homecomings after that experience.

I can take my social security money and stay in Brooklyn and play pool and be happy. I do not have to spend $2,000 to be miserable away from home at some football classic between Fort Valley State University and Albany State University!

But I shall never forget what Fort Valley State College did for me between September 1950 and June 1954. Fort Valley State, Fort Valley State, my life to thee I dedicate!

The Mississippi Valley State College (University) Alumni Association

Why this college alumni association when I was never a student there? Years after I did not go back to MVSC, one of the business employee's nephews was living in Brooklyn and wanted to begin an alumni association here in the New York area. Her name was Christine Brenda Bender and her nephew was Sandy Bender. Christine had told Sandy about me, and he introduced me to some of the others who were thinking about the new association. Among that group were the Darden brothers, whom I had as students when I was dean. Later other students I knew who now lived in the New York area joined. Because of this acquaintance, they wanted me to be their *adviser* (the spelling they wanted to use).

I thought it was an honor for them to want me to serve in that capacity. The State of Mississippi has an Annual Upstate New York Picnic in Central Park each year. I got one of my carpenter neighbors, Richard Walters, to build a Mississippi Valley State College booth for the park. They won a prize for it. For fund-raisers, this Association had boat rides and home cookouts. The association became very successful membership-wise and financially. Alumni T-shirts were made for the group and worn proudly at most of their affairs.

One summer at the picnic as I was passing where they had this fried chicken on display for the fried chicken contest, I went to my lunch basket and took out a chicken breast and put it on the table and won first prize. I was given a Mississippi cookbook.

One from our group, Ann Wilson, was a graduate of Mississippi Valley State College, an alumni member, and a parent of one of my counselees in Englewood, New Jersey.

I made many new friends by being the vice president of the Fort Valley State National Alumni Association, the New York area chapter, and the adviser to the Mississippi Valley State National Alumni Association, the New York area chapter.

Both groups support each other in all their affairs, especially fund-raisers. Both groups need to work on membership. It is hard to get the new graduates to join.

Pool (Billiards)

When I was Billy, Saul, Mr. Bethay, Dean Bethay, and many of my other names before I was John, it would not have been the thing to do or the place to go to spend respectful time with friends.

Only certain type of people played pool across the tracks, especially on Saturday and Saturday night in most small towns, Nashville included. Billy could not even go into the poolroom. Many places they were drinking and gambling. Every now and then, someone would curse when they missed a shot. There were worse things Billy could or should not have done, but he did.

Airman Bethay shot a few balls in Hawaii once or twice. During the seventies, Mr. Bethay would have lunch in Bergenfield, New Jersey, with two of his colleagues, Dr. David Lampron and Alan Brodsky, and would try his hand at shooting. I could hardly put a ball in the pocket with my hands then.

McKinley Smith, Smitty, was on vacation in Brooklyn during the early part of the turn of the century (2000), and we stopped into a new bar on Atlantic Avenue. While Smitty was having a drink, I got on the pool table and started shooting a few balls by myself. No one else was in the bar except the owner, the bartender, and security. The owner said, "Come back Thursday night after 11:00 p.m. and there would be others here. By the way, what is your name?"

I remembered the name I had used some years ago at the municipal building restroom, downtown Brooklyn, and I said, "John." I did not think that I would ever be coming back to this bar after Smitty left. Not only did I come back that Thursday night, I was there every Thursday night and many other nights when I would be leaving the earlier bars. The bars close at 4:00 a.m. in New York. How convenient.

Other patrons came and drank more and more alcohol. I came and played and played more and more pool. I began winning a few games. People like to watch me play because I was never trained and I would try to use all types of "body english" to get the ball to fall into the hole. They would get a kick out of this.

Later I learned that most bars had pools tables. Now I am a bar hopper just to play pool; I don't even drink $3 bottles of water in the bars. If I were to get thirsty or hungry, I go outside and get myself a slice of pizza and a soda.

I purchased a pool stick, someone gave me a pool stick, and my goddaughter, Pamel Sue Rivers, gave me a folding pool table with pool sticks which is still in the box. I have a pool table with sticks on a neck chain, which I now wear. Thanks to Sarah Cheatham.

The reason I have not unpacked the pool table is because I need playing pool as much for socialization as I do for recreation. It gives me a reason to go to the Y and do my four Ss: Steam Room, Sauna, Shave, and Shower. Every now and then, I might add another S to my activity—swim.

Practice makes perfect sometimes. I got better the more I played and at the different bars. One has to put his name on a board to play when his/her time comes. Now whenever I walk in, someone immediately puts "John" on the board. There is another John who plays often and is quite good. I remember he did not recognize his own signature and thought my "John" was his. Different players began giving me different names. That is why I am called at certain bars and by certain players—Pops, 1914, Handsome, and Dancer.

My pool playing has come to the point where everyone wants to play me, especially the top pool players, because I am a challenge because I can make a shot they would not think of or try. I am known to have good eyes.

My scheduled activities includes the following:

> The Senior Citizen Hall for lunch, Monday–Friday
> The YMCA
> The poolrooms (between 4:00 and 7:00 arrival time)

The theatres on weekends
The lunches with former colleagues each month
Scrabble night on Monday

    I joined the senior citizen place on Fulton Street near the Y, where I could stop by for the unseasoned $1 lunch during the week; nothing there but old folk. One day I stopped by the poolroom, which has two tables, one regular and one small. What I was most impressed by was the quality of the players' game—far better than most games I had seen in the other bars.

    I began trying my hand playing pool with them. Not only has my game gotten better at the Senior Citizen Hall, it is better at the other bars as well. Because I jump around when I shoot, I am called the Dancer at the Senior Citizen Hall.

    You know who shoots billiards!

Let's Not Forget...

Mama Marie Bethay

As I LOOK BACK at those days when the only money we had for the twenty-five pounds of flour, the mullet fish, and the grits was the money Mama had made taking in washing and in cooking Sunday dinners in you know whose house. She made a few dollars from the rent the teachers paid if it were during school season. There was not always something to sell living on the farm in all seasons, especially during the winter months. Mama bridged the financial gap.

As I said at Mama's funeral January 19, 1994, my sixtieth birthday, she made dresses for my sisters and my underwear from those flour sacks. She cooked those biscuits three times a day (for ten of us most of the time and the nephews and nieces during the summers), along with the other food and still worked in the fields. We were well fed with much of our own food we had on the farm—chickens, eggs, sausages, ham, bacon, chitterlings, and vegetables.

In the last thirty-plus years, Mama was able to live in her own home with all the necessary modern facilities. She had a new dress for all special occasions. She was among the best-dressed ladies in Miami. She was able to attend any church meeting locally and out of town. She flew whenever she made trips out of town at some distance. My sister Alline would be the one to accompany her. When she needed someone with her at home, there was never a time she was alone. She was a faithful church mother, a position she held during her membership. Before she became the honorary Church Mother, it was a fund-raising position one earned. I made certain that she raised the most money each year with the help of my friends' ads taken out in the church's bulletin, which I had printed many years in Brooklyn.

I had a friend at Medgar Evers College, Ed Hinds, who was in charge of the printing shop there, and he worked tirelessly and at the last minute many a year to get the bulletins ready for the Emanuel Church of God in Christ and then the Holy Ghost Training Center.

One Saturday night, I got a passenger at Kennedy Airport to take the bulletins on the plane with him to Miami, and someone met him at the airport in Miami in order for the bulletins to be there for the service. That could not be done today for security reasons, nor would anyone trust you to that extent.

Mama's legs began to fail and needed the support of a wheelchair, and someone had to be with her at all times for movement purpose. While everyone was still working, we hired a lady, Sister Annie Turner* (died December 22, 2017), to stay with her during the day, and Zipha was the main one to care for her most of the other times at home. Thank God, my other sisters were there to help also.

We are still grateful to Sister Turner for all she did to make Mama comfortable and to have someone to talk to.

It is not easy being a caregiver. When I would take my week vacation during the summer, I gave everyone who looked after Mama the week off. It made me appreciate what they had been doing full-time. Mama was the best person to wait on. She made no demands and was always concerned about your welfare while caring for her.

One time I had come to Miami and Mama could hardly talk from all the medicine she had been given by the different doctors. I took it upon myself to get rid of any medicine which did not pertain to something we knew was not needed, and in a few days Mama's speech was back to normal. Doctors have a practice of giving older people some type of medicine every time they come in just to get that money from the insurance company. Clinic doctors don't always look to see what the patient is already taking. I know because it was tried on me here in New York. A new doctor wanted to prescribe about seven different medicines without examining me. I have never been back to see him. At the time of this writing, I take no prescription medicine.

Once I was home with Mama and she began crying stating how she was thinking about their letting me ride that bicycle those miles back and forth to school in all types of weather when I was attending high school in Adel, Georgia—leaving so early in the morning and coming home some days after dark if I took it upon myself to stay for an after-school activity like basketball.

I told Mama the main thing you did was not stop me from attending school regardless of the circumstances. Where would I be today without the schooling I was able to get then and later? Also let's not forget the last of the summer money ($100) for me to enroll in Fort Valley State College in 1950.

Also, I remember those envelops with the three-cent stamps I received with a few dollars tucked inside. I knew where that money was made and how.

Mama knew that I appreciated every sacrifice she made on my behalf all those many years; she did this for me, having other children to be concerned with. Thank you, Mama. May your soul rest in peace forever. I love you!

Dr. O. E. Hicks

It was he who in 1950 saw this sixteen-year-old student away from home for the first time and needing a family. A member of his family I became, and after sixty-four years I still am.

First, he was my professor, then he became my father, followed by being my best friend.

He and his family made sure that college would be an educational and memorable experience for me. On my first job in Gray, Georgia, near Fort Valley, it was those delicious Sunday meals Mama Hicks prepared with extra special detail, knowing that I would be there to enjoy them with the family. They still wanted to make sure that I had at least one good meal each week as they did my freshman year when I lived across the streets from them in Fort Valley.

It was Daddy Hicks who took out bank loans for me when I needed extra money in New York. I do not know why I did not take out my own loans or why I needed them in the first place now.

Daddy Hicks helped me choose a graduate school and major, and he supported me all the way through. I ended up living in the same dormitory as he when we studied at Columbia University, Whittier Hall.

It was Dr. Hicks who wanted to give me a special Oldsmobile car he had, but I did not want to take a chance driving by myself to Brooklyn. He gave it to my adopted brother, his other son, Dr. Bruce Fort, in Albany. I knew I was the favorite son.

It was prostate cancer which took him from us. A sad day for so many of us. I spoke at his funeral and told the audience what he had done for me. My son, Claude, and his wife, Patricia, joined me in Fort Valley at the funeral.

It was after Dr. Hicks's death that I learned that I was a good friend of his doctor's brother in Philadelphia. I knew his doctor while I was in Fort Valley. His doctor cried at his passing.

Dr. James N. Mitchell

Mentor, tutor, advisor, big brother, and friend are the names to our relationship beginning at Michigan State in 1959, and it lasted until his death in July 1985.

His family in Atlanta adopted me as brother and Uncle Saul—my family whenever I am in Atlanta today or whenever they visit Brooklyn.

As mentioned before, we ended up in New York. Jim was always there whenever I needed his sound advice and counsel. In addition to always being there for me in my pursuit of my master's and attempt toward my PhD, he helped me tremendously with Claude, Steve, and Monroa's "adoption." Success or survival. I could not have done it without him. Jim was my editor for many of my papers, and he served as my evaluator when I did the Mobil Project at Medgar Evers College.

Jim wrote a manuscript which predicted some of the political happenings from Nat Turner through the death of some of our Civil Rights leaders at the time, "No One Likes a Genius Child," which was never published maybe because of our Guardian Angels.

I must add Jim's name to my brilliant list with Dr. O. E Hicks, Dr. Claude Saint-Come, and Dr. Steven B. Carswell. He was a psychologist, minister and an excellent speaker and writer. Because of the prejudice at that time, he ended up having to change schools to complete his doctorate. His topic might have been some of the problem:

NAT TURNER: SLAVE, PREACHER, PROPHET, AND MESSIAH, 1800–1831: A STUDY OF THE CALL OF A BLACK SLAVE TO PROPHETHOOD AND TO THE MESSIAHSHIP OF THE SECOND COMING OF CHRIST

James Nathaniel Mitchell
Divinity School of Vanderbilt University
Nashville, Tennessee
May 5, 1975

Any success I received at Michigan State University and Columbia University I owe a great deal of gratitude to James N. Mitchell. He too helped me become the counselor I became. Thanks!

John Blanding

It began in 1969 playing bid whist. John (Johnny) was my neighbor who lived across the streets in front of my garage next to Richard Walters and his family. John soon let me know he could do almost anything around the house. My car needed fixing. John and Richard fixed it. I needed new ceiling put up in my house. John installed the new ceiling. The house began leaking. John put on a new roof on the house for me. The garage started leaking. John replaced the garage top. The walls in the house needed painting. John painted the inside of the house. The kitchen needed new tile on the floor. John put new tile on the floor. When Claude and Patricia were to have their wedding reception here, John installed a ceiling fan for the hot weather. When I began having the Crab Feast at 220 Rutland Road, John covered half of the garage top with a removable top to keep the sun off. When I needed lights put out on top of the garage, John strung lights all around the top. (Now I have all new roofs and all repairs up-to-date.) When the electrical system needed some repair work done, John put in new sockets, light switches, bulbs, etc. When I wanted to drive to the Family Reunion one year in Valdosta, Georgia, John drove me there and back.

John's wife and their three daughters along with the grandchildren adopted me. I to them am Saul, Mr. Bethay, and Uncle Saul.

One of John's grandsons drowned and John wanted me to have his 2001 Mercury. John died from cancer, and the family gave me Johnny's 1994 Cadillac.

Now I need a roof replacement on the house and the garage. I need the water-damaged closet and hallway repaired and painted. I need work done for the ceiling and the floor of my kitchen. Johnny, where are you? I know you are in heaven, looking down on me, knowing that my Guardian Angels will come to my rescue.

Monroa B. Goutier

Imagine having no known living relatives and you are not old yourself. Your mother and sister died and you have no one else but friends. That was Monroa's situation before he died. That was Monroa whose friendship I cherished.

My second apartment living in New York was sleeping on Monroa's and Smitty's couch during my second summer in school at Columbia. He was sharing an apartment in Brooklyn with my homeboy McKinley Smith, whom I met at my sister's graduation in 1958.

It was Monroa who got me the job at Medgar Evers College to help it get its accreditation, and it was a job I kept for more than fifteen years, serving in several different capacities.

It was Monroa who helped me move from 232 Rutland Road to 220 Rutland Road. It was Monroa who always made my desserts for my entertainment and peach cobblers for me on weekends, whether I was having company or not.

It was Monroa who would cook much of my meats when I was entertaining. Yes, Monroa was known for his good cooking. He worked in restaurants before he got his bachelor's and master's degrees.

Monroa was able to meet my mother in New York, and years later, I took him to my family reunion in Valdosta, where he could meet the remainder of my family, the ones he had not met in New York. He got a joy out of seeing and being among all my nephews, nieces, and cousins—the family he did not have.

His former roommate, Smitty, from Brooklyn had moved back to Valdosta, and he stayed with him that weekend, which was a great reunion for them as well.

Monroa was born in New Jersey but spent some time in California and knew nothing about the South. I showed him where I learned to swim, where I went to elementary and high school, and where I did my sharecropping farming, and we ended up in Jacksonville, where I was dean of students in 1960–1961.

For his certification to become a counselor, I was his mentor at Brooklyn College. At my retirement, he gave me a check with my name and his signature only. He told the audience that I could write in the amount.

Monroa took sick and needed home care. I was able to get Robert Tadlock to come in daily to take care of his needs. Later he had to have full nursing home care with his medication needs.

I had him cremated when he died. I was able to let my former student, Therone Evans from Brooklyn College, get his apartment. I have or had all his possessions—jewelry, paintings, books, and *ashes*.

Monroa B. Goutier, you were my good friend. May you again rejoin your family in heaven!

Laxman Inamke, Bombay, India

Laxman and two other students from India were at Michigan State working on their master's in agriculture. They had a bachelor's degree from Pune University in India. Thomas Castro and Tuli were the other two.

Laxman first. I do not remember how we became friends. He and my friend T. Ray Lawrence became better buddies at Michigan State because they were drinking partners. Laxman loved beer. My Indian friends would come by for dinner when Cecil and I had our apartment that summer off campus in East Lansing, Michigan. We all were in summer school.

I left Michigan the summer of 1960, but somehow we all kept in touch. When I became a New York resident, Laxman would visit me during the summers from India and Canada.

Laxman owned a sugar plantation in India, and the children of the workers had no schooling. He wanted me to come to India and set up an elementary school on his plantation. What he wanted would not be a problem for me to do because I could copy the American curriculum (system) with the basic education they needed, and the administration would not be a problem either. With my having a degree in agriculture myself and having grown up on a farm, the environment would not be new. Remember we grew sugarcane and Daddy made syrup in Georgia. I had it all, firsthand experience in farming and the education I needed as well.

I was going to take a leave of absence from the Englewood school system without any concern for my financial future because Laxman was rich with a capital *R*.

Before my Guardian Angels let me send in my resignation, in 1966, Indira Gandhi became Prime Minister of India and federalized the country. This prevented my being able to get permission to establish a school anywhere in India, especially on an isolated, rich sugar plantation. No citizen of India could bring more than $300 out of the country at any time. There went my principal job in India.

After this happened, Laxman wanted me to sponsor him for citizenship in this country, but I did not have a profession or business where I could legally employ him. He later moved to Toronto, Canada, and would visit me in Brooklyn during the summers, still trying to become a citizen. He, Al Hicks, and John Jordan went with me one summer to Miami to meet my family. While there, we visited some of the sugar farms in Florida for Laxman to compare.

Laxman gave me several trips to visit him in Toronto while he lived there. Toronto is the only city I have visited in Canada since. Tony Hardie and I have driven to Toronto several times since—a beautiful city. We were going to drive from Toronto to Montreal, but got halfway and realized it was too far. We returned to Toronto for the remainder of our vacation.

Because he could not get any of his money out of India, Laxman would have his Indian friends living in the United States send money to him in Brooklyn. He would have big bucks while in New York, and he would have his family in India give the money back to relatives living in India. Where there is a will, there is a way.

One summer Laxman was visiting me and had a diabetic attack and had to be taken to Kings County Hospital here in Brooklyn via ambulance. He was there for over a month, and later I got a bill for $40,000. I told the administrators at Kings County that we were school friends and he was visiting, and I had no responsibility for him medically. My address was used because he was my guest at the time of the attack.

He returned to Canada and India and later he visited me in Brooklyn. Laxman gave me those throw rugs I have from India and some of the art pieces. He had sent some other things from India to me, but I was not permitted to receive them. Thomas gave me that ship I have on my mantel.

Our friend Thomas Castro was now living with his family in Brazil, with a wife and five boys, with this big position with the government in insecticides. He wanted me to visit him and see if I would be interested in working with him. Time did not allow me.

Thomas was there for more than twenty years. He and his family would visit me in Brooklyn on their vacations. His wife and my sister Marian became friends somehow, and she visited Miami.

Thomas's wife took sick and died and he and family moved to Florida, and we somehow lost touch.

I learned that Laxman had to have a leg amputated, and he ultimately died from his diabetes. What a dear friend.

Unpublished Writings

Why I Cannot Afford to Die
by Saul Henry Bethay

Preface

I have often been called on to help make final funeral arrangements for a deceased family member who had never given any time or attention to his/her final hour on this earth. There has always been a need for such information because the ones who need it the most are the least to make any prearrangements for the afterlife. Everyone wants to go to heaven but no one wants to die or make preparation for death.

The outline for this information was done more than twenty years ago, and I have used it for several speeches. Why now? No good reason other than procrastination and laziness. But it is needed more now than ever due to the plight many of us find ourselves in during this economic crisis. This crisis is not new to many of us.

When you attend a funeral and see the family screaming, falling out, and sometimes having to be taken from the facility, it is not from the loss of their loved one but from the knowledge of that outstanding funeral debt they have been talked into by the funeral director's smooth, sympathetic talk, taking advantage of their bereavement and telling them that their loved one should be put away in the style in which she/he lived—at the same time knowing that they cannot afford such an elaborate funeral. But it's show-off time at the wake or going-home celebration for their loved one. With the lack of pre-planning on someone's part, emotion takes over logic. *This information* will help eliminate some of this unnecessary grief at your funeral.

I am hitching the mule behind the wagon. You find yourself at prayer meeting on Tuesday night, you attend Bible Study on Wednesday, you rehearse with the choir on Friday evenings, you help with the pastor's and church's fundraisers, you pay your tithe, you make a great report during Men's/Women's Day, you attend conferences in and out of the town/state in which you live, you teach Sunday school at 10:15 a.m. and are in your pew at 11:00 a.m. every Sunday—all in preparation for the afterlife. You are doing an excellent job with this. You would receive an A+ grade from me. But should you come down this moment with a debilitating stroke or illness, which will render you unable to talk or even move, not to mention the possibility that you end up in a coma or die on the spot, are you ready to die? Can you afford to die? How much of the following information have you considered or acted on with someone else's knowledge of your answers?

Medical

Who else knows about your medical condition? Your doctors? Dentist? Gynecologist/urologist? Would they know how to get in touch with your doctors? What medicines are you taking? For what? With what hospital is your doctor affiliated? How far is the hospital from where you live? Who is your medical proxy? Are your medical insurances up-to-date, and does someone else know where the cards are?

Life Insurance

Do you have life insurance? Where are the policies? Does your beneficiary know that he/she is named?

Finances

(The really big secret from everyone)
Where are the bankbooks? Who else knows where they are? Who else has access to your accounts? Who are you leaving your

money to? Do you have a legal/durable power of attorney? Is this covered in your will?

Property

Where are the deeds? Have they been kept current with necessary changes you desire? Is there a right-of-survivorship included? Is the will properly and professionally done? Does the executor/executrix know? Who has copies of the will and where is it filed? Is the property adequately insured—fire, theft, flood, contents (jewelry, art, clothing, furniture, kitchenware, etc.)?

Final Arrangements

(The most difficult part to deal with)

Does anyone know how you would like to be "put away"? Are you financially prepared? Through what means? What part have you played in your final prearrangements? What kind of service do you want—wake, church, funeral home, graveside, etc.? Do you want to be cremated or buried?

Information is no better than the use one makes of it. You can continue to say at this time, "When I am gone, it will not be my problem!" True!

Other Family and Dear Friends

THE NAMES OF THE deceased are followed by an asterisk (*).

It would take a huge book to include all my relatives and friends in this book, but I must at least list some of them who made an impact or donated toward the Fort Valley State University's fund-raisers over the many years:

Geneva Anderson, Clifford Alford, Maudell Alford Jackson*, Mable Jones Perkins Allen, Marion Anderson, George H. Andrews*, Fran Alongi, Rosemary Ashe. Joseph Barker, Deborah Barnes, Eddie* and Dorothy Barnett, Glistene Bethay, Joyce Bolds, Douglas Brown, Toussant Brown, Melanie Brown, Yvonne Byrd, Julius and Cheryl Brown, Marvin* and Dr. Theresa Brown, Espenola Bethay, Mr. and Mrs. Ed Boston, Cynthia Burrowes, Dewayne Bush, Keith Bussey, Michael Cadet, Gwenith Chase, Anthony Chiappette, Mr. & Mrs. Gregory Nathaniel and Theresa Cooley, Gregory Cooley II, Lance Corporal Donovon Nathaniel Cooley, Brianna Monet Cooley, John F. Childs, Josephine Cruise, Dr. Johnnette Cole, Rubell Coleman, Bernice Constance, Garland Core Jr., Jake Cuthbert, Michelle DeRoche, Andre Devero, Robert Dock, Butler Dowery, Lionel Dowling Jr., Ernie and Sandra Duncan, Jeani Fogarty, Dr. and Mrs. Bruce Fort, Mr. and Mrs. Robert, Sr.* and Irma Gadsden, Robert Gadsden, Jr., Robin Gadsden, George Ford, Mr. and Mrs. Charles B. and Dr. Juanita Fountain, Henry and Alma Gallmon, Lillian Hardison, Ed Hinds, Mr. and Mrs. George* and Mable* Hicks, Clara Hicks*, Loiuse Hicks Williams*, Alfred Hicks*, William Hicks*, Mr. Posey* and Mrs. George Ellen Williams, Clyde and Lucille* Hagwood,* Mama Ethel Higgins, Mr. and Mrs. Tyrone Higgins,

William Higgins, David Hall, Robert and Patricia* Harden, Anthony Hardie, Maxine Hawkins, Victor Herbert,* Thelma Husbands,* Don Jones, Dyane Jones, Gregory Jones, Nolan Jones, John and Sheneal Hughes, Harry Green, James Jarrell,* Benjamin Jenkins, Margaret John, Clara Kearse, Lorna Grant, Grantley King, Mr.* & Mrs. T'Angelo King, Dr. Edwin C. Knox, Frantz Lauture, Jim and Julia Leonard, Hilda Lopez, Curtis Lyles,* Patricia Lytle, E'Tiene Lytle, Mr. and Mrs. John Lister, Jacqueline Lee, Shirley Luck, Daisy Lyles,* Laurice Lyons, Dwight Peavy, Juanita Manor, Richard Marion, Hattie Mitchell, Annette Murray, Neil Mapp, Lloyd Matthew, Dr. Thomas* and Merline McCloud, Joe* and Glynn McCray, Linda McDuffie, Ann* and Russell* Nix, Evelyn McKenzie, Godfey Nolan, Curtis NeSmith, Dr. Karen Nicks, Robert and Geraldine Orr, Carolyn Outlaw, Mr. and Mrs. James Penny, Carol Pearson, Emma Peterson,* A. C. Polite, Cecilia Robert, Mr. and Mrs. Raymond and Thelma* Rounds, Ossie Randle, Jr. Dolores K. Ray, Eugene and Gladys Scott, Shenita Spencer, Cleavie Evelyn Seymour, Fred and Loraine Simpson, Rev. Robert O. Simpson, Alan Singleton, Clinton and Sharon Smith, Mammie Snead, Jean St. Come, Nicole St. Come, Robert Taylor, John Tilford, Dr. Marguerite C. Thompson, Paul Thompson, Robert Tadlock,* Jacquelyne Tatum, Warren Turner, Mr and Mrs. John Walker, Richard Walters* and Sylvia Walters, Otis Ward, Wayne Webb, Barbara Washington Grant, Shane Weaver, Dr. Ila Wells*, Dr. Wilbur Williams, Jr., Albert and Earlene Williams, Robert L. Williams, Jim Willis, Sterling Wood, Josephine Worrell, Mr. and Mrs. Mar Likika Yaqira, Thomas Zachery, Johnnie Bender, Robert Beckles, Mr. and Mrs. George* and Ann Bing, Mr. and Mrs. David* and Connie Johnson, Mr. and Dr. Alton Burton, Dawn Stevenson, Charles Terry, Leo Vantepool, Helen Jewel Coley, Dr. Joy Davis, Phyllis Gross, Mrs. Dorothy Johnson, Mr. and Mrs. Herman Jackson, Dorothy Rounds, and Carolyn Williams.

Mrs. Ella Mae Bethay*, Arkia Bethay, T'Anello Bethay, Hendy Blendman, Alan Brodsky,* Sandy and Joan Bender Jr., William T. Broadnax, Sonja Bethay, Al and Patrice Bethay, Sarah Cheatham, Byron Cheatham, Topper Cheatham, Allison Presscott, Toby Gonzalez, Raymonda Luginbhl, Patricia McCarrick, Bea

Maldonado, Drs. Henry and Zeta Pruitt, Teressa Johnson, Charlyne Slater, Cecil G. and Avery* Smith, Barbara Stroud, Joan Stroud, James Sam Smith, Sister Annie Turner* Lula Smith, Mr. Raymond* and Dorothy Bledsoe, Dr. Dee Catarina, Rick Celis, Eileen Cohen,* Christine Vaughn, Johnnie Mae Bender, Carol Drakeford Lee, Joseph Barker, Cynthia Burrowes, Harley Beckles, Reginald Bush, Calvin Clark, Margaret Gainey, George McGee*, Mr. and Mrs. Reggie and Patricia Hart, Dyane Jones, Mrs. Florence King,* Mr. and Mrs. Joe Lane, Daniel Leacock, Shirley Leacock,* Thelma Little,* Andra Marquez, Aubrey Marquez, Kirk Matthew, Beverly Sims, Mr. and Mrs. John* and Emma St. Bernard, Priscilla Stevens, Jacquelyn Tatum, Mr. and Mrs. Stanley Tatum, Sara B. Thornhill, Rosa Hollingshed, Lois Jordan, Lynn Thompson, Sally Cooper, Mr. and Mrs. George O. Darden, Goldie Hawkins, Ida Henderson, Don James, Marsha Lewis,* Janice Molloy, Dwight Peavy, Harry* and Sue* Rivers, Tommy Singleton, Jimmy Smith,* Dr. Leland Stokes,* Sandra and Arthur Tate, Dr. Dorris Williams,* Joyce Williams,* Julia Springer, Lillith Vanterpool,* Ruth Vanterpool Whiteside,* Robert Vanterpool,* Marc Whiteside,* Yvonne Straker, Earl and Dr. Ella Carter, Dennis and Dr. Juanita Carter. Phyllis Hundley, Rick Thomas, Drs. Roy A. and Eda F. Hastick, Mr. and Mrs. Russell Bethay Jr. and Alberta* Bethay; Russell Andrea Bethay, Shoan Bethay, Arthur J. Robinson,* Leo Richard Williams,* John T. Spruill, Sr.* Raymond Alexander, Dilward Allen, Mr. and Mrs. Nathan Allman, Mr.* and Mrs. Joe Allman, Patricia Ames, Gloria Anderson, Dessie Andrews, Sylvia Anderson, Marion W. Anderson, Frank Austin, Jeanette Bagby, Ola Mae Baker, Deborah Barnes, Donald C. Bartley, Janice E. Battle, Ruth E. Battle, Jerry Bennett, Michael A. Bennett, Richard Blanding, Joseph Blenman, Camille Bodden, Shirley Bolds, Lois Braitwaite,* Walter Broughton, Willie Mae Brown, Eula Brown, Ivy Brown, Daquan Bruce, Reginald D. Bush, Linda Campbell, Barbara Caravanos, Betty Chapman, Jacqueline Charlot, Loretta Chisholm, Ruby Combs, Maxcine Cooper, Barbara Coston,* Muriel Cox, Antoine Craigwell, Gremmel Cunningham, Janet Curley, Robin Daal, Sonja Davis, Douglas Dervin, Hoyle Fontt Douglas, Jackie Dumme, Careta Early-Lawrence, Florence Eddings, James Edwards, Sybel Ellsworth,

WHY I HAVE SO MANY NAMES

Diane Essandoh, Juanita Evelyn, Roxanne Fagan, Barbara Flemings, Beverly Foster, Karen Frances, Emmett Frances, Lynette Fromberger, Margaret Gainey, Alexis A. Gaithers, Karin Gapper, Lulu Garcia, Kevin Gaudin, Desiree George, June George, Grace Grannum, Olga Haggerty, Leila Hamilton, Carrie Hargrow, Marian Harris, Richard Harris, William Harris, Kenneth Hawkins, Dennis Hawkins, Ida Henderson, Edwin A. Henry, Alice Hill, Lawrence Hopper, Susan Hughes, Gwenn Hunter. Sophia Bethay, Charlotte Bethay, Darryl Bethay Jr., Brian Husbands, Keith Husbands, Gwendolyn E. Ivy, Jacqueline Jacques, Gloria Jenkins, Mary Jennings, Sonia John, Mr. and Mrs. Ed and Emogene* Johnson, Caroline Jones, Don James, Brother Joseph, Karin Knife, Dr. and Mrs. David Lampron, Joe and Marlene Lane, Daniel Leacock, Shirley Leacock,* Gladys Maingrette, Maria Maldonado, Drs. James and Rubie Malone, James W. Manear, Ransford N. Manigault, Mary Marrone-Archer, Dr. Wayne Mason, Kirk Matthews, Deborah McConnell, Pamela McKenzie, Susan E. Meehan, Dimitris M. Meredith, Julia Meskus, Rebecca Miller, Renee Mills, Deborah Moore, Ronald Moore, Larry Morgan,* Ruth Morris, Archie Muckle, Ian Narine, Dolores Nelson, Cecily Nurse,* Mattie D. Oliver, Mr. and Mrs. Thomas Palmer, Rose M. Pearce, Glenia Perkins, Sue Phillips, Maureen Pierce-Anyan, Dorothy Pruitt,* Karia Raife, Margaret Reilly, Christopher Robert, Claude Robinson, Beverly Sakofsky, Maxine Scope, Yvonne Scott, Earl Shaw, Gloria Shepherds, Gwendolyn C. Simpson, Beverly Sims, Tommie Singleton, Kirk Smith, Jimmy Smith,* Carolyn Staley, Priscilla Stevens, Bernice Street,* Chiquita Smith, Paul Smith, Cyrus Smith, Laura Soaries,* Joyce B. Stephenson,* Yvonne Straker, Sabrin Syville, Authur and Sandra Tate, Patricia Taylor, Richareanea Theodore-McIntosh, Charles Thomas, Clementine Thomas, Edjar Thomas, Enid Thomas, Iona Thomas, Pierre Thomas, John Tilford, Rehama Trimiew, Dolores Trimiew, Anderyer Tripp, Rose Brown Tully, Donna Tumer-Floyd, Kana Kojo Turrour-George, Semaj Vansant, Alex Vington, Willie Ward, Marsha Watson-Brown, Darryl Williams, Mr. and Mrs. Ralph, Sr.* and Mercedes* Williams, Wanda Williams, Sandy Williams, Ralph Williams, Jr.,* Michelle Williams, Mickey Williams, Maria Williams, Emanuel* and Helen Durden,*

Alice Green, James Wills, Dr. Odessa V. Hardison McNair* Mr. and Mrs. Willie James* and Julia Bethay* Mrs. Cornell Bethay Walker* Jesse Lee Bethay* Dr. Henry Oliver, Rev. Robert Brown, Gwendolyn Williams Holmes* Mr. & Mrs. Frank and Betty Wilson, Sam* and Helen* Franklin, Claytis L. Knox* Fred Martin, Jr.* Mr. & Mrs. Frank* and Arletha Miller* Lillian Royster, Dr.* & Mrs. Roosevelt Hodges, Sharon Hughes, Jeanese Riley, Inga Smith, Daniel Williams, Mr.* & Mrs.* Jerry Powell, Sr. Lloyd Frances, Jack Kelly, John H. Love, Kenny Nelson, Mrs. Monica Swiggum, Mrs. Dot Bender. Mr. and Mrs. Norman and Mae Walker, Reliegh Bethay, Bobonia Feater, and Courtney C. Cruise.

I want to thank those of you whom I am able to recall who made an impact on my life or donated financially toward the Fort Valley State University's fundraisers each year. If your name is missing, charge it to my head and not my heart. Funds from the sale of this book will be donated to the Fort Valley State University as was your donations toward the annual Crab Feasts. Anyone who donates $500 or more will receive a copy of *Now Lay Me Down to Sleep: Thoughts from the Mind*.

I tried to warn you that it would be a bumpy ride, reliving my first eighty years vicariously with me. Not using an outline, I began writing about my life, people, and incidents as they came to what mind I had left at eighty. Many things happened simultaneously, which made for much duplication, but I felt that replication would be better than omission. Now that you have read *Why I Have So Many Names*, what name do you have for me?

WHY I HAVE SO MANY NAMES

SAUL HENRY BETHAY

WHY I HAVE SO MANY NAMES

SAUL HENRY BETHAY

WHY I HAVE SO MANY NAMES

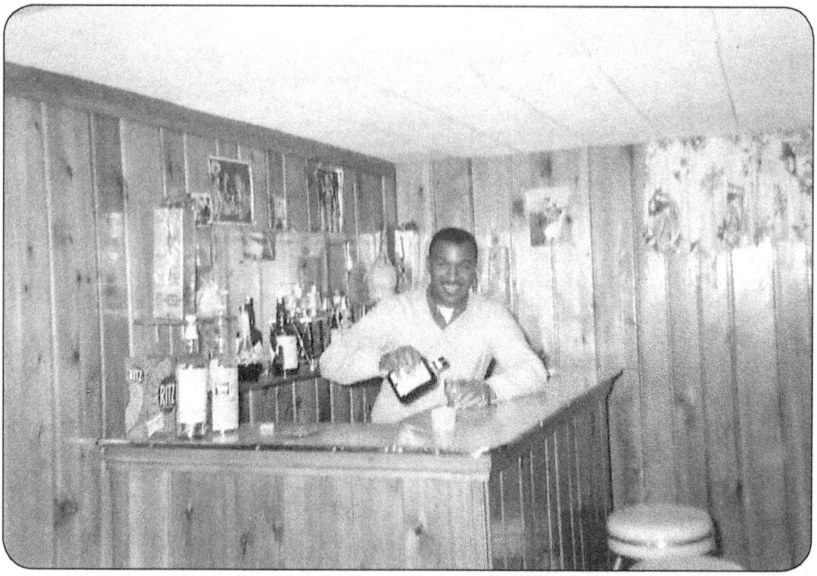

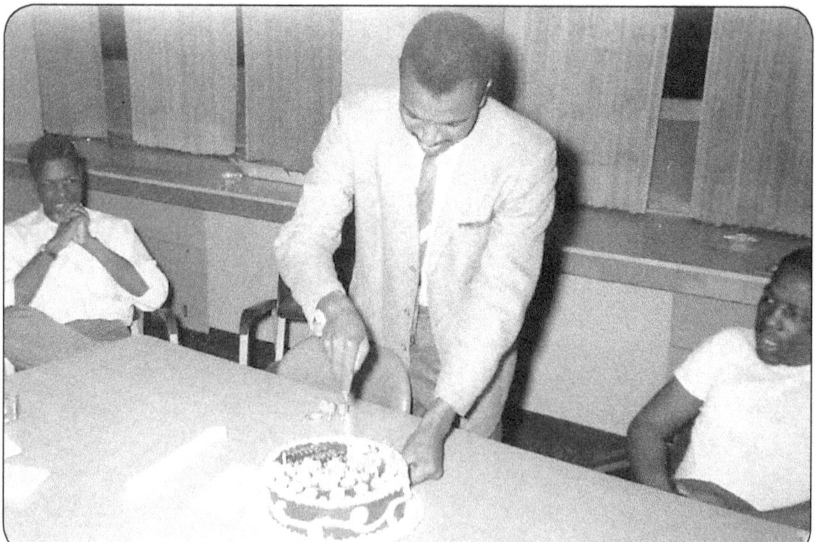

WHY I HAVE SO MANY NAMES

SAUL HENRY BETHAY

WHY I HAVE SO MANY NAMES

SAUL HENRY BETHAY

The Fort Valley State College
Fort Valley, Georgia

Know all men by these presents:

that by the authority of the Board of Regents of the University System of Georgia, and upon the recommendation of the Faculty of this Institution the degree of

Bachelor of Science in Agriculture

is hereby conferred upon

Saul Henry Bethay

who is entitled to enjoy all the rights and privileges pertaining to that degree. In testimony whereof, we have hereunto affixed the seal of the College and the signatures of the officers thereof. Given at Fort Valley, Georgia in the year of our Lord nineteen hundred and fifty-four, this the seventh day of June.

WHY I HAVE SO MANY NAMES

SAUL HENRY BETHAY

WHY I HAVE SO MANY NAMES

SAUL HENRY BETHAY

WHY I HAVE SO MANY NAMES

SAUL HENRY BETHAY

WHY I HAVE SO MANY NAMES

SAUL HENRY BETHAY

WHY I HAVE SO MANY NAMES